S0-ABB-075

BEHIND THE STAIRCASE

MICHAEL PETERSON

For more information and stories

http://www.behindthestaircase.com/

ACKNOWLEGEMENTS

Some names have been changed. A few characters are composites.

I would like to thank Al Zuckerman who has been my agent and friend for thirty years. He supported me throughout my struggle, and this book would not exist without his help and encouragement.

The copyright owner of this book has dedicated it to THE PUBLIC DOMAIN. Anyone and Everyone is free to copy, reproduce, and disseminate this book. There is no such thing as copyright infringement.

Copyright © Silenced LLC   2020

http://www.behindthestaircase.com/

DEDICATION

To my children: Margaret, Martha, Todd, Clayton and Rebecca

And to the future: Dorian and Lucian

PART I

2001-2003

1. DEATH

When I remember the horror of Kathleen's death—anywhere: at the post office, in a store, listening to music, reading quietly—I see and feel her dying in my arms, and though I want to cast away my anguish, pain that sears mind and body, physically hurts so that I have to brace myself against a door or wall, I force myself to remember because I cannot let her go; I don't want to forget any memory of her, even those last moments, her hair dripping blood onto my hands, the staircase floor and walls. Blood everywhere.

I clutched her as tightly as I could—No, No! Don't die. Please please!—but her breath was slipping away, her eyes growing vacant, dilating.

I didn't want to leave her in the stairwell, but I had to get help, so I gently rested her head on the floor and scrambled to the kitchen, grabbed the phone, my hands shaking so that I could barely punch in the numbers. It seemed forever before I heard "911. What is your emergency?" and I yelled "My wife fell down the stairs! She's dying."

"Calm down, sir," the woman said, but I couldn't. I could barely breathe as I rushed back to Kathleen with the phone. "Hurry! Hurry! She's dying!"

"How many stairs, sir?"

"What? What?"

"Calm down, Sir. How many stairs did she fall down?"

My call was recorded and played a thousand times on the Internet. I can't bear to listen to it. All I remember was wanting to know where EMS was, how much longer before they got there, demanding they hurry, and answering insane questions like "How many steps?", "Is she still breathing?" And endless urgings to be calm.

I ran to the front door to make sure it was unlocked then ran back to her, cradling her in my arms. Her last breath was a soft exhale. Then all was still except for my sobs.

That's how emergency workers found me moments later: holding her body, rocking in agony, unseeing, sobbing.

Kathleen died December 9, 2001. We were as much in love that Saturday night as the day we moved in together fourteen years earlier, the second marriage for us both, passionate from first day till last.

When her husband Fred left her in 1987—at Christmas!, Kathleen, unemployed with a five year old daughter, found an entry level job at Nortel, the former telecom giant. I was finishing my second novel, *A Time of War*. 1987 was stressful for us both.

Living only a block apart, our romance could be seen as a soap opera cliché where neighbors seek solace and sex. But our longing and lust soon turned to love, for we found in each other what we'd been missing and desperately wanted—closeness, joy, and fun.

Yet we had to jettison the baggage of our first marriages. She said Fred had controlled everything, even instructing her how to peel a potato, so she deferred to me more than I wanted. I finally told her, "I don't give a fuck how you peel a potato, or even if we have potatoes."

Then came the day I moved my fork at the set table and she moved it back. I told her to stop acting like Patty who cared about such things. She swept the fork off the table. "I don't care if you eat with your hands." Then her eyes narrowed and she added, "Or if you eat at all."

We laughed and that set the tone for us both. Every day was fun.

She was a petite dynamo, 5'2'', 120 pounds. And smart. Valedictorian of her high school with two engineering degrees from Duke. And funny.

"For God's sake, don't tell anyone your College Board scores," she'd said after I'd foolishly told them to her. "I don't want anyone to know I'm living with someone so stupid."

Her scores, of course, were much higher, which she loved to rub in. I didn't mind; I'd finished in the lower half of my Duke graduating class, a C student and not ashamed of it, rationalizing that I'd gotten A's in Fraternity and Extracurriculars.

That last night had ended like so many with us sitting outside at the pool happy and content, drinking wine, talking, our two English Bulldogs snoring at our feet. It was warm for December, nearly 60 degrees and clear, the pool fountain sparkling from the underwater light.

We had a large house built in 1940 on nearly four wooded acres in an old section of Durham, North Carolina.

7

After Kathleen's death it was always cruelly referred to by the media as "The mansion."

Around 1am, Kathleen had got up to go in the house. She had an 8 am conference call, an unpleasant unanticipated intrusion on our plan to put up Christmas decorations, an annual tradition that took all day.

Earlier that afternoon we'd brought them down from the attic—48 candles for our 48 windows, 36 nutcrackers for each step in the hallway, two large wood reindeer for outside, and all the lights and ornaments for the tree, this year a twelve foot Fraser Fir that with its star would graze the living room ceiling.

We loved decorating the house, especially the tree because each ornament was special and brought back a happy memory. We'd sip wine and joyfully retell stories of each. The star! Hers from her childhood in Lancaster, Pennsylvania. A bizarre fat angel in a bikini. Mine from the Christkindlesmark in Nuremberg. We'd discuss what we'd get the kids for Christmas—they were coming home from college the following week—and fastened reindeer antlers on the bulldogs. Christmas was special and she wanted the house perfect for the girls.

But Kathleen had received notice of the conference call from a colleague around midnight right after we had watched a DVD movie—*American Sweethearts*. She was not happy about the conference call—Sunday was decorating day, not a work day.

She had cooked pasta and we'd decided to spend the night in because we'd gone to a party the night before and had danced until it ended around 1 a.m. We were tired, wanted only to snuggle on the sofa, so I'd picked up the film at Blockbusters.

Around 10:30 pm my son Todd and a girlfriend stopped by. After talking with us a few minutes, they went to a party and we returned to the movie.

Watching movies together usually took much longer than the film's running time as we'd pause it to improvise our own dialogue or make fun of the movie's plot holes. Watching TV was for us interactive, especially during Duke Basketball games. Both Duke graduates, we were old Cameron "Crazies". During intense moments, one of us often left the room, not returning until the other shouted that Duke had either made a comeback or had fallen hopelessly behind.

After finishing the movie, when we went into the kitchen to put away the wine and close up, I saw the answering machine blinking and pressed it to hear a woman say she urgently needed to talk to Kathleen. Kathleen called her back.

Helen Presling in Canada informed her of a phone conference next morning for which Kathleen would need to review some documents beforehand. She asked Helen to email the documents to my computer because she'd left her laptop at her office, then she hung up.

"Shit," she muttered, a not so rare expletive at this interference of her decorating plans.

Pissed, she went to the refrigerator to retrieve the wine, now in what our five children and I called "Nortel mode." In only a few years she had risen to Director of Communications.

Her rise was thanks to her brilliance, but she jokingly claimed she owed it to mimicking male bosses: "Men always have answers. A man never admits he doesn't know something." So she always had an answer to any question, even total nonsense and passed it on with a straight face and authority.

Once travelling through rural South Carolina to the beach, we drove by barren fields with dilapidated wooden houses, cars on concrete blocks, roofless barns, and lean-to sheds.

"I wonder what they grow here," I'd asked.

"Sheds," she'd answered.

But her relationship with Nortel was love/hate. She loved the money, earning a quarter million dollars a year, but she hated the environment; by temperament she was not a corporate person—she was too independent. Regimentation did not suit her.

Forced to attend a "sensitivity" seminar conducted by a black man, she balked. When he'd ask a question, she'd raise her hand, but he'd ignore her. Sometimes she'd be the only one with an answer; he'd still ignore her.

She came home furious. "He pretends I'm not even there. I'm not going back."

When I suggested that his point was invisibility, that she was meant to learn how blacks felt, she snapped, "I know what it's like to be invisible—I'm a *woman*. Don't you remember that conference in Ottawa?"

Indeed I did. She had called me in outrage after a dinner when several male directors had offered to drop her at her hotel.

"That was nice," I said.

"NO! They dropped me off because they were going to a whore house across the river in Hull. That's the most sexist abomination I've ever encountered."

"Did you want to go with them?" I joked.

She slammed down the phone. When she got back home I had to talk her out of filing a grievance. "Let it go. Maybe they all got clap."

"I certainly hope so," she said.

She was still pissed at the memory, and tonight's message added to her aggravation with Nortel, so we went outside with the rest of the wine and settled on chaises by the pool.

I told her the tele-conference was a minor inconvenience; we'd decorate what we could after the call and finish when she returned from Toronto. She was leaving Monday morning for a director's meeting, returning Wednesday—still days before the girls came home; we had plenty of time to prepare the house.

What else did we talk about except Nortel? I can't remember: certainly the kids and what we'd get them for Christmas—their lists were long but not extravagant. We talked for perhaps an hour. Then she said she had to go to bed to be ready for the phone conference and I watched her go up the stone path towards the house.

Wilbur and Portia, our lethargic English Bulldogs raised their heavy heads to watch, but any effort to move was too much so they stayed with me, also too lethargic to move: it was a beautiful magical night with the pool shimmering and stars glistening. I settled contentedly on the chaise. I was so happy, my life so good: I loved my wife, I loved my children, I loved my work—I had just heard that a book of mine had been optioned for a movie— I loved my house, I loved my dogs. I wanted this moment to last forever.

What did I say to her as she disappeared up the stone pathway? Something innocuous, I'm sure: Good night, love. See you in the morning. I'll stay out here a little longer then put the dogs to bed. I'll be up shortly.

What *are* the last words you would say to your beloved wife about to die?

You'd comfort her and say you love her. You'd beg: No, please don't die. Don't go!

But what if you didn't know she was only moments, a few steps from death? Instead just going out the door to work or school, maybe only to the grocery or into the house to go to bed.

Later, remorse and guilt haunted me for all that I did not say and I suffered a thousand pangs of what ifs as I relived that final moment: Why did I let her go? Why didn't I clasp her tightly and protect her from the horror? If only, if only….

Instead, I dozed contentedly, oblivious to the encroaching horror.

When I went in around 2am, leaving the dogs out to relieve themselves, I rinsed our wine glasses, set them on the marble counter and went to turn off the lights and bring in the dogs through the den at the other end of the house, but as soon as I left the kitchen I saw her sprawled at the bottom of the back staircase in a pool of blood. Motionless. Eyes open.

Stunned as if electrocuted, my breathing stopped. This couldn't be. I had just seen her! Everything was fine.

What happened? Oh Jesus! Jesus! I closed my eyes to block out the terror, but when I opened them she still lay on the staircase floor and blood was everywhere.

I froze. Had she been attacked? Was someone in the house? We had had several break-ins recently. Once, Kathleen's Blackberry had been stolen from the kitchen while we were watching TV, and our cars had been ransacked in the driveway so often that I no longer locked my Porsche, but left coins in the ashtray as a toll/contribution—protection money.

Recoiling, I backed into the wall to distance myself from the horror, but then terror evaporated. Kathleen needed help. I ran to her and lifted her into my arms. She was limp. Dying.

I knew what death looked like—eyes vacant, mouth slack. I had seen it many times in Vietnam and one of my sergeants in Japan had died next to me in a terrible car crash.

For a moment I just held her, too overcome to move, then I lay her head back on the floor and rushed to the phone. After the call, I held her in my arms, staring into her sightless eyes, urging her silently to live, but by the time EMS arrived, which felt like hours, but really was only minutes, Kathleen was dead.

Immediately after EMS, Todd and his girlfriend arrived. It was 2 am, their party over. Todd pulled me gently from Kathleen's body and called his friend Ben whose wife Heather was a doctor. Both arrived within minutes. Beyond dazed and horrified—this nightmare could not be real!--I wandered around the kitchen as EMS tried to revive Kathleen. I couldn't think, speak, pray. Finally, Todd plunged me onto the sofa like a rag doll.

In Vietnam, I had been a Marine officer responsible for the lives of my platoon. During the 1969 Tet offensive, I'd called in artillery, directed my men, and saved our position near the DMZ, but now, what could I do? I was helpless.

Then the police arrived; at least twenty swarmed through the house. They immediately and roughly separated us, putting Heather and Todd's girlfriend in the living room and Todd, Ben, and myself in my den. Do not talk to one another, they ordered.

Slumped on the sofa, I was too distraught to notice much of anything, but Todd sensed right away that the police were acting so hostile because they thought Kathleen had been murdered and that I had done it. Concerned by their blatant hostility and by my near comatose state, he called his uncle, my brother Bill, an attorney in Reno.

Bill told him not to talk to the cops, repeated the warning to me, then he asked to speak to the chief officer on the scene, Detective Art Holland—about forty, short, squat, thick necked, brutal. Bill told him that he was representing me and that no one was to question me without a lawyer present.

Ever afterwards I lived with the accusation that the first suspicious thing I did was "lawyer up," obviously a sign of guilt, though anyone knowing the judicial system or who's watched TV crime shows knows better than to talk to the police without an attorney present. But I would have; I *wanted* to tell them that Kathleen and I had been outside, that she must have fallen down the stairs when she came in, yet Todd forced me quiet as he took charge.

"Dad! Uncle Bill said don't talk. Don't say anything."

I couldn't understand—Kathleen was dead; I had lost the woman I loved. Why were the police so hostile? Not a bit sympathetic, and why did they demand the clothes I was wearing and Todd's too?

An officer went upstairs for new clothes and put the ones we'd been wearing in paper bags as Holland threatened Todd with arrest if he spoke to me again; Holland was furious with him for having called Bill, but Todd wouldn't shut up: "This is a free country. Do not tell me what I can and can't do in my own house."

Their confrontation jarred me into realizing that the police were indeed treating me like a murder suspect. I jolted forward on the sofa, finally focused, now more worried about Todd than myself. I knew my 6 foot, 180 pound, twenty-five year old athletic son wanting to defend his father was not about to take any shit, police or not.

Roused from my stupor—I needed to protect him— I called a lawyer friend who had run my campaign for mayor two years earlier. She rushed over, but police would not let her onto the property. They detained her on the street.

In the den Holland, ignoring Bill's warning, put his arm around my shoulder in a "comforting" gesture coaxing me to talk, but I shook him off and stepped outside the French doors to get air on the patio. Beyond the rose garden, the pool still sparkled, but the dogs were gone. Shocked by the commotion—sirens, whistles, flashing lights, and cops everywhere—they'd run barking inside, but the cops had corralled them in the washroom.

I went back into the den to sit on the sofa beside a still fuming Todd. I put my hand on his knee to calm him, but he remained stiffly tense, eyes furiously on Holland.

That night was the most miserable of my life, worse than any in war, even the night during Tet when several of my men were killed and I numbly escorted their mangled bodies to Graves Registration in Da Nang.

I would have given my life to save those men, but Kathleen *was* my life. Now she was gone. I had not saved her. Twisting on the sofa with grief and guilt, I kept going to the den door to see Kathleen down the long corridor still crumpled on the floor surrounded by EMT and police, then photographers and a camera crew videotaping everything, but each time I would start towards her, an officer restrained me. "Sit *down*, sir."

Finally Todd came to my side. He put his arm around me roughly and said in a harsh tone—he knew if he'd spoken gently, I would have broken and cried, "C'mon, Dad, sit down,"

On the sofa, he nudged me and nodded towards Holland. "The cops are out to get you, Dad. Don't say anything."

In the morning after a sleepless night in the den, I watched Kathleen carried out in a zippered body bag to a hearse. That's when the hideous finality struck—she was never coming back. That body bag was more brutal and searing than seeing her on the floor or later in a coffin. All her joy and vibrancy, her love, humor, and intellect carted away like refuse. I closed my eyes and rested my head against the den window, my heart wrenching so that I could barely breathe.

When I walked outside an hour later, flashing cameras blinded me. I stumbled as reporters shouted questions. At the sight of yellow crime scene tape stretched all over the property I froze. Finally my attorney who'd had to wait outside all night hugged me and led me away. "It's going to get worse," she said.

I never imagined how bad it could get or how long it would last, nor how much my children would suffer.

I now knew the police did not believe Kathleen had fallen down the stairs; they said there was too much blood in the stairway, though when the medical examiner arrived, he ruled it "accidental death."

And that is how her death certificate read, but after the ME left, police summoned Duane Deaver, a State Bureau of Investigation blood spatter analyst. Within an hour, without tests of any kind, he determined from blood on the walls and staircase that Kathleen had been beaten to death. This was a homicide.

Exactly what the police wanted to hear. And believe.

For several years I'd written a twice weekly column in the *Durham Herald-Sun* that focused on city corruption, the state's highest crime rate, and the most out of control gangs.

The police had been my frequent targets of ridicule. So had some politicians and the District Attorney. One column lampooned the police for claiming that while there were 17 gangs in the city, there were only 42 gang bangers, about 2 1/2 per gang. Others ridiculed the DA for ignoring

17

gang warfare while concentrating on illegal bingo parlors and prosecuting an underage teen for voting in a city election. I had given him the weekly Stupid Award. Twice.

I stopped writing columns in 1999 and ran for Mayor when gangs burned down an elementary school playground after torching the dental practice of a dentist who had called the police when he observed drug dealings next door—in a house owned by a previous Mayor. Such was the city's corruption.

My animosity with the police had become personal a year earlier when my car had been broadsided in the post office parking lot by a postal employee racing to pick up his child at day care. I'd had to accelerate to get out of his way and not be killed. A witness called the police. The officer who arrived knew the postal employee and did not want to write an accident report claiming it was unnecessary because damage to my car was less than $100. Pissed, I pointed to the crumpled rear end of my Porsche and said a damaged gas cap would cost more than that.

He had made me wait three hours pacing the parking lot furiously before he reluctantly filled out a report. When my insurance company totaled the car I complained to police headquarters stating that officers should write reports not make insurance claim judgements. He was counseled and of course he was at the house the night Kathleen died.

More recently, the Chief of Police had emailed me that because my newspaper columns had so harmed police morale, she'd had to spend an inordinate amount of time tending to the wounded feelings of unhappy officers. So, I attributed their hostile manner that night to rancor about my columns, a simple case of what goes around comes around—payback—and a natural reaction to their superiors' animosity.

Believing—hoping—I had killed Kathleen, her death became murder; I the sole suspect.

As soon as I left the house, they sealed it as a crime scene and would not let anyone in.

I remember little of the following days where I stayed mostly in bed at the home of my lawyer friend, twisting and moaning, unable to function, unable to grasp the horror. My life had been completely upended and I felt impotent to right it. It would never be right again.

My sons living in the area--Clayton in college, Todd working in Raleigh--never left my side. My daughters Margaret and Martha and my step daughter Caitlin, all in college flew in the next day as did my brother Bill.

We celebrated Margaret's 20th birthday at another friend's house across the street from our own, a grim affair in which we watched out the window, the cake untouched as thirty police officers conducted a grid search of our property looking for a murder weapon.

Nothing was found.

That's when anger finally began to fester in me: this was so wrong, so unnecessary, and so grievously painful to my children.

On the second night, Bill and I walked from my friend's house to my own a few blocks away, but when I drew near I stopped and clutched Bill's arm for support.

Ten police cars, a mobile crime unit, and four media trucks with strobe lights lined the street. All the lights in the house were on as police shuttled in and our carrying "evidence" from my children's bedrooms and my den to their van.

This wasn't so much a crime scene as a war zone.

"Oh my God," I whispered. Kathleen's death had become a circus, beyond surreal, worse than a nightmare. Bill led me back to my lawyer's house.

On the third day police released the house. Walking through the debris they'd left, I grimaced at the violation: they'd gone through every room, all my personal items, one girl's diary, and even tore out the air vent in another girl's room where they'd found a little weed.

Our bedroom had been trashed, clothes and shoes scattered everywhere, dresser drawers rifled. I straightened up the room, remade the bed and slept there every night, comforted to be in the bedroom surrounded by Kathleen's things. It wasn't scary. No ghosts. I went and stood in her walk-in closet a long time trying to revive her, breathing in the smell of her perfumes, fingering dresses she had once worn.

I didn't want to be anywhere else but in that room with her. I didn't want to let her go. I wanted her back. Desperately. I sat on the bed and cried.

The house was still alive with her—the huge kitchen with fireplace, marble counters, and table where we all had spent hours eating, talking, and laughing, the dining room where we ate on special occasions, the living room filled with belongings we had bought over the years, every object a memory of London, Paris, Florence, Athens, Venice, Tokyo, Hong Kong, Hanoi.

I longed to be alone with her and our memories, but reality kept brutally crashing in, vicious jabs stirring anger and resentment. Every day I grew more bitter.

After an autopsy, the new medical examiner changed the first ME's report, declared Kathleen had been murdered, dying from blunt force trauma, a gratuitously cruel and unwarranted conclusion because she'd had no skull fracture, no brain damage, *no* injury of beating or blunt force trauma.

Horrified, I gasped and threw the report down. How could the ME say that? It was not true. I saw her at the bottom or the stairs. She'd fallen.

Years later, long after the trial, DA notes revealed that the ME did *not* believe that Kathleen had died of blunt force trauma, but she'd been ordered to write that by her boss, the Chief Medical Examiner. Why? Because he was part of the state's team: police, district attorneys, and medical examiners work together; they do not contradict one another.

To my gratitude and relief, Kathleen's sister Candace made all funeral arrangements, selecting the cemetery plot and arranging for service at Duke Chapel. I was of no use. I couldn't function until the funeral home director called to tell me that Holland and another detective had come to take a vaginal swab from Kathleen and comb her pubic hair.

That blew me out of torpor. The police? At the funeral home? A vaginal swab?

What the fuck? But all I could manage was a stunned, "Huh?"

He explained that they wanted access to Kathleen's body. "I've never encountered such a thing," he said. "I told them no because they didn't have a warrant. Besides, the body has been washed and embalmed so any tests would be pointless."

My mental picture of bullet headed Art Holland bursting into the funeral home for a vaginal swab from Kathleen's corpse sickened me. This was beyond bearing. Disgusting. I now hated the police. They were out of control, gone rogue in a phony attempt to make a case of murder against me. And it didn't stop at the funeral home.

On the night of Kathleen's wake, my daughter Martha and I were upstairs dressing when we were startled by thunderous knocking at our front door.

Opening the door, my brother Bill was confronted by twenty police lined up thirty yards from the door to the driveway.

Holland said he had a search warrant. "Get out of the way, sir," he ordered.

Bill, ever the lawyer, demanded to see it, read it, then handed it back. "This is flawed. A page is missing. It's not a valid search warrant."

A lawyer from the police department then stepped forward with another copy.

Bill, after reading it said, "This is flawed too; it's not valid."

As Martha and I watched over the balustrade from upstairs, Holland yelled at Bill to get out of the way or they'd knock him down.

I gasped at the outrage. They were going to hurt my brother. The cops were totally out of control, like the Gestapo, but there was nothing I could do.

Later, *years* after I had been convicted and sent to prison, the North Carolina Supreme Court ruled that that search warrant was unconstitutional: "Woefully inadequate."

Then as Martha and I watched, the police rushed in, fanned out in all directions with several running into my den. Thinking we would all be at the funeral home, they had waited until then to show up and would have broken down the door had it been locked.

When a few days later at Bill's urging I hired a lawyer—Bill was not licensed to practice in North Carolina—his first question was, "Do you think the police would like to see you convicted of murder?"

I said yes because I knew they were angered by my critical newspaper columns, but to the lawyer's second question, "Do you think the police would lie or cheat to get a conviction?" I answered, "No." I was part of the rich white establishment—I still believed they wouldn't do anything unlawful: they might be incompetent, but they weren't criminal.

That belief changed a few days later when I saw police pictures of the "crime scene."

I stared at bedroom photos in disbelief and fury. The bastards! They had actually doctored the scene to incriminate me.

The police photos were nothing like how we'd left the bedroom that night. On the night Kathleen died, when I brought back the Blockbuster DVD's, she was taking a bath. We had made love on the bed in the bedroom and then went downstairs where she cooked dinner which we brought into the family room to eat while we watched the movie.

In the police photos, the bed sheets we'd straightened were a jumbled mess, and strategically placed on the floor by Kathleen's side of the bed was a used condom.

I couldn't believe it. "Is that a rubber?" I asked, pointing it out to my lawyer.

"Yes."

I furiously sailed the photo across the room. "The cops planted that. Kathleen and I didn't use condoms. She couldn't have more children."

This gross tampering with the scene hurt worse than them bursting into the funeral home. They were determined to frame me; there was no other explanation.

Later I learned the police had found the condom long left behind a nightstand and planted it by the bed, photographed it, then took it to test for DNA, thinking—hoping—it would be mine and someone besides Kathleen's, or with Kathleen's DNA and someone's besides mine. They never mentioned the condom in any discovery turned over by the District Attorney. Except for the staged photo I wouldn't have known about it.

When my attorneys got the test results, it turned out to have been used by one of my sons' friends when Kathleen and I had visited her mother in Florida two weeks earlier. The guys had had a party in the house. The friend had taken a nurse up to our room, then discarded the condom behind a nightstand, but he was from a prominent Durham family and his secret kept.

For me, seeing that condom discredited everything the police did thereafter and I began to feel fear: they had only one goal—to convict me of murder.

When the police burst into our house the night of Kathleen's wake, Bill told me to stay and watch everything they did. So steeled for yet another phony move, I observed from the den's doorway as they went through my desk drawers, disconnected my computer and took it with them along with another old one upstairs that hadn't been used in years.

Martha was so distraught by the police intrusion that I told her to go to the funeral home and explain what had happened and tell everyone I'd be late.

Hours passed as the police searched. I struggled for patience, biting my lips, fisting my hands, knowing the wake would be over soon, but I also knew any intemperance on my part would result in even more delays. When finally they left, I rushed to the funeral home. Three hundred people had come to pay their respects and offer sympathy, but I arrived after everyone had gone except for my family.

Kathleen's coffin was in a dimly lit room with a heavy saccharine floral scent to mask the smell of mortality, but that odor only emphasized death, and the sight of Kathleen, cold and immobile, arranged like a doll felt as awful as when she died in my arms: I knew what the medical examiner had done to her body—they had carved her up and shaved her skull then replaced her hair like a wig.

The Friday before, she'd brought a special dress to the dry cleaners that I was to pick up before meeting her at the airport on Wednesday; she was to be returning that afternoon from Canada and wanted to wear it to a reception at the Governor's mansion for the North Carolina Ballet. She joked she would change clothes in the car, mooning everyone on I-40.

Now she lay buried in that dress.

Seeing her wearing it, remembering all that had been and what would never be, I felt that most of me lay in that coffin with her, and I might have fallen had my sons not held me.

In Vietnam I had seen so much death and sorrow that I long ago had given up prayers and pleas to God, not because He didn't care or couldn't help, or even because He didn't exist, but because I believed *we* didn't matter: Life was ephemeral, death certain, often horrifyingly swift—young Marines alive one moment, dismembered and dead a second later. I had no illusions about our meaning in the cosmos.

I took off the yellow Versace tie Kathleen had bought me in Ottawa on her last Nortel trip and laid it on her cold hands, then I stood numbly by the coffin until my sons led me away.

Burial was a grim gray day. Rain falling lightly. I sat beside Veronica Hunt, Kathleen's mother, holding her hand, wanting to cry as much for her as for Kathleen. My children had lost a loving mother, I the woman I loved, but I felt that paled to a mother's lost child.

Leaving the cemetery, seeing Kathleen's coffin waiting for the grave to swallow it, I turned away and took a deep breath struggling to brace myself against her loss, but also for what I saw ahead: they deemed me a murderer.

I turned for a last look at the coffin and clenched my teeth. I had to put aside grief to fight for my children. For my own life.

2. ANOTHER DEATH

Several days after Kathleen's burial, I was on the sofa in my den waiting for my attorney David Rudolf, the state's most celebrated defense attorney—about 50, short with black hair, incredibly assured and impeccably dressed, with a great sense of humor, but not about himself. He had not been amused when I'd compared him to Richard Gere's manipulative lawyer portrayal in *Chicago*. Nevertheless, I liked and admired David and we got along fine. My brother Bill who was not licensed to practice in North Carolina had recommended him and his partner Tom Maher, a more cerebral and less theatrical attorney; they were a great team.

Both had grilled me about Kathleen's death.

"Why do you think she fell?" Rudolf had asked.

"Because I found her at the bottom of the staircase!"

"There are other explanations," he pointed out. "The police think you killed her there."

I knew he was trying to provoke me if only to see how I would respond to adverse questioning on the witness stand, so I'd drawn a deep breath. "But I didn't," I said calmly.

"So why did she fall?" Maher probed.

I'd gone over it a hundred times in my mind. "Alcohol, plus valium and Flexeril."

"Tell us about that," Rudolf said.

"We had brought Martha to college in August; Margaret and Caitlin were sophomores, so all three girls were gone. To celebrate our new life without live-in children, we had an Empty Nest party on Saturday, September 9, 2001; about 100 people came. There was lots of drinking. Around 1 am, 20 of us ended up in the pool when Kathleen dove head first into the shallow end. Horrified, we pulled her out stunned and confused. The blow had been so hard that she had lost her diamond earrings in the water."

"Did she suffer a concussion? Are there medical records?"

"Yes. On Monday, September 11, she went to work. When I went down to my den, I turned on the computer and saw the Twin Towers catastrophe. Just then Kathleen called in tears, I thought upset by the terrorist attack, but it was her neck injury; she said the pain was unbearable, so I took her to Duke Emergency. We were there from 11am until 8 pm. Doctors gave her a neck brace, Vicodin, and valium. She didn't work for a week, and when she returned to Duke the following week, doctors told her to continue wearing the neck brace, gave her more valium, and prescribed Flexeril. They were in her system when she died along with the alcohol we'd drunk. The neck brace was packed in her suitcase for the trip to Canada."

Rudolf nodded. "Sounds reasonable. Good enough for reasonable doubt if they try you. Anything else?"

"Yes. Just before going to college, Martha dyed her hair a color previously unknown in the spectrum. When I came back from the gym one evening, Kathleen was furiously pacing the kitchen. 'Go upstairs and fix things with Martha. We had a terrible fight. It's her hair.'

'What's wrong with it?' I'd asked.

'My God, go look. I can't stand it.' Suddenly she stumbled, pressed her hands to her eyes and groped towards a stool at the kitchen counter. 'I can't see. I'm blind. Call Henry.'

'Henry Greene is our optometrist. He told me to put her on the line. He says it's an optical migraine, she relayed to me. I took the phone. You sure she's all right? I don't need to take her to the hospital? He said no, the symptoms would go away shortly; if not, call him back. I hung up. Kathleen was staring blindly towards the refrigerator. 'Well, at least now I won't have to see Martha's hair.' "

Rudolf laughed at that just as I had. "Dr. Greene will verify this?"

"Of course. That's why I think she fell—Valium, Flexeril, alcohol, and perhaps an optical migraine."

Rudolf and Maher both nodded, apparently satisfied.

Now I was anxiously waiting for Rudolf who had called to say he had news. Since he didn't tell me what it was, I assumed it was bad, but I had no idea how bad it would be.

Wilbur and Portia were at my feet. The bulldogs now followed me everywhere as if I might disappear like Kathleen suddenly had. They and my children were my solace during this awful period that I spent listless—almost somnambulant, trying not to think or remember, just waiting and hoping things would get better yet fearing they wouldn't. I'd wake—reach out for Kathleen, heave a heavy sigh at her absence, then I'd try to regain sleep, postponing another day I didn't want to face. I had begun to feel like a boxer pummeled by a stronger opponent, the referee, and everyone in the audience who jumped into the ring to land blows.

When Rudolf arrived, he somberly handed me a sheaf of papers. "The autopsy report."

Cause of Death—Blunt Force Trauma. *Homicide.* Kathleen had been beaten to death. Murdered. It could not have been worse.

Reading the report, I felt excruciating pain. I rubbed my temples but that didn't help. Neither did massaging my forehead. "Jesus, Jesus," I moaned, then I sank down on sofa, the closed my eyes and thrust back into the cushions, shaking my head in denial. "No! This can't be true."

"I don't think it is," Rudolf said. "There's no skull fracture or brain injury, *nothing* to suggest a beating or homicide. Worse, the ME explicitly ruled out a fall. That's never done. That's for the police to decide after an investigation. They are working together to get you."

"Can this get any worse?" I asked in despair. Then I looked up pleadingly. "Make this go away, David. Doesn't innocence matter?"

"Not when cops think you're guilty; lots of innocent men are in prison. The public hates defense lawyers trying to get them out, but have no problem with cops who put them there."

I felt nauseous, not like I'd been punched in the stomach, but as if I'd been poisoned. My entire body hurt. Kathleen beaten to death—and the police thought I killed her?

Rudolf did not sympathize. "It's going to get a lot worse," he said.

"How?" I cried.

"The media has the autopsy. It'll headline every newscast tonight and run front page tomorrow. Warn the kids."

Too late. TV didn't wait for 6pm but interrupted programming with Breaking News: "The Medical Examiner and State Bureau of Investigation have determined Kathleen Peterson was murdered. Police consider Michael Peterson a Person of Interest in her death. "

Person of Interest meant murderer. Me. The media could not get enough: a daily and nightly barrage on the murder of Kathleen Peterson--photos of her, of the house, lurid descriptions of her death. I stopped reading the paper and didn't turn on the TV. The pain of her loss, being accused of killing her was more than I could bear. I felt so beaten down that I didn't want to get out of bed in the morning. I wanted to stay under the covers until everything was better, but there was no letting up. It got much worse.

A few days later, David arrived without warning to ask, "Who's Elizabeth Ratliff?"

I was at my desk, the dogs at my feet as always. I turned to him in surprise. "Liz? She was a close friend.

Margaret's and Martha's biological mother. Clayton's godmother."

"How did she die?"

Nona Bart, my Italian great grandmother who had come from Torino used to say that when you shivered, it was someone walking on your grave. As a child I didn't understand—how could anyone walk on your grave if you weren't dead? Yet now, as shivers passed through me, I understood. I felt footsteps above me, my world quaking from a new terror.

"David," I said slowly, almost afraid to ask because I didn't think I could stand another blow. "What's this all about?"

"The police think you killed Elizabeth Ratliff too, Mike."

"What!" I was beyond shocked; it was as if a demon had suddenly leapt in front of me, something beyond belief, totally unexpected. And horrifying.

Liz had been my first wife Patricia's and my closest friend. We had known her since we went to Germany in 1973. We'd travelled throughout Europe together. Patricia and Liz taught at the same elementary school at Rhein Main Air Force Base where Liz met and married George Ratliff, an Air Force Captain in 1981. They had two children, Margaret and Martha before he died in the 1983—the first casualty in the Grenada invasion.

Widowed with two babies aged nine months and 23 months, Liz fell into deep depression, suffered a bleeding disorder called Von Willebrand's disease—a less severe form of hemophilia—and died from a cerebral hemorrhage two years later in 1985. She was 43.

I didn't understand. "Liz had a stroke *sixteen years ago*. German and American military police investigated. German and American doctors said it was stroke. Why would anyone think I had anything to do with her death?"

This was incomprehensible. It made no more sense to me than if someone had told me that my children weren't mine. That I had killed my mother who wasn't dead. That the world was make-believe. "What are you talking about?"

"Liz's sister Margaret Blair called Durham police and told them Liz was found in her home at the bottom of her stairs. Just like Kathleen. She said she'd always been suspicious of her death."

I exploded. "Jesus fucking Christ. That's complete bullshit. Liz had a stroke. She was unhappy, depressed, and unwell. Her death was natural. Not a murder. Not an accident. A *stroke*! Why would I have killed her? To raise her two infant children? That's insane."

I jumped up in fury. It felt good to be angry, to finally get over despair and grief. "God damn that lying bitch Margaret Blair!"

Rudolf held up his hands like a traffic cop. "Mike, Mike, take it easy."

"My ass I will!"

Finally focused on something besides sorrow and pain, I stepped over the startled dogs and began to pace the den. Accused of murdering Kathleen was horrific, but now accused of murdering one of my best friends, the biological mother of my daughters was beyond bearing. I would not sit still and take this bullshit.

"If people think I killed Liz they'll think I killed Kathleen. Jesus, now I'm an international serial killer—the staircase murderer. You've got to stop this, David."

"Tell me about Liz and I will," Rudolf said calmly.

I dropped back on the sofa exhausted and out of breath. I could not put my mind around this new nightmare. I could barely breathe. It took a long moment for me to recover from this latest devastating blow. Finally I looked up, no longer angry, just sorrowful.

"Liz—Liz McKee was born in Rhode Island, raised devout Catholic. Black Irish Catholic. When she graduated from Salve Regina, a woman's college in Providence, she got a job teaching for the Department of Defense, first in Japan then Germany. That's where Patty and I met her in 1973. We were all the same age. Best friends."

Rudolf put down the pen he'd been taking notes with. "Was your relationship sexual?"

"No. We were like brother/sister. When her father died, the Department of Defense called *me* to tell her. We were that close. When we returned to the States in 1976, she stayed with us one whole summer. After Liz went back to teach, she met George Ratliff, an Air Force navigator. By the time we returned to Germany in 1980, they were living together."

"Ok. Now tell me about George."

Thinking of George dissipated my anger. Suddenly he was alive again, a good happy decent man full of life and love. My thoughts and voice softened at his memory.

"He was a big Texas Teddy Bear. He and Liz were very much in love. He was patient and gentle and she introduced him to a new world beyond the officers' club—

strange food and museums even. Liz had always been Auntie Liz to Clayton and Todd; when they married he became Uncle George."

"What were you doing in Germany?"

"I'd just published *The Immortal Dragon* and was writing *A Time of War*. When I was in Vietnam, Patty had gone to Europe to teach. She always wanted to go back. We were young, had money--why not live in Europe? So we went. That's where Clayton and Todd were born."

Rudolf nodded. "George died in 1983. How?"

I cringed, twisting on the sofa, still hurting from that memory. "George flew for 'The Secret Squadron'. Its mission was to fly the Frankfurt/Berlin corridor over East Germany. In 1979 they were sent to help the Contras overthrow the Marxist government in Nicaragua. Very Top Secret. George left in April 1983, leaving Liz with two babies, Margaret 14 months old, Martha two months."

I'd rarely spoken of these events 18 years earlier, but with them as vivid in memory and sorrow as if they'd happened yesterday, I bowed my head and closed my eyes. "On October 23, 1983—my 40th birthday—I got an official call telling me that George was dead. I hadn't seen him in 6 months. He was 33, a military officer in excellent shape. I couldn't believe it. When I asked where and how he died, I got no details. I was just told to tell Liz her husband was dead."

"Why you?"

"Because no one else wanted to tell her and I knew her best. No one knew what had happened, but then word leaked that the Squadron had been involved in the Grenada Invasion. 8000 troops invaded the island. 19 KIA, plus

36

George who died hours before the invasion. He was to be navigator in one of the planes leading the invasion. His death sent panic up the chain of command. Had he been poisoned? Was the invasion compromised?

"The Air Force cut orders for me to take Liz and the girls to Texas where George was to be buried. It took a week for his body to come from Central America. Liz was too distraught to go into the funeral home. I made all the arrangements."

I was silent a moment recalling that sorrow, placing Martha's felt bunny in his coffin, tucking it into his uniform, feeling the empty cavity of his chest: all the organs had been removed for a complete toxicology.

I shuddered, casting off that memory.

"Two days later, the little war over, other squadron officers arrived for the funeral. They drew me aside and told me that in his Will, George had designated me and Patty to be guardians for his children if anything happened to him and Liz. I was surprised because we'd never discussed that."

"So how did he die?"

I spread my hands and shrugged. "No one knows for sure—it became a conspiracy theory. One was that the CIA killed him. Complete nut stuff—why would the CIA kill an Air Force officer just before a war? The best reason was the one his fellow officers gave me."

"Which was?"

"That George had gone running the day before. He got bad sunburn. That night he groaned so loudly in his sleep his roommate asked if he was all right. George mumbled yes, but when his roommate tried to wake him at

4:30 a.m., he was dead. They believed he had an electrolyte imbalance from the sunburn and died of a heart attack."

"Do you believe that?"

"I do because the autopsy later showed he had scarring on his heart."

I lowered my head and didn't say anything more.

After a moment Rudolf nodded. "Ok, now tell me about Elizabeth."

"She never recovered. A 41 year old widow with two infants. She moved to a home near Patty and me in Germany, hired a nanny, Barbara O'Hare and resumed teaching. But her health declined, she lost weight and in November 1985 suffered such severe headaches that she called her mother in Rhode Island to tell her how much they hurt.

"A few days later, Barbara arrived around 7a.m. and found Liz at the bottom of her steps—the bedrooms were upstairs. She ran to our house. We rushed over. She was dead, her body still warm. Barbara called German police and an ambulance and I called military authorities."

"There was a complete investigation?"

"By both German police and the American military police. The German doctor said she'd had a cerebral hemorrhage. A pathologist at Frankfurt General Hospital did an autopsy and confirmed it. Half her brain was sent to Walter Reed in Washington which agreed with the findings. I escorted her body back to Texas where she was buried in Bay City beside George. That's the whole story."

Rudolf shook his head as if he were the one suffering. "Another woman dead at the bottom of the stairs. No question, the DA will summon a grand jury.

38

They'll indict you for murder. You have about a week before you have to turn yourself in."

"But I didn't kill Kathleen, and I just told you about Liz."

Rudolf headed for the door. "Two dead women, Mike."

I sank back into the cushions but waited until Rudolf let himself out before burying my face in my hands in despair. How could I break this to Margaret and Martha? Tell them I was now accused of killing their mother? And tell them and my sons that I was going to be indicted for murder? I was going to jail.

How could that be? I looked up to the ceiling as if an answer was there. My mind could not take this in. Ten days ago my world had been wonderful. In love. Happy. Now my world was shattered. Nothing would ever be right again.

Then the phone rang. I glanced at the Caller ID. How did she do it? Always when I most needed her. I wiped away my tears and tried to sound strong. "Hi mom."

"I'm calling to see how you are." Her voice was not that of an eighty one year old woman suffering unbearable pain from rheumatoid arthritis, but of a woman half her age in the best of health.

"I'm good. Everything's fine."

She knew better. "I love you," she said simply.

"I know, mom. I love you too. How's Dad?"

"Sober, but it's not yet noon. He loves you too."

I smiled. "I know."

There was silence, then mom said, "Well, that's all I wanted to say," and she hung up.

I reached down and patted the dogs. And smiled.

For now everything was all right again. My mother loved me. Dad too. I could face anything.

\

3. QUEER!

Some things that look easy end up difficult: opening a jar of peanut butter; telling the truth, while some things that appear difficult end up easy: going to war; rejecting God.

I didn't know what to expect when I faced my four children in my den to tell them that I was going to be indicted for Kathleen's murder and that the police thought I had killed Liz too. I sat nervously at my desk; they faced me anxiously from the sofa.

I did not bother to tell them I was innocent; it wasn't necessary.

"What can we do to help you, Dad?" Clayton asked. He had turned 27 a week earlier, the day of Kathleen's wake. Hard to celebrate over a coffin.

"Nothing," I said. "Rudolf says I'll have to turn myself in and spend some time in jail. Probably Christmas and New Year's."

"So we don't have to get you a present?" Todd asked. Always the comedian.

Margaret and Martha started to cry, then they got up and put their arms around me. I stiffened, not from physical pain but to shield myself from sorrow—mine and theirs.

"Is there anything you need to know?" I asked them. We had often talked about their biological father George dying and all the circumstances surrounding Liz's death.

They shook their heads. "Just tell us what we can do to help."

"I want you to decorate the house for Christmas. Kathleen and I got everything down from the attic. Put it all up, please. And stay strong." That proved unnecessary too.

Kathleen dead, a second woman found dead in similar circumstances. The media were brutal: "Another staircase murder!" Lightening had struck twice. It couldn't be coincidence—I had beaten two women to death and left their bleeding bodies at the bottom of a staircase.

As Rudolf had predicted, District Attorney Jim Hardin summoned the Grand Jury back from Christmas vacation, a first in city history. Only the Medical Examiner and chief detective were allowed to testify. Knowing the old joke that a Grand Jury would indict a ham sandwich, I was prepared for the result and turned myself in to the county jail on December 23, 2001.

The house I left was decorated for Christmas, but there was nothing festive when I appeared before a Superior Court judge. Hardin said he had not decided whether to seek the death penalty, so I was not allowed to post bond. Instead I was stripped, searched, given an orange jumpsuit and placed on the protective custody block of the Durham County Jail.

My children had to spend that sorrowful holiday alone, but for me the time passed quickly without incident in a single cell. It was almost a relief to be locked up away from the media. I adjusted easily knowing that it was temporary because Rudolf had assured me that Hardin would not seek the death penalty; he was just trying to make my life miserable. Bond could be posted with $1,000,000 in property at the next hearing.

But Hardin made a spectacle of the bond hearing, milking it for publicity which backfired on him when he unexpectedly called Todd to the stand.

Todd, surprised, wary, and pissed hunkered down in the witness chair and glared at the DA. Hostile witness? Oh yeah. No comedian now.

Hardin wanted to know about a Power of Attorney I had executed for Todd and Clayton to pay house bills—mortgage, electricity, water—living expenses, and next semester's tuition for the girls, but the DA tried to turn it into something nefarious: I wanted Todd to sell all my assets so that I could flee the country, therefore no bond should be allowed.

Not sure where this was going and unsure how to protect me, Todd decided that knowing nothing, admitting nothing was the best way to defend his father.

DA Hardin: Mr Peterson, let me show you State's Exhibit A and ask whether you're familiar with this document?

Todd: At this time I couldn't tell you.

DA: Has your father executed other powers of attorney to you in the past?

Todd: At this time I could not tell you that either.

DA: You don't know whether your father has executed other powers of attorney to you?

Todd: Are you asking me the same question twice?

DA: Well, this power of attorney was executed on the 10th of December 2001. Is that what you see?

Todd: Yes, of course I see it. You just handed it to me."

DA: Was this power of attorney executed by your father on the 10th of December.

Todd: Are you telling me that, sir. Or are you asking me did he sign this, or what?

DA: Yes.

Todd: I could not tell you at this time.

And on and on it went for another fifteen minutes until the Judge finally shouted in exasperation, "Answer the dad gum question."

Todd: What was the question?

I buried my face in my hands to keep from laughing. Rudolf was the lawyer I wanted to defend me, but Todd was indeed the Praetorian I wanted beside me in this war.

Hardin was furious. And unforgiving. Todd had been so hostile and uncooperative that Hardin decided that *he* must have murdered Kathleen and that I was covering up for him, so he had the police investigate Todd thoroughly. They spoke with everyone at the party where he'd been that night. A hundred people. Todd was the ultimate fraternity/party animal, hard to miss. Had he ever left the party? A hundred witnesses said no. They talked with the girl he was with. She swore he was with her the entire time.

Years later, *15 years* later, Hardin told the BBC that he still believed Todd had something to do with it. That wasn't his worst though. While I was in jail, the police searched the house yet again unsuccessfully for a murder weapon. Margaret asked to get two Blockbuster videos that

44

needed to be returned. The police said no. Send the late fee bill to the DA, they sneered. So she did. The result? Hardin tested the stamp she licked on the envelope for DNA to compare with mine to see to see if she was my biological daughter. Of course the result was negative. And he didn't pay the late fee.

I posted bond with property. The homecoming was warm but didn't last long—the girls returned to college, Martha at the University of San Francisco, Margaret to Tulane. Clayton lived with Becky a few miles away, and Todd moved in with me.

Just after my release Rudolf asked, "Who's Brad?"

We were in my den. The trite clichés that your breathing stops, your chest is ripped open and your heart squeezed with crippling pain didn't capture what I felt: a huge hand crushing down, grinding me to nothing.

I didn't say anything for a moment, staring unseeing straight ahead.

Like a good lawyer, Rudolf knew the answer to the question he'd asked. "Tell me everything, Mike."

The secret I had sought to hide my whole life— about to be exposed. Brad was a military policeman at Fort Bragg. He was also a male escort.

I discovered I was bisexual at 11 though I didn't know the term for it then. I was madly in love with Melanie, a girl in my 6th grade class. I fantasized about her, but one night the shortstop on my baseball team popped into a masturbatory fantasy. I was very confused. I'd never had a male/male sexual thought before. I had no idea where it came from, but I realized then that I was attracted to guys as well as girls.

"The police found gay porn on your computer," Rudolf said. "And an email exchange with 'Brad'."

I cringed inwardly. "It had nothing to do with Kathleen's death."

"But it looks terrible. The media will go crazy. Help me out with this, Mike."

"There's no helping, David. I'm bisexual."

"Kathleen dead, Liz dead, gay pornography, a male escort. Could you make this any more difficult for me?" David asked.

Despite my pain and embarrassment, I laughed. "This isn't about you, David." But of course it was. Defendants are incidental to big time defense lawyers—it's *their* case, *their* reputations, not the defendant's life. Or death.

So I explained the best I could. "When I was young, you were straight—normal—or queer. There was no alternative lifestyle. Homosexual activity was the butt of jokes—and illegal—so *any* gay activity was hidden. But "gay" was not the word then: you were queer, homo, a faggot--or worse, so those of us who could hide their nature did; those who couldn't were reviled. Homosexuals were effeminate mincing queens."

Rudolf heaved a heavy sigh. "Mike, I'm Jewish; I know discrimination. I grew up in New Jersey, but your jury is here—the Deep South. Not an enlightened venue."

That proved true with this newest media bombshell—a devastating front page and prime time outing: I had lied about my sexuality, so I must have lied about not killing Kathleen. This became the lynchpin of

46

the prosecution's case—everything I said was a lie because it was not possible to be bi-sexual and happily married.

All my neighbors shunned me. All my friends save a couple deserted me.

At first I was shocked—these were professional people, liberal Democrats, people who had known Kathleen and me for years—had been to our house; we'd been to theirs. They knew us a devoted loving couple. Fucking hypocrites!

It's such a cliché–boy discovers he likes boys. He's told it's an abomination, hears the jokes and degradations and tells them himself. That's what I did. I hid my desires and led a life of lies. I was a coward.

Should I have been honest at eleven when I discovered my inclinations? What if I had told the shortstop about my feelings? All I know for sure is that I wouldn't have been on the ball team any longer. And I liked playing ball.

In the fifties and sixties growing up in a military environment (my father was career Army), playing sports, living in a fraternity, as a Marine, homosexuality was an unlawful detestable perversion. Perhaps in a cosmopolitan environment I would have been accepted, but not on military bases and certainly not in the Marines. Before Don't Ask, Don't Tell—it was just Don't.

You can't retrace the road taken. I took the well-travelled one--deception. Had I taken the less travelled--truth, I would not have had the love of wonderful women nor had my lovely children. There would have been no Marines, no books like I wrote, no sons, no daughters. My life would have been completely different—maybe not worse, maybe better…but I'm glad I didn't travel that road for there would not have been Clayton, Todd, Margaret, and Martha in my life. There would not have been Kathleen or Patricia.

I hadn't been brave; I lived a lie all my life. I could not overcome my upbringing when homosexuality was a perversion. I could intellectualize but not emotionalize my bi-sexuality. Perhaps cowardly, but not murderous.

I could have ended the deception at any time, but why reveal a "dirty" secret if it could remain secret? The lie had become second nature—the lie *was* me.

Moreover, I did not want to change or be "reprogrammed". I loved loving women and I liked liking guys; I enjoyed sex with both. I didn't want to give up one for the other.

It was the most intimate part of me, and I did not want to lose it. Besides, there was no changing—maybe biology or genetics, but in any case beyond my control.

I'm glad I hid the truth about myself from Sigma Nu, for I would not have had those men as my fraternity brothers. I'm glad I withheld it from the Marines for I loved the Marines, was a good officer and saved numerous lives in Vietnam.

But I was wrong to deceive Kathleen. I didn't tell her; I cheated her of a deeper and more profound marriage. I know she would have accepted the truth because she was wise, understanding, generous, and loving. She loved without restrictions or prejudices and she could have brought me a peace that I had never had.

Did the deception make me a bad person? The police, DA, and most of my friends thought so. The lie about my bi-sexuality disgusted them, but I also think the bi-sexuality itself disgusted them. That's what I had been afraid of.

They would not accept that a bi-sexual could have a loving marriage. Only Kathleen could have convinced them, but she was dead, so they accepted the DA's Domino theory: I had lied about my bi-sexuality; therefore I was lying about everything. Kathleen had discovered the secret when she saw the Internet porn and I killed her. A simple tidy scenario. Completely false.

The lie didn't have anything to do with her death, but it took on gargantuan dimensions. The lie proved my undoing.

Sex and murder, money too—we lived in a mansion; we were rich—the media could not get enough: Murderer; Liar; Pervert. Hammer blows day after day. I didn't feel shame as much as embarrassment, but that soon turned to anger. How could people judge me without knowing me or the facts?

Thank god for Todd who moved in with me. He never let me leave the house alone for wherever I went, people stared with accusation and condemnation. Todd would tense, ready to intercede if necessary and no one ever approached.

Nevertheless, the toll was grueling. I felt old and tired sometimes unable to go on; sometimes not wanting to go on.

Holding my head up was hard with blows constantly raining down--Murderer! Queer! Liar! But I would steel myself, yet when I saw those condemning looks, I'd think with dread: these are my "peers". They'll be on my jury. I'd try not to be afraid, but fear would squeeze me, and in private I would feel cold.

I'd shiver, and feel footsteps on my grave.

4. PRE-TRIAL

In Kafka's *The Metamorphosis*, George Samsa wakes one morning to find himself turned into cockroach or dung beetle, some kind of horrible vermin. He has no idea how it happened, and he comes to a miserable end without ever learning why it happened.

I spent nearly two years being transformed by the media, police, and DA into vermin, came to a miserable end, and it made no more sense to me that it had to Samsa.

My transformation wasn't overnight, but like Dorian Grey's portrait--gradually growing more grotesque until there was a monster on the canvas.

In trials there are two artists, the DA and the defense attorney. The defense attorney uses a soft brush with pastels to paint a sympathetic portrait. The DA slashes brushstrokes with vivid clashing colors to paint a gruesome frightening portrait.

While it is not necessary to prove motive in 1st Degree Murder—just that it was willful and premeditated—juries want to know *why* the accused committed the crime, so DA's always supply a motive. In my trial, DA Jim Hardin provided two: sex and money. Explosive reds and greens, blacks and yellows.

One day during pre-trial which went on for over a year, Gladys Parker, our housekeeper for ten years, a lovely woman about my age, ran—a full out run--shouting into my den where I was at my computer. She'd been eating lunch in the family room as she watched TV.

"Mr. Peterson, Mr. Peterson, you're on TV!"

I didn't bother to turn around; I'd been front page and prime time TV every day for six months. "Mrs. Parker, I am always on TV," I said calmly.

"NO! You have to see this," she insisted.

So I followed her and saw my picture plastered on the screen as two mutilated bodies were dredged from the Pacific Ocean, a woman's and a baby's. What the fuck?

It was the Scott Peterson case; the network had mixed our photos.

I just shuddered and wondered who had the better libel lawsuit—Scott or myself?

There were over a dozen pre-trial hearings. In one, Candace Zamperini accused me of using a blow poke to kill her sister. She had given Kathleen the 3 foot long hollow copper fireplace tool when Kathleen and Fred were married. When she came to Kathleen's funeral, she noticed that the blowpoke was missing. She told the DA it must have the murder weapon.

The blowpoke weighed about a pound and could have been bent in half by a child. No one had seen it for four years, including Kathleen's daughter Caitlin. Though the idea that it could have been used to kill Kathleen was ridiculous, Hardin, desperate for a murder weapon, bought Candace's theory. The blowpoke became the murder weapon!

When the ME agreed that it could have been, I began to worry. It was missing! And a thorough search of the house and yard did not turn it up.

The DA and police believed that I'd hidden the blowpoke after beating Kathleen with it. The idea was so ludicrous that I went online and ordered three more for Rudolf to demonstrate to a jury that it was impossible to beat anyone to death with it.

But that proved unnecessary because near the end of the trial, the blowpoke was found. Clayton was working in the garage late one night restoring his 1966 Mustang when he saw it propped in a dark corner covered with cobwebs. He showed his sister Margaret and together they woke me. I immediately called Rudolf and Tom Maher. Maher rushed over on his motorcycle. He and Rudolf photographed it in the corner and called Judge Hudson.

The next morning, Hudson came to the house, authorized Rudolf to retrieve it, and David sent it for testing which proved that it was not dented and there was no blood on it.

Once it was introduced in court and handed to Detective Holland, the prosecution, after extolling the blowpoke theory for a year, never mentioned it again.

This and everything else noteworthy in the case was filmed by a French film crew that was practically embedded with our family during pre-trial and trial.

Jean de Lestrade won an Academy Award for Best Documentary in 2001. *Murder on a Sunday Morning* was a film about a fifteen year old black wrongly accused of murdering a white woman in Jacksonville, Florida. The police brutally beat a confession out of him. When that was exposed and the youth's alibi confirmed, the defendant was released.

Now Lestrade wanted to compare how justice worked in the American judicial system for a poor black and a wealthy white. He read about my case and contacted Judge Orlando Hudson, DA Jim Hardin, and my attorney to propose a film that would document a trial from the prosecution, defense, and judicial points of view. No money would be paid.

We all agreed and promised to give the film crew full access to our deliberations.

I in particular wanted this because I had been writing newspaper columns critical of police, the DA, and city politicians for years and had little faith in Durham's police and judicial system. I worried that I would not get a fair trial and wanted the entire process documented.

When we first spoke, Jean de Lestrade said he did not know whether or not I was guilty, but the documentary would reveal the truth. I told him he could film anything he wanted, ask me anything, but in the end, I was confident the documentary would show that I was innocent.

Within a month, Hardin backed out, and since there was little to film of Judge Hudson before the trial began, the French crew concentrated on me and my legal team. They would show up unannounced at the house and film my conversations with my kids, brothers and lawyers. We never denied them or held anything back.

At first it felt uncomfortable being filmed, but the crew was so unobtrusively ubiquitous, that after a while we ignored the camera. We were in a reality show, but we weren't acting.

Allowing them to film everything was the wisest decision I made, for during the trial, witnesses lied and committed perjury to convict me; it was all on film.

Six months after Kathleen died, in the middle of pre-trial hearings, my brother Bill called to tell me Mom had suffered pulmonary aspiration and was on life support. There was no hope.

I flew to Reno, took a cab to St. Mary's, raced to her bedside and stood over her with my brothers. We embraced, stroked her hand and forehead, whispered good-bye, and a nurse turned off the machine. My brothers cried; I couldn't; I had no tears left after Kathleen's death.

Then tragedy turned to comedy. Bill dropped me at the funeral home two days later to oversee arrangements for the wake that night. "I'll be back in fifteen minutes," he said.

I went into the viewing room, saw mom in the coffin and bowed my head. Hours passed—*four hours* in the room with my mother in her coffin. I felt like Meursault in Camus's *The Stranger* and finally curled up on a pew to sleep. An hour later, Bill shook me awake.

"How can you sleep with your mother dead in front of you?"

"Where have you been?" I yelled loudly enough for the funeral director to rush in.

"At the office."

"Your mother's in a coffin and you're at the office? My God, the wake starts in an hour. I'll just wait here until everybody shows up."

An hour later my brothers sat Dad beside me. He was pissed. "Why am I here?"

"It's for mom," I said.

"She's dead," snapped the old colonel. A fatalist—dead was dead; the bullet with her name on it had found its mark as would the one for him—he had no interest in the proceedings. He wanted to go home and drink. At least now mom wouldn't be there to bitch at him.

As my brothers greeted family and friends, Dad grew more restless. Despite warnings—Dad was 85 and definitely slipping—many came to express condolences to the bereaved widower, but Dad was having none of it. Practically yelling at each mourner who approached, he'd shout "What an asshole!"; "Your mother never liked her."; "They cheated at bridge."

As they'd recoil, I'd say, "Thanks for stopping by."

The next day was the burial and the following day I flew back to Durham. Just in time for another volcanic eruption. After the media exploded with news that Liz Ratliff had been found at the bottom of her stairs in Germany seventeen years earlier, DA Hardin sent Assistant DA Freda Black and Detective Art Holland to investigate Liz's death.

I watched their festive send off on TV in disgust. At the airport, a throng of well-wishers cheered Freda and Holland like troops being sent off to war, even presenting Freda with a good luck teddy bear.

The circus had gone international.

Freda and her team talked with German officials who had investigated Liz's death and had found nothing suspicious. They took pictures of the house and staircase, interviewed a neighbor, talked with Barbara Malagnino, nee O'Hara, the girls' nanny who had married the taxi driver who'd driven her to the house that fateful morning, and spoke with friends who had gone to the house after Liz was found dead.

When Freda et al. returned to Durham, fanning the flames of the media inferno, DA Hardin sought to exhume Liz's body, buried 18 years in Bay City, Texas. Judge Hudson gave permission for the exhumation and for the body to be transported to North Carolina so the medical examiner who'd autopsied Kathleen could re-autopsy Liz to determine if she too had been murdered.

We were caught in the middle: an exhumation was a gross violation which would shatter Margaret and Martha, but to oppose it would make it appear that we were hiding something, so we didn't contest it.

An exhumation!

The media went into frenzy. Every local station sent a camera crew to film the event.

Mrs. Parker and I were glued to TV the day Liz's coffin was lifted from the grave as church bells tolled twelve noon. God himself couldn't have been staged it better had He been DA: A cemetery, church bells, resurrection. They might as well shoot me now, I thought.

After loading Liz's coffin into a hearse, Detective Holland drove it 1250 miles to Chapel Hill, filmed all the way by the French. A highlight was a scene of him in his room at a motel where they had stopped for the night peering from behind curtains to make sure that I wasn't in the parking lot hearse-jacking Liz's corpse.

The arrival of the hearse and unloading the coffin at the medical examiner's office was televised live on every channel. Of course after the autopsy, the medical examiner concluded Liz had been beaten to death exactly like Kathleen though half her brain was missing—sent eighteen years earlier to Walter Reed which had confirmed natural death: cerebral hemorrhage.

I had predicted this result to Rudolf and told him that I wouldn't be surprised if they "discovered" a blowpoke in the coffin.

The media was orgasmic—the most sensational trial in North Carolina history: Murder! Exhumation! And for the piece de resistance--Porn! Not regular porn, fellatio and sodomy for "normal" people, but Gay porn! Men with men sodomy and fellatio. Abominations!

Poor Mrs. Parker! And my poor children.

If I could have fled or disappeared, I would have, but there was no escape; all I could do was steel myself each day for new humiliations. Grit my teeth. Hold my head up.

One day in the middle of the horror show, my PI Ron Guerette, a former Charlotte, North Carolina police officer who'd investigated over a hundred murders--silver hair, silver mustache, tough and intelligent, Hollywood's dream PI--came to the house with a copy of Detective Art Holland's interview notes with Dennis Rowe.

"Did you know Rowe?" Ron asked.

"Yes. He was a close friend of Kathleen's sister Lori. The Rowe's were neighbors in Lancaster, Pa. When Kathleen was in high school, she baby sat the four Rowe boys. Dennis came to our house several times to see Lori and Kathleen's mother when they visited us."

"Did you have sex with him?"

No. Not my type."

"Not a Marine?"

"Hardly. He's slight and effeminate. And a cripple."

"Well, he claims he had sex with you. But he won't testify at your trial."

"I guess not. That would be perjury!"

Ron handed me the note: "If you want to know about Mike Peterson and the gay community, ask Tyrone Lacour."

Perplexed, I looked at Guerette. "Who's Tyrone Lacour?"

"You don't know him?"

"Never heard of him. I have no idea why Rowe said that. What does Lacour say?"

"Either Holland didn't follow up, or it was a dead end because there's no record of any interview with Lacour."

That was the end of it. Neither Dennis Rowe nor Tyrone Lacour were mentioned at trial, but one year *after* I went to prison, Tyrone Lacour murdered Dennis Rowe— beat him brutally with a bar bell, duct taped his head together, and stuffed him upside down in a garbage can.

When I learned that, I didn't know what to think. Coincidence? It remains a mystery.

While Dennis Rowe was a footnote in my trial, "Brad" became a headliner.

Brent Wolgamott was an MP at Fort Bragg who augmented his income as a male hustler—or perhaps he augmented hustling with his military salary. His nom de plume was Brad, his website—Soldierboy, with pictures and lots of references from satisfied customers.

I found him on an Internet search of male escorts. He was exactly what I was looking for: young, blond, military, and attractive. We exchanged emails; I wrote that I was in love with my wife, but wanted sex without involvement. We set a date to meet, but at the last minute he cancelled. He emailed me an apology, but I didn't respond. There was no further contact.

The police discovered our emails in the computer search and tracked him down. They threatened him with criminal prosecution unless he cooperated.

"Cooperate how? We never had sex; we never *met*," I told Rudolf and Guerette.

"That's not the point," Guerette said. "It's to smear you. If there'd been a rumor you'd had sex with an animal, they'd put your picture on TV with a pig's. They'd subpoena farmers."

They did subpoena Brent and threatened him with violations of the Uniform Code of Military Justice as well as civilian prosecution for crimes against nature if he didn't appear.

He contracted Rudolf for help. David engaged a lawyer for him who negotiated a deal—immunity from all prosecution if he would testify.

"Testify to *what*," I asked Rudolf. "Nothing happened."

"It's just to get him on the stand. That's all they want."

Brad and I would finally meet. In court. On TV!

To close off the money motive, we hired a former FBI financial expert to examine our assets that included six rental properties which brought in $5,000 a month, our

60

incomes, savings and investments, income tax forms, and all our liabilities—car payments and credit card debt.

"Your credit card debt is too high; you should pay it off," he advised.

"But were they financially healthy?" Rudolf asked.

"Very," he said. "More than most. More than me. Worth about $2,000,000."

My lawyers and children cautioned me against reading Internet comments on the case, but like rubber necking a car wreck, I couldn't help myself. I wanted to see what people were saying. Bad decision; the bloodlust of vitriolic message board posters was worse than the murderous frenzy of a Roman Forum crowd.

Evil, sick, creepy were common troll descriptions of me. I was shocked at the malice.

Worse were distorted facts—that I had murdered my first wife Patricia (who sat front row in court every day in support of me), drowned my dog, beaten my children, had an affair with Liz, fathered Margaret and Martha, etc. etc. Christ, *I* would have convicted me.

At night I'd go to bed not caring if I woke for I knew tomorrow would be another day of torment—not just for me, but for my children seeing their father trashed: murderer, liar, queer, etc. It was so depressing, so discouraging, so wrong that I could barely drag myself through the seemingly endless days. Weeks. Months.

Wilbur helped pull me through. I'd sit slumped on the sofa in my den, and the old bulldog, twelve then, would waddle in. He'd look at me, sense my unhappiness and put his heavy head on my thigh gazing up with sorrowful eyes more forlorn than mine.

I would laugh: I can't have my *dog* feeling sorry for me, so I'd pat his head and say, Treats!, and together we'd pad to the kitchen to recover.

Jury selection went on for two months. I participated every day in their selection--seven women and five men who claimed to be impartial. Surely they would see my innocence.

There was no motive, no murder weapon, no domestic abuse, nothing to prove that I had killed Kathleen. We had experts—Henry Lee, one of the most famous crime scene investigators and forensic scientists in the world, Jan Leestma, author of the text *Forensic Neuropathology*, and Dr. Faris Bandak, Director of Head Injury Research at the Department of Transportation, a mechanical engineer who had written numerous texts on the mechanics of brain injury.

But the prosecution was ready too. After creating a mudslide, they had a second woman dead at the bottom of a staircase. They had bi-sexuality. They had Brad.

And they had SBI Special Agent Dwayne Deaver.

5. TRIAL

Entering the courtroom on the first day of my trial felt like walking into a packed theater for a Broadway play. Or to blockbuster movie; a horror show.

Right away I spotted the Internet trolls, gruesome looking women sitting like Madam Defarges, only without knitting needles. They glared at me the whole time then went home to post poison.

The French film crew was there along with Court TV, cameras from local stations, and newspaper reporters. My kids sat behind me with my brothers, my first wife Patricia, and numerous friends. Sitting behind the prosecutors were Caitlin, and Kathleen's two sisters Candace and Lori with their husbands.

It was like a football game with fans on opposing sides.

When the jury filed in, I gripped the edge of the Defense table so tightly that my knuckles turned white. My life was at stake, in the hands of twelve "peers" with only two possible verdicts—Guilty or Not Guilty.

Nervous doesn't capture the terror I felt, though Rudolf told me to sit calmly and look intent. Don't react to anything, he said.

He seemed relaxed and confident, but then—it wasn't his life at stake. Just his reputation, which I think meant just as much to him. Looking every bit an intelligent intense attorney from New Jersey, there was nothing slow, measured, or southern about him

The prosecutors seemed relaxed and confident too.

DA Jim Hardin was—no other words for it: a good ol' boy, or as everyone seemed to agree—a Boy Scout. His expressions were non-existent and his speech measured. Slow. Excruciatingly slow. His mother, Mama Hardin sat a few rows back and brought cookies daily to those on the correct, prosecution side.

Assistant DA Freda Black was—for no better word, enthusiastic: flamboyantly dressed with lots of make-up, her facial expressions exaggerated and her speech…Southern. Todd said he thought grits were going to fall out of her mouth every time she opened it.

Superior Court Judge Hudson, a former prosecutor, was perfect for TV—looking benignly judicial with flashes of humor.

The jury, a mix of whites, blacks, men and women sat upright interested and fair.

The prosecution opened exactly as we expected: they would prove that I had beaten Kathleen with a blowpoke, let her lie on the floor at the bottom of the staircase, and then beat her again when she stood. All the elements for 1st Degree murder.

Rudolf began with what many considered a great mistake. He said Kathleen and I were a devoted loving couple: soulmates.

That was what the DA had hoped Rudolf would say because it immediately allowed rebuttal. Having introduced our relationship as loving and devoted, Hardin could bring in evidence to prove it wasn't. Bi-sexuality. Gay porn. The emails to Brad. Brad!

How could there be a loving relationship with all that?

But I didn't fault Rudolf. Kathleen and I *were* a loving couple, soulmates: bi-sexuality had nothing to do with that. How could Rudolf talk about us without saying that we were in love and devoted to one another?

I wanted him to say that, but neither of us anticipated the vitriol and homophobia which emerged. We misread the audience, those jurors.

Perhaps another mistake Rudolf made was trying to prove that Kathleen fell down the stairs. I believed that she did—she was found at the bottom of the staircase; it was the most logical conclusion.

But once he attempted to prove that, he set himself up.

All he had to do was present reasonable doubt that I'd bludgeoned Kathleen to death. He didn't need to present an alternative theory, but once he stated emphatically that she fell, he had to prove it, so the trial became a battle between two theories for the jury to decide—beating or fall.

It might have been better to simply cast doubt on the beating. By putting forth an alternative theory, he had to defend it. He made the DA's job easier by opening the defense to attack.

But Rudolf was magnificent attacking the prosecution's case.

He asserted that Kathleen and I were a devoted loving prominent public couple. No one could say we had ever argued, had a problem, or were anything but loving.

No one, and God knows the prosecution had looked, he said.

There had never been a hint of domestic abuse.

To counter money as motive, he didn't have to present our former FBI expert. He got the *prosecution's* financial expert to admit there that we were wealthy, living within our means, and had no money problems. We had credit card debt, but Kathleen had been deferring 80% of her salary into a savings program. If we needed money or wanted to pay off credit cards, she could have reduced the amount she deferred.

For me, Rudolf's greatest coup was destroying the prosecution's theory that Kathleen had viewed pornography on my computer after her call from Canada about the next morning's teleconference. Hardin argued that when she had accessed the computer to see the Nortel emails, she saw the porn, and horrified, confronted me. We fought and I killed her.

Over Rudolf's strenuous objection—my computer had been seized in an unconstitutional search (the NC Supreme Court later unanimously ruled the search had been unconstitutional)—Hudson allowed in the pornography found on the computer.

"Pure T Filth," shrieked Freda Black, waving photos of men with men sex before shocked matronly jurors, then she triumphantly handed them the photos.

When Hardin put his computer expert on the stand to verify that there were hundreds of pornographic images on my computer, Rudolf sprung his trap.

When was the computer last accessed? He asked.

4 pm, the witness replied.

Were the Nortel files that had been sent to Kathleen opened? No.

Could Kathleen have seen any pornographic images that night? No.

He reaffirmed that: You are telling this court that Kathleen Peterson did not go on Michael Peterson's computer that night. She did not open the Nortel files or see any pornography.

That is correct, the computer expert stated.

So much for the fight.

There was no money problem and we hadn't fought. I wanted to pump my fists after these revelations, but of course I sat stoically.

That however, proved difficult when Hardin brought up Elizabeth Ratliff's death.

To me and my children, the most disgusting moment in the trial came when Freda Black introduced into evidence pictures of Liz in her coffin, exhumed after 18 years in the grave.

Parading the photos around the courtroom, she thrust them into Margaret and Martha's faces. They ran sobbing out of the courtroom. I ran to comfort them.

It was an obscene demonstration. Vicious and heartless.

Fifteen years later, after Freda was found dead in her house, Margaret and I talked about that trial moment. Neither of us took satisfaction in Freda's death and we both felt sorrow for her daughters, but Margaret told me that now, finally, she could get over her anger for what Freda had done to her and Martha. They had had nightmares ever since her display.

Liz's death occupied the trial for days. The Army pathologist who had done the autopsy on Liz in 1985 was put on the stand. Reading from his autopsy report, he said she died of a cerebral hemorrhage.

Hardin questioned the credentials of the Army doctor and asked if he might have made a mistake. Could he have missed a slight skull fracture? He agreed that it was possible.

Jan Leestma, one of the foremost pathologists in the county studied the slides of Liz's brain that had been sent to Walter Reed Hospital in Washington along with half of her brain.

Leetsma read from Walter Reed's report confirming that Elizabeth Ratliff had died from a stroke.

Do you agree with that finding? Rudolf asked. Yes.

Only medical examiner Deborah Radisch disagreed. She said death resulted from blunt force trauma.

Rudolf showed her *Forensic Pathology*, the standard text in medical schools and asked her if she'd read it. She said yes, of course.

He pointed to Leetsma. "But you don't agree with the man who wrote the book?"

No I don't, she answered.

For a reason I never understood, Hardin called the military crime scene investigator who had gone to Liz's house after her death. On the stand under oath, he read from notes he'd taken that morning eighteen years ago: There was no blood on the floor and nothing suspicious about the death of Elizabeth Ratliff.

Rudolf asked him to verify those facts. No blood? Nothing suspicious?

No. Nothing suspicious.

Did the German police and German doctor on the scene see any blood or find anything suspicious? No.

Unaccountably, to refute his own expert witness, Hardin called several of Liz's neighbors and friends who came to the house the morning after her death.

All these witnesses had been flown in and housed at State expense. They testified that there had been blood everywhere—floor, walls, stairs. An abattoir.

"Why have you waited eighteen years to bring this up?" Rudolf asked with incredulity. "Why didn't you say something at the time?" They had no answer.

"Why didn't the police see any blood?" They had no answer.

One witness said that she only saw the blood now because of "flashbacks."

As soon as she said that, realizing how damaging it was, Hardin called for a recess. Flashbacks are not reliable; they aren't memories, but like dreams. Yet the next day the witness repeated that her recollection of events resulted from flashbacks.

Her husband, an Air Force Major at the time, the ranking man at the scene of Liz's death did not testify. He didn't even come to court.

Though seeing blood now, the flashbacking witness said she never had any suspicion that I had anything to do with Liz's death.

Barbara Malagnino, the girls' nanny in Germany, testified that when she found Liz's body, it was warm. She ran to our house a block away and woke Patricia, who woke me. We both rushed over.

Rudolf pressed her on those points: Liz's body was still warm? Yes.

There was no rigor mortis? No.

Michael was at his own house asleep? Yes.

Did you suspect Michael had anything to do with Liz's death? No.

The next question was obvious: then why are you here as a prosecution witness?

It had to do with a Chat Noir poster. Chat Noir was the first modern cabaret; it dated from the 1880's in Paris's Montmartre district. A Chat Noir poster hung in the stairwell where Kathleen died.

Photos of the stairwell with the poster had appeared in newspapers, on TV, and on the Internet. Seeing a photo, Barbara remembered the same poster had hung in Liz's house.

The implication was that I had taken it and many other items (they belonged to Margaret and Martha as Liz's heirs; I was the Executor of Liz's Estate) and placed the poster in the stairwell where there was another killing.

The next day Rudolf introduced the poster as a defense exhibit.

"You're sure this is the same poster," he asked Barbara. She said it was.

Then he took it out of its frame and had Barbara read the copyright date—1998. She could not explain how a poster printed in 1998 bought at the World Market in Durham was in her German bedroom in 1985.

I am still dumbfounded by those eyewitnesses I'd known well in Germany, and to this day, after their lies were exposed, I don't know why they did it.

But all that was minor theater compared to Brad's court appearance. Standing room only that day. A Gay Hustler! Unnatural Sex! Prostitution!

We could have sold tickets.

Brent Wolgamott took the stand with complete confidence.

"Should I smile at him? Wave?" I whispered to Rudolf.

"Just don't flirt," he whispered back. I didn't, but Freda seemed to; she moved as close as she could and batted heavily made up eyes at him. He smiled condescendingly, but he had nothing to offer on the case. He testified that he'd never met me.

He said we'd exchanged a few emails to set up a meeting, but it never took place, emails in which I said I was in love with my wife and that the meeting was strictly for sex.

Freda asked him what kind of sex was involved.

You could feel the courtroom audience leaning forward, holding its breath.

Oral and anal, he said as calmly as if someone had asked what toothpaste he used.

Who are your clients? She persisted.

Most are married men, he answered. Doctors, lawyers, even judges.

"Not this judge," Hudson said to laughter.

And that was it. No meeting. No sex.

Under Rudolf's cross examination, he repeated that there had been no meeting and no sex. He didn't know "diddly" about anything.

I knew the damage was done by his mere presence. Perversion! Filth!

The prosecution had scored enough to offset their financial and computer setbacks.

When he left the stand, I didn't acknowledge him. I wish I had. He'd been much braver than I'd been. We both knew who we were, but only he had had the courage to admit who he was.

With all side issues dealt with, the trial moved to the central issue: Kathleen's death.

The DA summoned Deborah Radisch, the medical examiner who had autopsied Kathleen and Liz. She testified that Kathleen died from blunt force trauma, but under Rudolf's cross examination, she couldn't explain why Kathleen alone in the history of North Carolina blunt force deaths had not suffered skull fracture, brain damage, or *any* injury associated with a beating, a beating supposedly inflicted by a blowpoke that no one had seen for years.

In a revealing demonstration, he stacked the histories of several hundred blunt force victims in North Carolina. All of them had skull fractures or brain damage.

Then he held up the case history for Kathleen. "This is the only one without those injuries. Can you explain that?'

She couldn't.

But the jury didn't blink at the inconsistency, or at the lies the witnesses had told.

Worst of all, they were mesmerized by the prosecution's main witness, the key figure in my conviction—State Bureau of Investigation blood spatter expert Duane Deaver.

Brad had been a star—young, blond, handsome, personable, the high school quarterback. Deaver was bald, middle-aged, dull, the nerd who never showered after gym class.

He was a supercilious know-it-all. *BUT* he was a special agent of the State Bureau of Investigation. North Carolina's expert on blood spatter.

Deaver testified that Kathleen had not fallen down the stairs; I had beaten her to death. I beat her to the floor, then waited until she stood (there was blood on the soles of her feet) and then I beat her again. That proved pre-meditation: First Degree murder.

He testified for eight days pointing to charts he had made of blood spatter and describing asinine experiments.

In one, on video tape, he hit a blood soaked sponge representing Kathleen's head **34 times** with a stick the length of the blowpoke to reproduce a cast off drop of blood on the shorts I'd been wearing. When he finally got the desired result after 33 unsuccessful attempts, his assistant did a victory dance and they high fived.

He did a similar experiment to reproduce a drop of blood on one of my shoes.

His most outrageous experiment was "proof" with string showing where I had struck Kathleen in the back staircase. He selected a few blood drops on the wall, traced them back with string to an intersecting spot and said this was the "Point of Origin out in space" where her head had been.

Of course he could have selected other drops and gotten different points of origin. What he did was like finding a football in the end zone and "proving" with string that Tom Brady had thrown it from the 17 yard line. Impossible. He might not have thrown it, might not even been in the game—a tight end could have run the ball in or the ref dropped it there.

There is no way to prove how a football gets into an end zone unless it's been filmed or there are witnesses. And there is no way to prove a point in space where a head had been.

His experiments were mindlessly stupid, patently ridiculous: junk science. I'd gotten a D in chemistry and didn't even bother to take physics, but I knew this was horseshit. Not even factoring in that I was innocent and not in the stairwell.

Yet the jury raptly listened to him. He was so assured, so "expert".

Court TV filmed the entire trial. A circus tent was set up outside the judicial building for the cameras. People stood in line to comment.

When court ended for the day, everyone rushed home to see the wrap up. As soon as we got in the house, my kids ran to the TV room.

"Jesus!" I yelled the first time that happened as I headed to my den with Wilbur and Portia. "You were in court all day. You saw the whole damn thing."

"It's a different trial on TV, Dad," Todd said. "Nancy Grace, lawyers, and psychiatrists are saying you're a psychopath guilty as shit. One psychiatrist said that when you shift your shoulder to the left, you're admitting guilt.

Another said that when you put your hand to your mouth, you're hiding a smirk. Nancy Grace says anyone can see you're a deranged monster."

Clayton nodded. "They're like a rabid Colosseum crowd giving you thumbs down. It's best you wear a hood in court, Dad. Better yet, don't go."

Margaret felt sure Judge Hudson, the DA, Rudolf, and the jurors rushed home to watch TV too. "It's the biggest thing in their lives. Great entertainment! Beats every soap opera and game show. No matter what they say, they're watching themselves."

Yet through it all, I was convinced I'd be acquitted: innocent men aren't convicted.

That doesn't happen in America.

6. GUILTY

When I first saw photos of Kathleen's shaved skull prepared for autopsy, I recoiled in shock.

My God, what happened? The long slashing lacerations were horrifying. It absolutely looked like she'd been brutally beaten. No wonder Caitlin, Candace, Lori, and the prosecution believed that. I understood. I would have believed it myself—except that I knew it didn't happen. Or at least knew that I didn't do it.

Could an intruder have done it? Did someone break into the house, startle her, and then beat her as he escaped? But nothing was missing. There was no sign of an intruder.

The mystery was that with so much trauma to her skull there was no fracture or brain damage. Though I had found her at the bottom the stairs, after I saw those photos, even I began to question whether she had fallen.

Nevertheless, our biomechanics expert and forensic pathologist went to great lengths to show how the wounds could have come from a fall. What else could have happened if there was no beating and no intruder?

But all their technical explanations and demonstrations could not stand up to the prosecution's simple admonishment: use your common sense; do you really think a fall could cause those lacerations? Many people had fallen, probably some on the jury. I had. None of us had seen wounds like that.

And all that blood. Splashed on the floor with hundreds of drops on the walls. So much blood. Dr. Henry Lee demonstrated how it could have happened. He compared cast off droplets of blood when she shook her head to what happens when dogs shake off water; it's flung everywhere.

But again—*that* much blood? Use common sense.

Yet there was no cast off from a weapon, no evidence that any weapon had been used. While the prosecution stuck to the blowpoke theory, Rudolf asked to have the jury visit the stairwell in the house which had been boarded up and preserved for the past year and a half. His idea was to show jurors that it would be impossible for me to wield any weapon in that confined space without leaving cast off blood on the ceiling.

When a weapon strikes an object creating blood and is brought back up, cast off drops are flung. With so many blows (according to Deaver), the blowpoke or any other weapon would have sent cast off blood onto the ceiling. But there wasn't any.

Hudson authorized the visit. Another media extravaganza.

Jurors and alternates came down the long driveway in special buses that stopped in the circle in front of the house. With them were sheriff deputies, my lawyers, DA Hardin and Assistant DA Freda Black, Judge Hudson, court officials, and of course TV cameras and reporters.

I barricaded myself in my upstairs bedroom as everyone trooped through the house, went out to the pool where Kathleen and I had talked that night, then jurors went into the stairwell.

They did not see any cast off. They saw a confined stairwell where Kathleen had lain. They saw a wealthy rich couple's house luxurious beyond their means.

And they saw dried blood on the walls, stairs, and floor.

They were shocked at the amount of blood. What Rudolf had hoped to prove backfired disastrously.

Common sense: there was too much blood for a fall.

One man had an explanation for the wounds and blood.

When my neighbor Larry Pollard, an attorney and hunter saw pictures of the lacerations, he thought they looked like a turkey track. Then he studied the photos more carefully and concluded that the wounds looked like what owl talons might cause.

Owls were in his backyard, ours, and across the street.

Most years there were two owls in the wooded area on our property; one year there were three, their baby I assumed. They used our swimming pool as their supermarket when small animals—voles, etc.—went to the pool at night to drink. Owls are nocturnal raptors that make no noise when they fly. They are efficient lethal predators with razor sharp talons.

Sometimes an owl perched on a porch railing and would follow us walking to the pool by swiveling its head, not completely around like in The Exorcist, but almost. Kathleen thought owls spooky, but she wasn't afraid of them.

Indeed, they often amused us as we watched them torment Wilbur and Portia. They would hoot from a tree and the dogs would rush out barking. As soon as the dogs were confident they had frightened off the intruder calling Whoo Whoo, they returned to the kitchen. The owls would immediately start hooting again and the dogs would again rush out. This went on and on. Kathleen and I would laugh. The birds were smarter than our bulldogs.

Once, when I took out the trash, a neighbor across the street rushed screaming from her backyard onto the street. She told me she had been terrified of a big owl staring at her.

Larry concluded that Kathleen had gone outside that evening after leaving me at the pool and before going upstairs to bed. She had put up the balsa wood reindeer that we placed in the driveway circle every year to decorate for Christmas (they were there the next morning draped with crime scene tape). Larry believed an owl swooped down, struck her with its talons, and she, bleeding (there were drops of blood on the brick path leading to the front door), ran into the house and then to the stairwell where she collapsed.

Larry went to the DA with his theory.

Nonsense, said Hardin. Where are the feathers?

Larry then went to Rudolf. Nonsense, he said.

I knew nothing about the theory until Larry called me in prison a year later to explain what he thought had happened.

Nonsense, I thought.

It was too bizarre to believe an owl had caused Kathleen's death, but then Larry sent me a magazine photo of Kathleen's scalp lacerations with an owl talon superimposed over them. The talons matched the lacerations perfectly. I began to wonder—could it be true?

Long after I had been convicted, slides prepared by the SBI from hair samples taken by the medical examiner showed feathers clutched in Kathleen's hand with bloody hair that she had ripped from her head by the roots. A bark fragment had also been found in her hair.

Though I have no idea if Kathleen had been attacked by an owl, Rudolf now believes it is the most plausible explanation for her lacerations, but the only way to prove it would be with an exhumation to test for owl DNA in her wounds.

At trial, there was no mention of an owl attack, so jurors were left to choose between beating or fall: science or common sense.

After three months in court, everyone was worn out.

But the prosecution rallied for the closing, especially Freda.

Parading the courtroom waving porn pictures, shoving them in jurors' faces, she shouted, "Filth. Pure T Filth."

And for Dwayne Deaver, that "poor man" who had undergone days of cross examination by Rudolf, she referred to him as a "tried and true" public servant. He worked for you, she told the jury. He was a state employee who would never lie.

As opposed to those "outsiders"—the defense experts: Jan Leetsme who had come from the University of Chicago; Faris Bandak from Washington, D.C. who looked foreign and had a foreign name, and finally, Henry Lee from Connecticut who definitely was a foreigner—Chinese! She ridiculed his accent and his statement that there was "too much" blood for a beating.

These experts weren't from North Carolina. They were *paid* for their testimony. Paid experts would say anything for money while prosecution experts, state employees, would only tell the truth.

Hardin closed in a more reserved, almost sorrowful manner. He told the jurors that the bloody walls they'd seen in the stairwell were talking for Kathleen. They were demanding justice: a guilty verdict.

The night before Rudolf's closing argument, the defense team gathered in his office.

Should I testify was a main question. Should my children be put on the stand?

Margie Fargo, our jury consultant, told Rudolf that it was necessary to give a personal touch to my case. So far, she argued, it's been nothing but science. You're throwing a textbook at the jury while the prosecution has given them a trashy novel.

Let Mike testify, she said. Let the kids go on the stand to tell about his relationship with Kathleen and how much he loved her, and what a devoted father he has been.

Make it personal, she insisted.

Rudolf didn't think it was necessary. He felt that he had decimated the prosecution's witnesses and exposed all the fallacies in their completely circumstantial case.

He had, but Margie didn't think that was enough. Make Mike human, she said. Bring in the family.

The final decision was left to me. I wanted to testify, especially because Rudolf felt it too risky. He worried that I might not be able to withstand cross examination by Hardin and Freda. I wanted to prove him wrong. Of course I could stand up to them. I had nothing to fear or hide.

But in the end, I went along with Rudolf. He was my attorney. Why pay him all that money (around $750,000) and then ignore his advice?

So I didn't testify.

The next morning, Rudolf gave an impassioned speech, a closing that went over the defects in the prosecution's case. It was all about Reasonable Doubt, he emphasized. There was more than enough. The jury had to acquit me.

Judge Hudson gave the jury its instructions. There were only two possible verdicts—Guilty of 1st Degree Murder, that I had willfully and intentionally with premeditation murdered Kathleen, or Not Guilty.

The jury was sent out to deliberate.

Four excruciatingly anxious days followed. We sat in the courtroom Monday through Thursday until Hudson would dismiss us. I spent most of that time talking with my children.

We debated whether it was it a good or bad sign that the jury was out so long; we concluded it was a good sign.

Rudolf thought at worst there would be a hung jury.

Only Todd thought I would be found guilty.

The jury had been out four days when I was saying good night in his bedroom.

"The jury's going to convict you tomorrow, Dad. It's going to be one of those Friday verdicts because those people want to go home this weekend. But they are not going home to families, friends, and neighbors to live with everybody thinking they let a serial killer go free."

"I didn't kill Kathleen! I didn't kill Liz. I didn't kill anyone."

He hugged me—almost like a goodbye hug. "I know, Dad, but it isn't about Reasonable Doubt. There's no such thing; they're just words. The DA didn't have to prove you killed Kathleen; you had to prove you *didn't*. The burden was on you to prove your innocence. You had to prove absolutely that you didn't kill Kathleen. You had to leave no doubt. You had to prove a negative. That's impossible. Plus there's been 18 months of media trash. Tomorrow that jury will come back with a verdict convicting you."

In the morning there was another harbinger—Wilbur at the door when I went to court. The old bulldog slept most of the day and had never seen me off. I reached down to pat him, then closed and locked the door behind me. That was the last I ever saw him.

Within an hour of court convening, the bailiff announced that the jury had reached a verdict.

As they filed in, I felt detached: an out of body experience as though watching from another dimension, thinking Not Guilty would be good, but Guilty would be all right. This wasn't my life; it wasn't even me any longer.

Guilty, the clerk read.

I felt the blow, but it was too much to absorb. I understood, but it made no sense. Guilty? I had killed Kathleen? No. NO!

The judge immediately sentenced me to Life without Parole.

All I could think about were my children behind me. As I was being cuffed, I turned to them. Margaret's and Martha's faces were twisted in an agony that made Munch's *The Scream* look like minor angst. My sons stared straight ahead, stoic.

"It's ok, it's ok," I said, but I knew none of us would ever be ok again. Our lives were destroyed.

I was taken to the basement and put in a dank cell waiting to be transferred to Central Prison.

As I looked through the bars, horror gripped me.

I had lost my children.

I was condemned to die in prison.

7. The Psycho Ward

War is terrifying, but I don't remember being afraid my first day in combat when I went up the Cua Viet River to join my unit on the DMZ. Huddled on the river craft with twenty other Marines, enemy snipers fired on us from densely overgrown banks, but I knew I would be all right. No fear at all. Of course then I was a young second lieutenant charged with bravado.

Nor was I afraid later that day when enemy mortars shelled the battalion compound and I saw the Sergeant Major run out of the wooden shitter with his trousers around his ankles. He tripped and fell, cutting himself on a nail. I later learned he put himself in for a Purple Heart. And got it.

What I remember most that first day as I dove for cover was thinking, "Holy shit, this is going to be either a very long or very short war." Either way, I was excited. War!

Thirty five years later, chained and shackled in the back of a police car on the highway to Central Prison, I was no longer young and bravado was gone. Slumped in the seat fighting tears, I felt beaten. Lost. Defeated.

As the car pulled up that dazzling bright October afternoon to Central Prison, a massive castle-like edifice housing 1000 inmates and the state's Death Row, I saw rabid gawkers, some with signs—GUILTY! MURDERER. The Forum crowd had followed me here.

You're wrong, I wanted to yell, I'm innocent. Instead, I closed my eyes and bowed my head awaiting the next blows.

Passing through a series of tall iron razor wired gates with armed guards, a strange phenomenon occurred: color disappeared; everything turned gray. That was my first impression of prison—I had entered a world bleached of color.

The Sheriff's deputies brought me to Receiving, a gigantic barren room where two Department of Corrections officers accepted me as if I were toxic waste.

After they strip searched me—"lift your nuts, bend over, spread your cheeks, cough"—they handed me a brown jumpsuit and thrust me into a holding cell. There was no place to sit, so I stood, hands folded staring at the iron bars, my mind blank, not knowing what to expect. Not caring either. The worst had been done to me and my children.

I knew I was in shock, like being conscious of being unconscious, but I didn't want to think. Or wake. I could have remained like this forever—without pain, thought, or memory.

Footsteps broke the spell; a casually dressed man of about fifty, short, puffy faced, wearing glasses approached. Only when he entered the cell without a key did I realize it hadn't been locked. I could have escaped. But where?

He introduced himself as the prison psychiatrist. "How are you?" he asked pleasantly.

I just stared at him. Was he serious? What kind of psychiatrist was this?

"On a scale of 1-10, ten being the worst, how do you feel?" he pressed.

Kathleen was dead; I had just been convicted of murdering her. I had lost my children, everything I owned, freedom--condemned to live in prison for the rest of my life and die here.

"10? That isn't a big enough number. How about 100 or 1000? Ten thousand?"

For that frippery, I was immediately brought upstairs in a caged elevator to the psych ward and thrust naked into a starkly lit cell under suicide watch. That was my first prison lesson: Never tell the truth to an official. Even when they're trying to help, they'll fuck you.

Looking about the cell barren except for a metal bunk with a worn slim mattress, I sank down in exhausted defeat, curled into a fetal position, and pressed my face against the brick wall to shut out everything. I wanted it all to go away. I wanted sleep. Without dreams. Oblivion.

A loud voice ordered me to roll over.

Looking up to the ceiling, I saw a speaker and a camera.

That's when I broke. Naked under camera observation like an animal or madman, I gave up: the police, the DA, jurors, friends who'd abandoned me, all who'd separated me from my children and put me here had won. I pressed my face against the cold concrete wall and sobbed.

That night was the lowest in my life, worse than any in combat because then I knew, just knew I would survive battle—I was young and in love; my whole life was before me.

I felt worse than the night Kathleen died, which had been horror beyond anything I'd experienced, but Todd had been there to support me, and I had my children to live for.

Worse than when I lay near death on the ICU ward at Zama combat evacuation Hospital in Japan; medication relieved that pain and smothered thought. I'd been critically injured returning to Atsugi Naval Air Station where I commanded a Marine guard platoon after Vietnam.

Remembering the agony on that awful ward, I was jolted from self-pity. Guilt and shame overcame me. How could I feel sorry for myself when Kathleen had died? What did my suffering compare to her death? How could I feel sorry for myself after witnessing the suffering of others in that hospital?

A Japanese truck trying to beat a train at a railroad crossing had slammed into my vehicle, pinning me to the wheel, crushing my chest, collapsing a lung. I was unable to move as my sergeant beside me cried, Help me, Lieutenant, help me. He died. The last thing I remember as I was carried into the hospital was a corpsman saying, "This one isn't going to make it either."

But I did, though in so much pain that I became a Demerol addict. We all did on that ward except for a young Army sergeant beside me whose suffering was beyond medication.

Greg Schmidt's injuries were so bad—a land mine had blown off half his body—that he screamed relentlessly: Please God let me die. Had he been able to kill himself, he would have.

That first night in prison, I felt like Greg. Had I a way to kill myself, I would have, but there was nothing in that cell—no rope, sheets, nothing, so I lay on my back like I had for weeks in ICU, staring at the ceiling, thinking of Greg and Vic and others who had suffered more.

After stabilizing in ICU, I was moved to the 60 man Orthopedic Ward, the only officer, the only Marine, and the only non-amputee. Because I was an officer and had been in Vietnam, the staff put the worst incoming cases next to me thinking I could comfort them, though I was badly injured and doped on Demerol.

One middle of the night I woke to moaning beside me, "Help me, Help me." The bed had been empty when I fell asleep, but now a guy writhing with pain was in it.

"There's a button behind your head," I said. "Press it. A nurse will come."

He held up two stumps--arms severed at the elbows. "I can't," he cried.

"Jesus!" I yelled and mashed my button. When the nurse ran in, I pointed to the guy and ranted about putting him there with no way to call for help. They rigged a coat hanger into a hoop to place a stump to trigger the button. He was a big Hawaiian named Vic.

But Vic's injuries weren't the worst. Red had lost both legs *and* his dick. He won Most Fucked Up. When the plastic surgeon came to discuss Red's replacement dick, the rest of us joined in the consult. Make it Big we shouted. Long, Thick, Long *and* Thick. We debated dick size merits all day. That's what I remember more than pain about that ward: humor. And that no one ever felt sorry for himself because there was always someone who suffered more.

But here I had succumbed to self-pity. I had forgotten Greg, Vic, and Red, but also my great grandmother Teresa Bartolino from Turin--Nonna Bart--who used to say, "Never think things can't get worse. Don't test God. He'll find a way."

In the Marines, self-pity certainly wasn't encouraged. Before PTSD counseling there was Court Martial. I spent four years in the Corps and retired a Captain.

Kathleen wouldn't tolerate self-pity either. "Get a grip. Move on," was her rebuke to anyone who indulged. So I did. And exhausted—it'd been a full day--I fell asleep.

In the morning the psychiatrist returned. When he asked how I was, I still had nothing to say, but when he offered pills to sedate me, I said yes. Eagerly. I spent that day and night zonked. The next morning I was let out to take a shower and given back my brown jumpsuit.

Twenty of us were on the ward, all considered deranged and dangerous. I and a few others were allowed out of our cells for two hours in a large Day Room that had a couple metal tables and chairs. The other loonies were considered too risky to others or themselves so they remained in their cells medicated like in *One Flew over the Cuckoo's Nest*.

The guy in the cell beside mine walked in circles until his feet bled. Leroy, on my other side looked like a rat and had a deep southern accent. Utterly mad, he screamed constantly.

They gave me zonk pills too. I hid them under the mattress in case I changed my mind about suicide, but in

90

the end I flushed them down the toilet. I wasn't in a Death Camp. Primo Levi had called the horror he endured at Auschwitz an "adventure", not an ordeal. How could I compare my suffering to his?

Perhaps Milton's Lucifer was right—better to reign in Hell than serve in Heaven, but I wasn't going to reign in Hell: I was going *serve* here. Nevertheless, I was alive, fed, housed, and clothed. Beatings and rape had not yet occurred to me.

Brown uniforms were "General Population—me; yellow for those on their way to trial; green for honor grade, those soon to go home, and red—Death Row.

One red suit was on the ward; I encountered him my fourth day. Accompanied by a guard, I was returning from medical/dental in-processing as he was leaving with two guards, heavily shackled—hands, feet, and a chain around his waist. He'd "acted up" on Death Row.

How could you act up on Death Row? I wondered. But if you could, why not? Since they intended to kill you, why not go down fighting?

I waited behind three sets of metal gates as he was brought to the elevator, a black man in his late twenties wearing glasses, about my height. We stood a few feet apart.

His eyes, not a bit hostile, appraised me. "How you doing?" he asked solicitously.

"Better than you," I said, trying to smile.

"Good luck. Take it easy," he said, disappearing into the elevator.

We were two Titanics passing close, plowing to separate icebergs, doomed, both under death sentences, his death quickly by lethal injection, mine a slow decaying one. I bowed my head for us both.

That evening I encountered RJ, the first child molester I met in prison. Weighing more than 350 pounds, he looked like the pie eating fat guy in *Stand by Me* who explodes--a mess and a simpleton, pathetic even considering his crimes. At 27, he'd been convicted three times for child molestation, most recently for violating two little girls.

Born in Portsmouth, Virginia to a crack addict mother, he'd been raised by his grandmother. Seeing me alone at a table writing a letter to my children, RJ shyly asked if he could sit with me. Everyone shunned him, so he was happy when I said yes and put aside my letter. Like on that ICU ward, here was someone whose suffering was worse than mine.

A simple man/boy eager for company and grateful to have a listener, he told me he was getting out next month. "I'm going home to my grandma. She's 80. But I'm afraid."

"Why?"

"The sheriff said he'd kill me."

One could only imagine that hideous home coming for this immense soft sex offender-- the little girls had been under 10. Doomed from birth, born in poverty to a crack addled whore, unwanted, uncared for, soon to be released to a future more doomed than his past. His last release lasted only a few hours. Let out at 11:15 am, he returned for self-commitment at 4 pm. He said he was suicidal.

Indeed, why go on?—a pathetic youth facing society's disgust and a sheriff who wanted to kill him.

"I get a candy bar here," he said, as if that made up for everything.

His job, wiping tables, mopping, earned one candy bar a day. That's what he lived for. He had no love or joy, past, present or future. His past was pain, his future terror. His life might better have been unlived, death a blessing— for him and society.

During the day I wrote letters, ate meals, showered, and shaved with a dull disposable razor I had to return. At night, I could not keep dark thoughts at bay: I will never get out, I will not see my lovely children again; I will die here.

Tossing on my mattress, I wanted to yell, This can't be. It's wrong! Yet all around me I could see injustice-- man or God's. How to explain RJ? His victims, those little girls?

The next day I was given a written test for...I didn't know what. Hundreds of questions—math, science, grammar that took me hours to answer. Did I want to do well? Would they cut my sentence? Should I play stupid and get everything wrong? They couldn't add to my sentence. Finally, I filled in the blanks randomly, but made sure I did well enough so that I wouldn't be considered Special Needs and end up in the state bin at Dorothea Dix.

That evening in the Day Room, Rabbit sidled up to me. Young, white, and quick, Rabbit was the Trustee, which I soon learned meant "snitch", our Kapo who did the guard's bidding. He'd advised me earlier, "Play fucked up and they won't send you to the real shit places."

He said he was on the ward only pretending to be nuts. I saw why—a handsome guy not muscular enough to protect himself in those "shit places," he'd likely become a punch board for sexual predators.

"Guards say you're going to Nash Correctional Institution tomorrow," he whispered.

"You're too high profile."

He pointed out the barred window. "WRAL TV is across the street. The *N&O* a couple blocks away. They don't want the media hanging around; they want to bury your ass."

Did I care? What difference would it make where I was sent? Was the seventh ring of Hell worse than the sixth, or better than the eighth?

When I in-processed, an officer asked which high security prison I'd like to go to.

I asked if any had special advantages--TV's, refrigerators, microwaves? Room service?

"No," he said in triumph. As if I'd been serious.

"Then you choose," I said. They chose Nash near redneck Rocky Mount 50 miles away.

The next morning I was shackled, put in a police car, and driven to Nash for what I thought would be the rest of my life. I sat silently in the back seat watching the world rush by--farmers in their fields, travelers on the highway, children playing, stores, houses, trees.

This last sight of the world was too much. Tears welled. I wiped them away with my hands, but the metal cuffs scraped my face. I concentrated on the back of the heads of the guards—thick necked, buzz haired. They looked like Marines. I let out my breath slowly, and suddenly I felt as I had forty five years earlier on the boat traveling upriver to war.

But unlike in Vietnam, this time I was alone, no longer young, going where everyone would be the enemy. Bravado was gone.

I closed my eyes and sat rigid: no more looking at the world I was leaving. No looking back at all.

8. PRISON

The trip from Central to Nash took an hour, a journey not so much in time as dimension, as if travelling to an unknown planet of horrific aliens. Sitting tensely upright fists clenched in the backseat of the squad car, I saw a sprawling complex of concrete buildings behind three high rows of concertina wire looming closer.

Almost afraid to look, but unable to help myself, I pressed against the window to see "home" for the rest of my life—a barren expanse surrounded by razor wire with arc lights and a guard tower just like in prison movies. All I knew about prison was from those movies where bad things happened to bad people.

As the prison drew closer, I felt conflicting emotions: overwhelming depression that my life with those I loved ended here, yet also strange exhilaration like I'd felt going to war: Would I be brave? Survive? Yet deeper than depression and exhilaration lay fear. My stomach knotted so painfully that I had to stretch back to relieve the cramps, yet I was still shaking when the car stopped at the fifteen foot tall iron mesh gate.

Armed Guards peered in, checked the engine compartment and trunk, then ran a large mirror under the chassis. This just to get *in*.

I held my breath with clenched jaws and cuffed hands tightened into fists as the car passed through a series of gates topped with razor wire, but once beyond the gates,

I saw manicured lawns, flower beds, and unshackled men casually walking about. I relaxed somewhat, yet wondered, why is a TV news truck here?

When the car pulled up before Receiving, a long concrete building, I was roughly pulled out and thrust into a large sterile grim room where I was unshackled, stripped, handed ill-fitting brown clothes and black boots. I put them on, still dazed and not fully comprehending that this was real. Once dressed, a guard said, "Follow me," and I dumbly trailed out the door after him.

The guard led me across what he called the "campus"—as if Hell were a college: ten treeless acres with four housing units of 150 men each, a chow hall, small infirmary, gym, chapel, and an isolated unit on a hill surrounded by two barbed fences—Segregation: The Hole.

'You're prisoner number 640," he said. "Unit 1 is for chow hall workers, 3 and 4 plant workers. You'll be in 2, the school unit."

School? Was there school for prison? A curriculum for survival? I hoped so—the only good news so far.

In zombie like trance, I was led to a concrete building at the end of an open grassy acre called The Yard. Men in brown uniforms stared at me menacingly. I felt small and vulnerable.

At Unit 2, I was brought into the main office where six steel-toed jackbooted guards towered over a short middle-aged white woman in beige dress and pink tennis shoes.

The nightmare had turned surreal. I felt like Alice at the Mad Hatter's tea party except the men staring stonily at me were no Dormice and The Queen wore pink tennis shoes. *Pink!*

Raising my eyes when she addressed me, I saw moving lips, but I didn't hear a word. When she stopped talking, she motioned me to follow her.

Shell shocked, like in a walking coma, I followed her down a long grey painted corridor to a half-football field size room labeled in huge black letters Cell Block B. An iron door slid open. When we entered, a guard jumped to attention and 50 brown uniformed inmates milling about backed away except for one massive black with long dreads who ran up to me and thrust his furious face into mine.

I jerked back, almost falling and brought up my hands for protection, but the woman made a slight papal motion and the guy slinked away, then she tugged on my sleeve and led me to a cell, pointed inside, directing me like a dog into its cage. Then she left.

I was home.

But immediately, the black guy, twenty years younger, a half foot taller and outweighing me by at least 50 pounds rushed to the door and snarled, "Come on out, motherfucker."

Yeah right, I thought, pushing against the cell door to make sure it was locked.

Fully conscious at last, I couldn't catch my breath: I was in prison. In a cell. This was real. Forever. I hugged myself tightly yet I couldn't stop shaking.

Nothing was going to make this go away. Or the guy outside my iron door.

Sooner or later I'd have to face him, but putting it off as long as possible, I gazed about my cell and walked off its dimensions; it didn't take long—9x12 feet. The walls, concrete floor, and ceiling were gray along with the metal toilet, sink, table with stool, and bunk built into the wall.

The iron door had a narrow perpendicular triple paned window; at the opposite end of the cell, a vertically barred window looked out on a small rec yard the size of an elementary school playground with a miniature concrete basketball court, dirt volleyball court, track, and weight lifting area—Hell with a little jungle gym.

Inside was gray, outside brown with tattooed behemoths lifting hundreds of pounds on the weight pile. Outside looked more dangerous than the cell block.

I didn't want to go out there, but I also didn't want to fight the black guy outside my cell where fifty men waited to see the famous rich guy who'd murdered his wife, probably two women, and solicited a male hustler.

I had no good options, but I couldn't remain in my cell forever.

This was worse than travelling up the Cua Viet River under enemy fire, but I'd volunteered for that. I was young, hard charging, and unafraid. I had a rifle and the men with me were other Marines looking out for one other. Here I was unarmed and no one was looking out for me; I was old, tired, completely on my own, and no match for the black guy or the monsters on the weight pile.

I dropped down on the hard bunk's thin worn mattress, lay back and closed my eyes. This was the rest of my life. I wanted to cry, but what good would that do?

Taking a deep breath, I let it out slowly then sat up. Might as well get this over with and take my beating, so reluctantly I stood and went to the door. I pushed a button on the wall for a guard in the booth to let me out.

Steeled for a fight, I walked into the day room as if it were a boxing ring, but the guy with dreads had disappeared—apparently bored or with a short attention span, and the group of fifty had broken up. Only a few guys stood around. I relaxed and loosened my posture for they seemed friendly and introduced themselves with bumped fists to explain the simple rules of block life: we were locked in cells only at night, never allowed in another's, and had to stand in front of our own at Count Time three times a day. They told me when we ate, how to get to the chow hall, and the hours for canteen, rec yard, and showers.

"Who was that woman who brought me in?" was my first question.

A heavily scarred nearly toothless guy spat, "The warden. *Mrs*. Wynette."

"The *warden*? In pink tennis shoes?" I was incredulous, but felt it a good omen; she was protecting me.

Nope. "That bitch just planted her Dorothy shoes up your ass. She never brought anyone to his cell before. You're special."

"Special" dripped sarcasm. The guy was bitter. Uh oh, I thought.

Another near toothless brute resentfully added, "*No one* gets a cell right away. The rest of us had to wait months on a bunk out here before we got one."

So that's why the guy with dreads had been hostile--the warden had treated me like a VIP. After only thirty minutes, I had a target on my back.

I was about to offer amends—hey, it wasn't my doing--when the loud speaker suddenly boomed, "Lock Down!"

Iron doors slammed shut as ten guards rushed into the block screaming LOCK DOWN! LOCK DOWN! LOCK DOWN!

One yelled at me, "It's *you*, Peterson. A TV crew is here for the news tonight. Lock Down until they leave."

Guys ran to their cells and bunks, leaving me alone in the middle of the Day Room. I stood stunned until a guard snarled in my face, "Lock down, asshole. Get in your cell."

After I ran in, the lock bolted behind me and I dropped onto my bunk, pulse racing, heart pounding. Holy shit! How long had I been here? Thirty minutes at most.

I lay forlornly until lock down ended an hour later with the shout "Clear", then I ventured nervously back into the day room, but catching hostile glances from the guys in the day room and thinking it might be safer outside, I went out to the rec yard.

I didn't get five feet before a bald behemoth with swastika tattoos ran towards me screaming, "Peterson!" I froze.

No sense running, there was no place to go, so I rooted myself to fight, but the monster threw open his massive arms, yelled "Homie", and embraced me in a suffocating WWE hug.

"Durm," he whispered lovingly in my ear.

It took a stunned second to understand that I was not being assaulted. "Durm" was Durham, and "Homie" our geographical bond. I almost wilted in his arms, never so happy to be hugged by a guy. Salvation! Protection!

Finally releasing me from his crushing grip, the monster gestured to the fearsome troop of six guys who'd followed him, heavily muscled and scarred, heads shaved, most missing teeth, all tattooed with Confederate flags, crosses, and swastikas. "All Durm," he said proudly.

Stepping back to thrust out his pumped chest, he boasted, "Underwood": six feet, 200 pounds—none fat--about 30, a gruesome sight with knife scarred face, broken nose, and a mouth no dentist had ever worked on.

The others, pure brawn bumped fists, introduced themselves, and welcomed me to the Durm hood. Relief swept me. Yes I was In Hell, but it appeared I had a few bad ass devils on my side.

That night lying on my bunk I took stock. Things are rarely as bad as they first seem. I didn't think I'd make it at Central Prison, but I did. Boot camp, war and the ICU had been that way too. And I figured that if Underwood and the others could manage this, I could too.

Communal living was not new: I'd lived three years in a fraternity house at Duke with 80 guys whose living habits were probably grosser than here and in a 60 man Marine barracks among guys a lot tougher. But I'd never been in a group this diverse: young, old, black, white, Native American, Hispanic, Asians; psychopaths, murderers, gang bangers, drug dealers, thieves, punks, snitches, and child molesters.

It was like being a zoo animal with all the animals in the same cage--some dangerous predators. I would have to be on my guard every minute.

The block had 60 cells on two levels with four open shower stalls. In the middle was a huge day room. Two televisions mounted on poles were at one end, an officer's desk and glassed guard booth at the other; sixteen bunks stood in the center because of overcrowding.

A guards' booth controlled a sliding iron door leading to another door where two more iron doors led to the canteen and a classroom. Another opened to yet another which led to the staff offices. A final iron door opened onto the main yard patrolled by guards and surrounded by razor wire. A thoroughly controlled environment which made me feel like I was supposed to—in prison.

Wake up was 5:30, breakfast 6:30, lunch around noon, dinner 4:30, and lock down at 11:30 when lights were dimmed, never turned off.

For five days I kept to myself observing routines and the hierarchy--who ruled, who was to be avoided (those who talked to guards—snitches), and who might be trusted: No one!

On my fifth night, I sat at a table in the day room with "Pops". After 50, inmates were called Pops or Old Man; all Hispanics were Amigo and Native Americans Chief. Blacks called whites Honky, Cracker, and Redneck; whites called blacks Nigger. Motherfucker as noun, verb, gerund, adverb and adjective prefaced everything and usually followed: Motherfucking Cracker motherfucker.

Pops, decrepit yet ten years younger, had a few widely spaced teeth, long white hair, but alert eyes that took in everything. He'd been "down" twenty years. I'd sought him out for survival tips. His advice: "keep a low profile; stay out of the way," which didn't help since I was the most high profile inmate at Nash, especially since my first night when another inmate had been interviewed about me.

The show everyone watched showed a typical grim cell, "Mike Peterson's new home," having lost his 12,000 square foot "Mansion" after murdering one woman, maybe two, and soliciting sex from "Brad", a male hustler. With each appalling revelation, guys had turned to stare at me. I kept a stoic look but cringed inwardly. I hadn't killed anyone, and my involvement with Brad made me a sitting duck among lots of duck hunters.

In the interview, the "typical" inmate, a ruined morose old black man said, "Now he's nobody like the rest of us." I found that sad; who had told him that he was a "nobody"? I wasn't. I was the inmate TV had come to mock, the one the warden had escorted to a cell which *no* new inmate had ever gotten.

After that, I felt comfortable only with Pops and a few other older men because younger inmates seemed to circle like wolves waiting for an opportunity to hustle me. Or worse.

As Pops and I sat that evening, he pointed to the black muscular inmate with dreads who'd confronted me, prowling the room like a leopard. "Something's jumping off tonight. Larry Wade's going to check off."

Puzzled, I asked, "Check off?" I'd learned "Car" meant your radio; "Gunning down" was masturbating while staring at a female guard; "Woofing" was pretending ferocity, like dogs barking instead of biting; "Bugs" were inmates flat nuts; "Brown eye" was your asshole. I had not learned "Check off."

But I'd kept my eye on Wade and noticed he'd block the paths of white guys to stare threateningly into their faces like he had me.

"He's a Five Percenter," Pops explained. "Black racists--Nation of God. They pray to Allah and hate whites. Watch out for them. Wade's been in 50 fights and won them all."

I believed it; he was massive, and I saw another fight coming because Homie Underwood and his (our!) rednecks had been yelling at him all day: "Want to fight, Nigger? Come on out."

Earlier, he'd confronted one of them. The others had chased him back to B block. Underwood and his men were in C; inmates weren't allowed in a cell block other than their own.

Before the yard closed this night, their taunts had escalated. "You're dead, Nigger."

Pops said, "Wade's got to check off or Underwood will kill him."

Good, I thought—one for the Homies, but I still didn't understand Check off.

"He'll do something to get off the unit, but he can't ask guards for protection."

Pops stared at me meaningfully. "You NEVER go to guards for help."

Got it: Don't Tattle. "So what will he do?" I asked as Wade stalked the room.

"Pick a fight so they'll take him to The Hole—the isolation unit on the hill. It's his only out. Guys check off

105

when they owe someone and can't pay, or they're afraid, just any reason to get moved, but we're safe—there's no status for him to jump us; we're too old. He'll take down a young white kid."

Lulled by Pops' words, I went to my cell when guards called Count Time at 7:30, a three times a day ritual that sometimes went on for hours because guards could not locate all prisoners, or more often, count us accurately. Until count "cleared", inmate movement was not allowed.

This night's count cleared quickly. As I lay on my bunk reading a magazine, a hulking guy walked into my cell—Wade. My blood froze. I'd left my door open after being warned a lunatic was prowling for a victim. How could I have been so stupid?

Bolting upright, I looked for something to protect myself, but all I had was the magazine to swat him with.

"Do you know who Allah is?" Wade demanded, fury in his eyes.

"What? Get the fuck out," I said, swinging my legs off the bunk.

He rushed me, face grimacing, teeth bared. I only had time to raise an arm to deflect his blow and turn my head or he would have blinded me. His gloved punch threw me against the wall. I spun, hurt and scared, then ran, a natural survival technique. I wasn't about to fight a guy twenty years younger, 50 pounds heavier. Later I learned he had concrete chips in his gloves.

He hadn't shut the door, automatically locking the cell trapping me inside, so I ran out, barely able to see through blood streaming my face and staggered to the officer's desk.

The unit broke into uproar as guards rushed me to Medical. They cuffed Wade and dragged him to The Hole as Pops had predicted.

At Medical, a one room clinic, a nurse examined me as I bled on the floor under the relishing gaze of the large black middle-aged Assistant Warden.

I asked him to call my children to tell them I was all right because I knew I wasn't hurt badly and this incident would be on the news; I didn't want them to worry.

"No one will ever hear of this," he said smugly.

Idiot, I thought angrily: You can't keep this quiet; everyone will know within an hour.

The nurse insisted I go to the county hospital, so I was cuffed, feet and waist chained and put in the backseat of a squad car. I was pissed: *I* was the victim; *I* had been attacked; *I*--to my shame--hadn't hurt anyone. Why was *I* in chains?

On the 10 mile drive to Rocky Mount, I tried to fathom what had happened. Wade's attack had caught me off guard, but I should have anticipated it—a lunatic looking for a victim, me the obvious one. I'd been a fool. I could have been blinded, maimed, killed. So angry at myself for being such an idiot—leaving my door unlocked!—I twisted and squirmed on the back seat until we got to the hospital where I was pulled roughly out of the squad car, thrust into a wheelchair and pushed through the front door.

Patients, their friends and family who'd all watched me on TV for months gasped and whipped out cell phones as I was wheeled into Emergency, admitted as "Joe Nash."

A doctor told reluctant guards to unshackle me for a CAT scan. He found no serious damage, so I was reshackled, put back in the squad car and returned to Nash at 2 am. The block was dark and quiet and I was completely drained; all I wanted was sleep, but when I entered my blood splattered cell, a guard handed me a mop, wash bucket, paper towels, and red toxic waste bags. "Clean it up," he ordered.

I was shocked. It hadn't occurred to me that *I* would have to do this. Had I expected room service to do it? Taking the cleaning gear, I spent the next hour mopping and wiping my blood from the floor and walls. I tossed my clothes in the bags along with my sheets and pillowcase, then, exhausted and still hurting—I'd been given two ibuprophen--fell asleep.

When I woke, I discovered I'd been locked in my cell until further notice. My face hurt and my head throbbed, but most of all I was pissed and I banged on the door angrily: "Why am *I* being punished? For what? Let me out!"

Of course I was ignored until Pops crept to the door and said I'd headlined last night's News at Eleven on all networks: "Peterson in fight"; "Peterson in hospital after fight"; "Peterson in trouble again."

"You look like shit," he said. "He really tore you a new one," then he ran off when a guard pushed a metal breakfast tray through the door slot—gruel and cold coffee.

In the metal mirror, I did look like shit—black and blue, face swollen almost beyond recognition, and I hurt like hell, so I lay on my bunk and decided it was better to be confined—I was mortified at how badly I looked and didn't want to talk to anyone.

Later that morning, an officer informed me that I was under "investigation."

"For what?" I shouted. "The guy came in my cell and hit me. I was lying on my bunk."

"It might not have been that simple," he said darkly. "We need statements."

The investigation took eight days locked in my cell brooding on my stupidity and peril. Wade could have killed me. Someone would soon unless I figured out how to survive.

My face throbbed so badly I had trouble eating. I was lonely and miserable. I wanted Kathleen. I wanted my children. I *had* to get out of here, but the only hope was my appeal before the North Carolina Court of Appeals. There had been so many errors, so much injustice, surely my conviction would be overturned, but the court's decision might take months.

Until then, I had to plan as if I would be here forever.

Feeling sorry for myself did no good, nor did thinking of the past, so I resolutely put all that away to solve the problem of survival.

I spent hours at my barred window observing guys working out, playing basketball, interacting, preening and woofing. They had adapted; they'd survived. How?

In gangs! The same way they'd survived on The Street—in black, white, and Hispanic gangs that marked off their territory and provided protection for members.

One black gang dominated. Underwood and his (our!) thugs kept their distance and yielded their territory when they approached. My homies didn't top the pecking order.

Those not in gangs, obvious losers and pariahs probably since elementary playground days, huddled together out of everyone's way.

Two guys, however, stood out; they seemed to rule the yard. When on the weight bench, no one approached. When they finished, they returned to C block without speaking to anyone. Only then did others work out. I watched this daily, but couldn't figure out why no one bothered these two. *They* had the secret to survival. I needed it!

The two were white, young, incredibly muscled and heavily tattooed, remarkably handsome, six feet, chiseled like fitness magazine models, with olive skin and black curly hair. They joked constantly and pummeled each other with blows that would have felled me.

Fascinated, I asked the guard who came daily to see if I was still alive who they were.

"Gino Gambatti and Mario Biagini," he said with a tinge of respect. He pointed to my face. "Larry Wade fucked you up good, but you don't want to see what those assholes can do. Stay away from them, Peterson."

"How come they have the workout equipment to themselves and no one bothers them?"

"Connections." he said simply. *"Family* connections. New Jersey."

Of course. *That* family. Indeed, they did look like young enforcers in a Scorsese mobster movie. No wonder no one messed with them. Good to know; I'd keep my distance too.

But learning their secret didn't help; I didn't have connections. Or a gang—I wasn't about to get a Nazi tattoo to join my homies. There was no Old White Guy gang—not that it would have helped, nor a gang of Liberal Democrats, which would have been even more impotent, like being armed with celery in a knife fight.

I had only one weapon, my Marine retirement money. But money, like any weapon, could be taken away--no point having a gun if someone could grab it out of your hands and shoot you with it. I needed an ally—my life depended on it.

The young Sopranos weren't going to help, and Underwood with our homie gang wasn't enough. I needed the most powerful gang, the black one. But how could I ally myself with them?

I pondered for days, pacing the cell relentlessly, growing more and more anxious, but I couldn't come up with anything.

On the eighth day the investigation ended; I was cleared and released back to General Population, but I still had no plan.

Help came from a most unlikely source.

9. Weightlifting with Mobsters

"God *damn*! You look like shit," Pops exclaimed when I emerged from my cell. After eight days healing! The swelling had gone down, purple bruises had turned yellow, and I didn't hurt any more, but I tried to cover my face in embarrassment because I looked like I'd been mauled and hadn't put up a fight. I hadn't.

"You should have locked your door," he said.

"*You* told me there was nothing to worry about. *You* said he wouldn't attack us because we were too old."

Pops's face crinkled in amusement. "Never trust a con." Then he wagged an instructive finger. "Good lesson there."

But I was in no mood for lessons or humor; I was still pissed at my own idiocy, so I went out for fresh air, yet as soon as I got on the rec yard, massive iron weights clanged to the ground.

Looking towards the weight pile, I was shocked to see one of the two monsters I'd watched from my window stomping towards me. Shit! Another beat down? Already?

As he approached with very determined look, I tried to hide my fear by not flinching, standing straight and meeting his gaze, yet when he reached me, he smiled dazzlingly with perfect white teeth, itself unusual--missing or deformed teeth were the norm.

"Gino," he said, extending a hand, not bumping fists, my first civil interaction. I almost collapsed in relief.

Then he shrugged, head cocked slightly to the right, palms open, the Italian gesture stating the obvious, what everybody was supposed to know—his name. "Gambatti. Need help, don't you." It was not a question.

Then he scared the shit out of me again by tossing a muscled arm around my shoulder, steering me to a corner of the yard—deserted now because the nerds clustered there had scattered like geese at his approach. As I watched them flutter away, Gambatti said, "Let's talk."

I didn't resist--*couldn't*--yet my worries were unnecessary for he disarmed me immediately, rather like: "Hi, I'm Al Capone. How's it going? Need help? Maybe I can do something for you." As soon as we were alone, he told me with a thick, but friendly New Jersey accent that he was from New Jersey.

Swallowing my relief because I didn't want him to know how worried I'd been—animals smell fear, and this guy looked all animal—I nodded with a faint smile. "I can tell."

He spoke so softly I strained to hear, but didn't move closer for his stance, legs spread slightly, rocking lightly on the balls of his feet, signaled: Stay away! Danger!

He opened with, "I can help you (youse). I'm here cause (cuz) I got caught on business (bidnis) for my Uncles. They're in construction (struckshun) and sanitation (centayshun)."

"Your *Uncles*? What were you caught for?"

"Trafficking."

Bravely I ventured a joke. "Trafficking what—lumber? Toilets?"

He smiled *very* faintly. "Cute. My Uncles used juice (juz) to get me sent here. It's a soft shithole."

I pointed to the weight bench. "The other Soprano too?"

"Mario?" He nodded. He's my cousin (cusn), my *compare*."

Contemplating me a moment, the tiger appraising a rabbit, he decided against the meal and tousled my hair—roughly; concussion worthy. " 'Lumber. Toilets,' " and he smiled. "I figured you were smart, funny too." Then he nodded approvingly, "We'll get along good. If I'd known what that nigger had going down, I would have killed him."

He shrugged modestly. "Or had somebody do it."

Believing it and realizing this *might* be fine, I relaxed slightly, breathing more easily and ventured another joke. "Why didn't you know? I needed muscle."

He smiled indulgently. "We say 'juz."

"Ok. Juice. It's the least you could have done for a paisano."

He sneered, "Peterson isn't wop."

"It's Swedish, on my dad's side, but Swedish is a recessive gene."

He didn't get it, so I added—"dormant". That didn't register either. "Bartolino," I finally said. "On my mother's side. My Nonna came from Torino, up north where Italians are blond, blue eyed, and handsome."

"Gay."

What a dick. "Cute, but you know, Gambatti, my Nonna hated my Uncle Henry—Francisconi. He married

114

my aunt Marie. Nonna couldn't stand him because he came from Sienna. She said it got worse the further south you went in Italy. Rome was terrible, Naples nothing but criminals, and Sicily—that wasn't even Italy, that was Africa."

I pointed to his curly black hair. "Looks African to me."

Now he laughed and yelled to his *compare* Thor. "Hey Mario, come here. We got another dago in the unit— a gay one."

Mario, just as big and dark, swaggered over (neither walked, they strutted), shook hands and said, nodding at Gino—"Oh shit, not another queer."

That prompted a terrific blow from Gino, but it didn't shake Mario and they threw themselves on each other like Transformers for a couple minutes.

I backed away to watch with cautious amusement as they battled to a draw, then Gino told Mario to go to back his "pussy weights;" he needed to talk to me.

After wiping sweat from his face and chest, he turned an intense gaze on me, but it wasn't threatening. I relaxed; it *was* going to be ok, so I waited.

"I been wanting to talk to you," he said. "I saw your trial on Court TV. What a fuckfest. I couldn't believe you got convicted." His eyes glinted maliciously. "Course it didn't help when they paraded out your blond gigolo soldier. He from Northern Italy too?"

Guessing that head on was the best way to deal with him, I risked, "Fuck you."

He nodded. Yep, this was the way to handle him.

"It'll make a great story when you write it, Peterson. At least you can. None of the assholes here could write theirs, even if they were innocent."

"Can't you? Schlepping shitters from New Jersey sounds like a TV movie to me."

He shook his head. "I wasn't innocent," then he jerked an index finger to his lips. "You didn't hear that. In fact, I didn't say it."

I whispered, "Omerta."

"*Molto bene*. Your Nonna teach you that?'

"Mario Puzo. *The Godfather*."

"Great movie! I seen it fifty times. Reminded me of Uncle Frank."

"A role model."

He frowned. "Naah. Uncle Louie whacked him. Money. Or drugs. Or cunt. Probably all three."

"Ah, family. *Famiglia*."

In only ten minutes we'd hit it off, a most unlikely couple. I felt safe with him from that beginning though I had no idea why he welcomed me: he seemed to have no ulterior motive for befriending me. There was nothing I could offer him, but there was so much he could do for me.

I must have glowed with pleasure for he seemed amused and tweaked my cheeks painfully. "Ok, I'm gonna look after you." His eyes narrowed. "But don't get any ideas."

What an arrogant asshole. "Not to worry. You're not my type."

His thick black eyebrows rose alarmingly. "Why not?"

"You're too dark."

116

He grinned. "Right. *Blond* gigolos. Ok, now I'm gonna set you straight on how to make it in here." He held up a finger. "First rule: Don't say anything personal to anyone. They'll run to the hacks. Snitches. So don't tell anybody your business."

"I haven't got any business."

He shrugged his knowing shrug, palms slightly raised, lower lip protruding. "You will. It's the only way to survive. Put *your* juice to work."

"What juice?"

"Money and connections: what juice is always about. Muscle too, but…well, at least you got money and connections. Two out of three aint bad."

I ignored the slur. "Money buys muscle. How much do you want?"

"You (youse) don't have that much money, Peterson; I aint for sale or rent," then he gestured towards the weight pile. "But talk to Mario. He'll do *anything* for a honey bun."

"I'll tell him you referred him, plus the price—a honey bun. Fifty cents in the canteen."

"Seriously," he went on, "How long did it take you to get on TV after the hit? Before the blood dried. And they kept you in your cell because they didn't want anyone to see how fucked up you were. They wanted to hide you. You scare them. You're the only inmate who can get media involved."

He added off handedly, "They wanted to send you to protective custody, didn't they?"

"How'd you know?" I asked in surprise. While locked in my cell, the assistant warden told me that the only

117

way DOC could safeguard me was in "protective custody" at a remote prison. In general population at Nash, I'd be subject to assaults.

Protective custody was for convicted law enforcement officers, snitches, and high profile cases who needed extra protection. I'd said no; better beaten down than hidden away.

"They wanted you in PC because they don't want your ass here. Whatever happens to you is front page and on TV. You're too high profile. I'm sure Wynette got her snatch scorched for your beat down."

He let that sink in, then added, "High profile means you can get away with more than anyone, but it also means they watch you carefully."

Thus began his classes in Prison Survival. Gino, with ancestors probably dating to Spartacus, knew all the ins and outs. "You got a lot to learn, Peterson, so pay attention."

He held up a finger. "One: like I said, beware of snitches. These guys hate you. They're jealous. You're famous. You have money. They'd stab you in a hard on, so don't ever let your guard down. "

A second finger went up. "Never call a guard out or embarrass them; they never forget and will get you for it eventually. Most don't give a fuck about rules; they're just here for the paycheck. So, if rules say you can't have more than 25 stamps, have a 100. Or a 1000. Just don't rub them in a guard's face. Same with shanks, porn…."

He grinned maliciously. "And punks—lots of blond gigolos here."

I ignored the gay taunt; protesting would just invite more.

A third finger again. "Don't let anything bother you, and *never* let on if it does." He smiled. "Like the way you just handled that gay gigolo thing. That was good."

Another smile. "For a gay guy."

"You asshole."

Third finger. "Don't let anyone get in your head. Let shit slide unless someone comes at you. You can't let that go because they'll keep coming, but otherwise *never* let anyone get in your head. If that happens, they own you. You're their punk."

Then he patted me—more like hammer blows--on the head, class over. "Now I gotta get back to the weight pile before that cunt Mario gets any stronger."

Grateful for his help, I thanked him, but he waved it off. "*Figurati.*" It's nothing. Then he shook my hand, a ritual performed every time we met and parted.

He had surprising Old World elegance for someone so young—he and Mario were only 22—yet I saw ferocity in the intense look that occasionally flashed across his face; it left no doubt that he'd tear you apart and eat the pieces if you fucked with him. Mario too. They were very big bad boys and I was delighted they'd befriended me. Maybe we bonded as notorious outsiders—their "family" and my high profile status, but whatever the reason, I was thankful for their protection.

A few days later Gino handed me several hand written papers scrawled with what looked like hieroglyphics. They contained the signs, markings, codes, and tattoos of the different gangs.

"Study them so you'll know who you're dealing with. You gotta know this," he said.

I crammed that night like for a major college test, studying as if my life depended on learning the signs. It did.

In the morning on the weight pile, I pointed to Gino's tattoos—a pitchfork on his right arm, the number 6 on his left, and bizarrely, a Star of David on his always no matter the weather pumped bare chest. "Folk Nation."

He nodded. "*Bene.*" He gestured towards Underwood. "What about your homie?"

"How'd you know we were homies?"

Gino flicked my forehead with a finger; it was like a bullet. "Me and Mario make it a point to know everything. You better too if you want to survive here."

"Ok, ok. Aryan Brotherhood. Swastikas."

"What about the 88 on his redneck neck?"

"Heil Hitler. H, the eighth letter in the alphabet."

"Bloods and Crips?"

I pointed to the dominant group I'd watched from my window. "Bloods: regular star with a 5 inside it. And dog paws."

He nodded. "*Buono.* But two tattoos you probably learned don't mean shit— a tear drop coming from an eye and a spider web on the elbow."

"I thought it meant the guy's in for murder."

Gino snorted. "They wish, but it's just woofing to scare you. Mario's got one on his ass—he's scared someone will take it."

He turned to Mario, "Show Peterson the spider web on your asshole."

Of course that prompted a major skirmish. I backed far away to laugh; I did not want to become collateral damage as they fought fiercely cursing one another in Italian.

One of my great regrets is that I never learned Italian because Nonna didn't pass it on. America was her country from when she landed at Ellis Island and she spoke only heavily accented English except when vexed with Uncle Henry; then she lapsed into machinegun Italian, hands slashing the air. Nonna was going to assimilate and demanded her children do also: only English.

My grandfather who didn't finish the fourth grade and couldn't finish a sentence without god damn and sonofabitch never spoke Italian to my mother. He could barely read and write, but he took me every Sunday to The Penguin Soda Shop to buy the *Nevada State Journal*. He loved the comic strip *The Katzenjammer Kids*, especially when Mama pounded wayward Fritz and Hans; it was the story of Nonna, himself and his brothers John and Frank. German, Italian--immigrants all; he understood that strip even though he couldn't read it.

In my grandparents' house there was a photo on the wall in the living room of Granddad in a WWI doughboy uniform. He was 19 with a bewildered look on his face—a perplexed mostly illiterate youth on his way to a war he knew nothing about in 1917. But I know Nonna was proud—her oldest son fighting for America only a few years after her arrival from "the old country," not a word of English on her tongue.

But granddad never made it to war. He caught influenza during the 1918 pandemic and almost died during basic training at Fort Lewis, but Nonna went to Washington to nurse him with whiskey and water. After the army, he returned to Reno, married my grandmother in 1919, and they lived with Nonna in her house. In 1920 my mother was stillborn.

Nonna plunged her into a pail of cold water, then hot water, then cold water, then hot water until she gasped for air. She saved my grandfather then she saved my mother. I am twice indebted to Nonna for life.

Though Gino and Mario spent a lot of time on the weight pile, they went inside every day to watch *The Young and The Restless* and *The Bold and the Beautiful*, followed by *Jeopardy* and *The Price is Right*, and they ended afternoons with *Jerry Springer* and *Maury Povich*.

I teased them about it, but they were immune to ridicule: "It's real life," Gino said. "Better than the one here," Mario added.

I didn't watch daytime TV; I'd go to the library, a room the size of three cells with about 3,000 public library cast offs. Though Gino and Mario never read anything except porn, other inmates read voraciously. Danielle Steele (!), Louis L'Amour, and George R.R. Martin were favorites. "Good" literature--Hawthorne, Conrad, Dickens, etc.—went unread. My system for selections was to choose a book that appeared new and avoid the well-thumbed ones.

The inmate librarian told me my books had once been there but *The Immortal Dragon* had been stolen because it was so "dirty". Officials had removed *A Time of War* and *A Bitter Peace* when they learned I'd be arriving.

The first books I checked out were the *Lord of the Rings*, figuring the trilogy would last a month. I wanted to reserve a couple Phillip Roth novels, but the librarian said it wasn't necessary: none had ever been checked out.

I also started a diary and made an entry every night. My life was reading, writing, going to the chow hall and spending time with Gino and Mario. There was no stress and I was not unhappy. I was in prison, had lost everything including my children and freedom, and yet I was not miserable. How could that be? Candace and the DA would be so pissed.

One afternoon after *Jerry Springer*, Gino warned me about a "shake-down" the following morning, a guard search of all cells and lockers.

I figured a bribed guard had told him, but I didn't think I had anything to worry about so I was shocked when guards swept through and confiscated Gino's gang symbol papers that I'd left in plain view. They screamed at me for having dangerous contraband and locked me in my cell for another investigation.

How could I have been so stupid! Again. Gang contraband!

I couldn't blame Gino for not warning me: did I need to be told not to have cocaine or a gun? Jesus! My second lock down in less than a month. I wanted to bang my head against the wall, but instead dropped on my bunk in disgust.

How long would this lock down last, I wondered, but my cell door suddenly burst open and two guards rushed in.

"Get up, asshole," they screamed, then they cuffed and dragged me ou

10. Security Threat

Filled with dread, I knew I was on my way to The Hole, but instead I was frog marched in a cold light November rain to the main office and tossed in a barren brightly lit room with a metal table and two chairs just like in TV cop shows. No point asking for a lawyer, I thought, trying to appear brave as they slammed me into a chair, but almost immediately, a seven foot jug eared Frankenstein in a guard uniform filled the doorway, then he clumped towards me.

No good cop bad cop, this was going to be *all* bad cop.

"Stand up, asshole," he screamed in a high pitched southern drawl. The sight of him was terrifying, but his helium squeal was even more unnerving.

Holy shit, I thought jumping up, courage gone. As he loomed over me, I backed away, but he swatted the table aside as if it were a doll's and advanced towards me, pinning me against the wall like a collector's dead butterfly, which is how I felt before the monster.

"I'm the STG Captain and *you* are fucked."

STG I knew meant the fearsome Security Threat Group that dealt with gangs. He was the commander, and no doubt about it, I was fucked.

Braced against the wall, it took all of my will power to stop quivering and stay upright.

"Where'd you get these?" he yelled, bitch slapping me with the gang papers.

"Someone gave them to me before he left," I stammered. "He's not here any longer."

"Bullshit! Bullshit! Bullshit!" he shrieked. "Gino Gambatti gave them to you. And he's still here."

Quivering, I managed a feeble, "Who?"

Frankenstein slammed me against the wall and thrust his face furiously into mine. "Yeah, right. Do you know what that piece of shit is in here for? Him and his asshole buddy Biagini? Drugs! Heroin! Cocaine! They bring that shit down from New York or some Yankee fuckplace. They're gangsters. Are they recruiting you?"

He grabbed my shirt and ripped it. "Do I need to check you for mob tattoos?"

I was afraid he was going to, but instead he suddenly laughed and let me go. It was too absurd, even for him—me, a little old white man as a security threat.

The helium seemingly gone from his balloon, I exhaled. He was just putting on a show; I'd seen DI's do better, and *they* never laughed.

"Goddamn you, Peterson, you've already caused enough trouble. Ms. Wynette has worn out a pair of tennis shoes pacing her office about you. She's going to have to go to Walmart to get another pair. Pink!"

Then he convulsed in laughter. I tried hard to keep a straight face, but the Inquisition was over. This was just theater that had turned into a comedy, yet it wasn't completely finished for the tree topping Savonarola whirled me around, unlocked the cuffs and shoved me towards the door. "You need a job, Peterson. If you're hanging out with Gambatti reading gang shit, you got too much time on your hands. Get out of here."

As I strolled towards the door with as much dignity as I could muster, he grabbed my arm and spun me to face him, his menacing eyes a promise. "I'll be watching you closely."

I took my time getting back to the unit, enjoying a few minutes away from its confines, a rare few minutes alone. The rain had stopped, but not my worries: I knew I'd reached authority's tolerance limit and had violated one of Gino's survival rules--taunting guards by leaving gang contraband out in front of them. I hadn't meant to, but stupidity was no alibi.

Gino was waiting on the rec yard like a pissed drill instructor. Grabbing my neck, he pushed me to the fence even more roughly than Frankenstein had mangled me; I thought he was going to ram me through it.

"Get your shit together, Peterson. Stop fucking up!" Then, whirling me around, he thrust another set of gang papers into my hands and shook me violently. "*Don't get caught with these.*"

My ass was pressed into the wire; I had no place to go. So this is what it's like to fuck up in his world. I looked to Mario on the weight pile for help, but baring his teeth, he drew a finger across his throat.

Jesus! I pushed Gino away with all my strength and unwedged my ass from the wire. "It won't happen again."

He stared at me a long moment debating what to do. There was no ocean to drop me cement footed into, so finally he shook his head dismissing my sacrilege, crisis over.

"Ok, as I was saying about gangs before you fucked up—for the *last* time."

His hand swept across the yard taking in about fifty guys clustered in numerous small groups. "Gangs here are bullshit little street corner sets, nothing like in New York, LA, and Chicago. Those gangs are real; they *rule* prisons. They own guards. Here, Lurch, that fucking redneck STG Captain, gets rid of dangerous bangers."

"Why hasn't he got rid of you and Mario?"

"We don't bang. We got better things to do."

"Like *The Young and Restless* and *The Price is Right*?"

He gave me the finger. "Besides, I already told you—juice."

Then he pointed to several guys in another corner. "MS-13. Salvadorians. Vicious motherfuckers, never cross them—they are scary dudes, but there are only a couple here because Lurch ships new ones who come in. The rest—Latin Kings, Folk Nation, Crips, Aryan Nation— are minor players. You don't need to worry about them. Bloods run this place; they're at the top, but they don't *rule*. Guards rule. Understand?"

He read my quizzical look. "Bloods control the yard, except for the weight pile—that's me and Mario's— but they don't control the units. Lurch, Wynette and the hacks run this place. But you don't want to fuck with Bloods because they owned the yard, they owned drugs, and gambling. They also have some hacks on their side because they bribe them."

I'd already determined from watching out my window that Bloods were the most powerful gang, so I asked what concerned me most. "How do I make them allies?"

He seemed annoyed. "Like with everything, it's how you carry yourself: don't act afraid; treat everyone with respect; mind your business; watch everything that goes on. And never back down, even if it means getting your ass kicked."

Nodding at my still bruised face, he deadpanned, "Again."

He closed his palms. "That's it. Blood gang leaders--shot callers--are watching you; when they think they can trust you not to snitch, they'll come to you to do business."

Again a quizzical look. "Why?"

Back on attack, he hammered my head as if it were a cinder block to be judoed in half. "Did Lurch give you a hard time? No. He just wanted to pucker your asshole. The *Po*-leese, even Lurch and Wynette aren't going to fuck with you because they're scared of the media. That makes you valuable to gangs. You got media juice."

Catching my doubtful look, he gestured to the guys milling around. "Can't you see?—they're watching you now."

I did notice eyes on us. "I think they're looking at you," I said.

He inflated a little more, pleased with his own notoriety. "It's both of us." Then he got serious. "I'm leaving next month. I want a copy of your book when you get out."

I blanched in surprise. "Am I getting out? You really think so?" He was the only guy who ever told me that. "How do you know?"

He opened his hands, pursed his lips, raising his shoulders like my Italian forebears. In today's vernacular, "There it is," or "What is Is,"--a self-evident truth.

I said excitedly, "You think I'll win my appeal? The Court of Appeals has it now."

His lips made the noise of a two year old spitting porridge. "*Merda.*"

"What! You don't think I'll win the appeal?"

More porridge spat. "Those cocksuckers won't overturn your case. Judges never overrule other judges. You got fucked; they're not going to unfuck you. You're gonna stay fucked. But you'll get out. You're not the type to stay here."

"I also happen to be innocent."

He pushed me, almost knocking me over. "*Stronzo*! Wake up! Peterson. That doesn't have anything to do with it. The judicial system isn't about justice. When were you born? Where have you lived? Join the real world. *This* world."

I must have looked like I was going to cry. I felt like it; I was going to lose my appeal. My head drooped, my shoulders fell, but he'd have none of it; he tousled my hair like a rag doll's and jerked up my chin, nearly snapping my neck. "You'll be all right. But until you get out, there's a lot you need to learn. So pay attention, I'm going to teach you how to make it in here."

Mimicking Don Corleone, head bowed as if talking to the ground, he started a mumbling lecture. "Murderers are at the top."

He dark eyes rose to meet mine. "At least you're first in something."

129

"I didn't kill anyone!"

"Doesn't matter. *Convicted* First Degree murderers are at the top—that's you. This is good, but it would have been better if you'd used your hands or a knife. What'd you use, a napkin? Not impressive. And it'd have looked better if you'd killed a cop or a cartel lord. Killing women with a dustpan don't get you many points."

"Fuck you!"

"After murderers come guys like me and Mario. *Maggiore Spacciatori*, major dealers."

"Then come B&E guys, arsonists, druggies—street corner pushers and users—rapists. And finally…." He paused, then spat the word, the bottom of the bottom. "Chesters. Kiddie fuckers. *Molestatori* like that new cocksucker on your block."

He meant Chris, an obese soft inmate in his early thirties who'd arrived a few days earlier claiming to be in for trafficking cocaine and heroin, pronounced "hair-on."

Gino had been outraged. "That fat cocksucker never dealt smack. He's a Chester." He'd fumed all day, his ferocity flashing constantly, but next morning he was relaxed, at peace, as if he'd just returned from church: a mass for the dead.

He and I had been talking near the fence that afternoon after *Jeopardy* and before *Jerry Springer* when Chris waddled onto the yard. Gino nodded to Mario in a prearranged signal. Mario went to Chris, put his arm around him in a friendly manner and steered him to Gino.

Mario—who looked like The Rock on steroids—stood so close to Chris that only I saw the blade he'd stuck in Chris's gut.

Shocked, I backed away. A shank! The first I'd seen, not taped up razor blades, but something from SEAL Surplus that could have boned an antelope. I didn't want to see this, but like a car wreck, I couldn't take my eyes off what was happening.

"Get on your knees, cocksucker," Gino ordered.

Chris dropped to the ground. Mario pressed the blade into his throat, drawing a trickle of blood. I backed further away, eyes wide unable to stop watching.

"Yell, I'm a Chester,'' Gino demanded.

"I'm a Chester," Chris yelled.

"Louder."

"I'M A CHESTER," Chris screamed.

"Now yell, I'm a queer Chester."

"I'M A QUEER CHESTER!"

Gino unbuttoned his fly and took out his dick. Everyone on the yard watched open mouthed, even guards, but they made no movement towards us.

"Now scream, I want to suck your cock."

"I WANT TO SUCK YOUR COCK!"

Gino kicked him over backwards. "You'd love it too much."

Then he put his arm around my shoulders, and said, "If I wanted a blow job, I'd get sweet lips Mario."

A tremendous hit from Mario to Gino almost knocked me over in ricochet, but it didn't faze Gino. He turned to Mario. They both laughed uproariously.

There were not going to be any fat queer dope dealers in their world.

"How did you know about him?" I stammered, still stunned by the incident.

131

He gave his all-knowing shrug with open slightly raised hands. A guard might have told him, or maybe he found out by using a cell phone, strictly forbidden and a serious offense. Owning one could result in an attempted escape charge—but of course he and Mario each had one. Yet if Gino had wanted me to know, he'd have told me. His motto was: Never ask questions. If you don't know anything, you can't be accused of snitching. However, the corollary was: Know everything. Pretend you know nothing, but know it all.

He'd bang me on the head and say, "You gotta learn that." Not only did I have to learn that, I had to get in better shape. "You need to toughen up, Peterson."

"I was tough when I was a Marine your age. I'm sixty years old."

"Uncle Frank was a monster at your age."

"You said your Uncle Louie whacked him."

"Yeah, but he looked great in the coffin." Then his eyelids drooped and he gave me a sleepy sensual look that must have devastated women. "Don't you want to look good for me in the coffin?"

"No, Casanova, I don't give a fuck about that. I plan to be cremated."

His eyes shot open. "Cremated?" He crossed himself.

Of course. Catholic. "It won't hurt, but where you're going—Hell—might."

Two weeks passed with bantering and jokes. One morning as I headed out to join Gino and Mario, I stopped at the door. Wait. This isn't right.

I went to a table and sat down. Prison was supposed to be awful. I missed my children desperately, but I wasn't miserable; I wasn't even unhappy. I felt comfortable, safe. I was reading, writing, and working out. Was it really possible that I could survive this? For now as Mario's and Gino's *compare*, yes, and soon my appeal would come through and I'd go home.

All I had to do was stay busy and not dwell in the past torturing myself with my lost children. I would not think about the trial. It was over. As the Buddha said, life is an endlessly flowing stream. You can't step into the same water twice; the past is gone.

I would avoid self-consuming anger. Above all, I would not hate. Not even Larry Wade who had clocked me. My wounds had healed and he was gone. Besides, as Gino had taught, when you're angry and filled with hate for someone, he's in your head; he owns you.

So, deciding to enjoy this as long as possible, I jumped up and ran eagerly out to the weight pile where Gino and Mario were gobbling raw yeast that they'd bribed (or strong armed) someone to steal from the chow hall kitchen.

"You need this, Peterson" Gino said, offering me a handful. "As good as steroids. It'll pump you up."

I waved it away. "Baking yeast? Forget it. I don't want to look like a cupcake."

They howled with laughter and started to pummel me. "Elder abuse!" I yelled.

At that moment the loud speaker blasted, "PETERSON, GO SEE MRS. SNOW. NOW!"

I looked quizzically to Gino and Mario.

Mario drew a finger across his throat, his voice doom. "You. Are. Fucked."

Gino nodded ominously, but his voice was almost chipper. "Ass Rape Time."

11. Mafia Queen

Lurch, making good on his promise to keep me under close watch, had decided I'd become too comfortable with Mario and Gino, so he used a sledgehammer to break up our triumvirate--the notorious Ms. Snow, a terror reputed worse than his own STG unit.

I'd heard fearsome stories about her since arrival. As the supervising counselor, she had more control over inmates than anyone and used her power to reward or punish—usually punish, but I didn't understand how.

Everyone feared her; even Gino spoke of her with rare respect. He said she was the most important official at Nash; not even the warden would tangle with her because she had enough "dirt" to bring anyone down.

In Gino's survival class on who to avoid, he put her at the top of the list. "She could be a Mafia queen," he'd said.

"Is there such a thing?" I'd asked in surprise.

"No, but if there was, it'd be that bitch."

"Why's she so powerful?"

"She controls all job assignments."

I was not impressed. "So?"

He shook his head in annoyance. "You don't understand anything about this place. You're like some fucking little princess who dropped in for a visit."

"Ok, so tell me what I need to know."

"Unlike you, me and Mario, most guys need money, but they can't earn any unless she gives them a job. 40 cents or 70 cents a day. *Capisce?*"

"Ok, got it."

"More importantly, even for me and Mario, is that you can't get a cell without a job. Without a cell, you live on a bunk in the day room with 15 other guys. You got NO privacy and share a shitter with cum and piss everywhere."

I grimaced. "Got that too."

"It gets worse. Without a job, you don't earn Gain Time--six days every month off your sentence: 20%. If a judge gives you 12-16 years, the max is 16, but gain time— a job--can bring it down to 12. See? She controls your money, whether you have a cell or live on a bunk, and your time served. If she favors you—if you kiss her fat ass-- your sentence is cut by years. That's why me and Mario have jobs."

"*You* have a job?" I asked in amazement, unable to imagine him working for anyone except--envisioning machineguns and squealing tires as cars made their getaway--his Uncles. "You're out here all goddamn day except when you're watching *The Young and the Restless* and *Jerry Springer* freak shows.

"I'm a janitor. 40 cents a day, but I subcontract; I pay a guy a dollar to do it."

Of course. "Sub-contracting. Like New Jersey."

The shrug. "My Uncles were good teachers. *But*, if Ms. Snow doesn't like you, you don't earn money or gain time. You live years longer on a bunk in cum and piss."

"I got it!"

"No, you still don't, so pay attention. Her price for helping you get a job, a cell, and your time cut is that you snitch for her. Her snitches are everywhere. You can't trust anyone *with* a job because they owe it to her; she owns them. And you can't trust anyone without a job because they'd do anything to get one. That's how she knows everything about everyone—inmates, guards, staff, and admin. *Everything*. She probably even knows when I jack off."

"Do you and Mario snitch for her?" I knew the answer of course; I just wanted to piss him off. I did. "Me and Mario got connections higher than that cunt," he said contemptuously. "You don't."

"But I don't need a job. I already have a cell and 20% off a life sentence doesn't mean shit. Six days a month off forever is still forever. Death minus a week is still death."

Mario, listening in as he lifted weights to expand shoulders and a chest that seemed impossible to broaden, said, "You won't stay in that cell much longer. Only guys with jobs get cells. Even the warden can't change that rule. Guys are already complaining about you. She'll give your cell to someone with a job."

Gino nodded with satisfaction. "Soon it'll be piss and cum time unless you get a job."

Though I'd been lulled into a sense of security with my cell, I knew I couldn't remain a privileged inmate forever, but I didn't want a job. I liked having the day to read, write, and work out with Gino and Mario. I didn't need money or a job, but I really wanted to keep my cell.

Only Wee Man had ever wanted to stay on a bunk in the day room, and that was because of Mario.

Wee Man was a diminutive guy terrified of being raped. It had happened at another prison; a couple guys had gone into his cell when he was asleep and raped him repeatedly. After that he felt safer in the open on a bunk with guards watching, so when Ms. Snow gave him a job, he reluctantly moved into a cell.

The first night, Mario slipped into it while Wee Man was at chow and hid under the bunk. When Wee Man came in and lay down, Mario waited until he heard snoring, then he jumped out, pounced on Wee Man and ripped off his trousers. Wee Man screamed, then fainted.

Mario slipped out leaving him naked.

When Wee Man came to, he ran out of the cell and wouldn't go back in.

"You got the tightest pussy I ever had," Mario told him.

"Did you really fuck him?" I asked Mario.

Mario laughed. "I don't fuck guys."

"He's a bottom, not a top," Gino said, prompting yet another major skirmish.

I now understood Gino's respect for Ms. Snow: she could take away my cell unless I worked for her, so when summoned to her office, I listened to Mario's and Gino's final advice.

"She's been here forever," Mario said. "They built the prison around her--it took *lots* of razor wire. Whatever you do, don't piss her off."

"Too late," Gino declared. "He's already fucked." Then to me, "You're white. The only whites she likes are young studs like Mario and me." Then the inevitable shrug. "You're old."

"But charming."

He smiled slyly. "You'll see."

So off I went unworried, more curious than concerned to see the person everyone feared, like wanting to see Godzilla up close despite the danger.

Her office was in A Section behind three iron sliding doors controlled by guards in an observation booth. A sign warned: **NO ENTRY UNLESS CALLED. WRITE UP!** Write ups were infractions resulting in loss of cell, gain time, and money, as well as a trip to The Hole, but having been called, I knocked boldly on the windowless door labeled, MS. LATOYA SNOW.

"Come in," a treacle voice sang.

And there she was, a huge colorful Mardi Gras float troweled in make-up wearing what had to be a wig (no hair could be that black or straight), teeth gleaming, cleavage about to burst open. She was in her forties—maybe; age was not what you noticed when you first saw her.

Regally motioning to a chair in front of her desk, she smiled like a talk show host--not Oprah, but one about to ruin whatever doomed career I might have had before this—and her stop sign red lips barely parted. "Why, Mr. Peterson, how nice to see you," she said, not at all pleased. "Have a seat. How are you transitioning? Everything going all right?"

"Yes. Thank you," I answered, perching on the edge of a chair searching for a safe place to center my gaze- -*not* on the cleavage.

Her phony smile widened; I thought of *Jaws*. "Ms. Wynette asked me to talk to you. She wants you to assist teaching GED classes." She batted her eyes encouragingly with lashes so heavily made up Mario would have struggled to lift them. "I believe Captain Deckerd spoke with her about a job for you so that you could keep your cell."

I knew it! Lurch *was* behind this. And Gino had been right, I could keep my cell only with a job, but teaching GED didn't seem so bad. It certainly sounded better than cleaning toilets and showers. If I had to have a job, this would be the best I could get. I could do something meaningful. "I'd be happy to help," I answered, trying to sound gracious.

Her voice continued as syrup. "Everyone should have a job, but no warden has ever contacted me about one for an inmate."

Then the trap sprung. "Until *you* came!" she screamed lifting out of her chair like a Saturn missile, eyes wide as searchlights, wig bouncing, cleavage heaving.

Shocked, I gripped the chair to keep from falling off.

Then, teeth bared, she hunkered down like an offensive linesman. I wanted to flee, but I was paralyzed, and no doubt she could have sacked me before I got to the door.

Gino had been right: I was fucked even before I'd knocked, but he'd been wrong about what doomed me. Ms. Snow might have favored black and young white inmates, but my doom was sealed with something equally not in my control--a turf war with the warden in which I was the turf. Just dirt.

She snarled, "*I* handle all job assignments. Many other qualified candidates have been here longer than you. I was about to place one in the Teacher Assistant position when Ms. Wynette told me to give you the job."

Uh oh, I thought, squirming uncomfortably, grabbing the arm rests. Though I saw the peril, I didn't state the obvious: of course the warden wanted me to teach; it would look good when reporters inquired about what I was doing. She could say, "He's helping other inmates get an education." That sounded so much better than, "He's lying on his ass all day reading books and gang shit, watching TV, listening to his radio, getting beat up, and hanging out with Mafia gangsters."

But that didn't matter to Ms. Snow. What mattered was interference in her fiefdom. That bastard Lurch had put me in harm's way about to be crushed by a Mardi Gras float and there was nothing I could do.

"You'll earn a dollar a day assisting the Nash Community College instructor. Work is 8:30 until 3:30 five days a week, plus two night classes from 7-9."

She pushed a contract across the desk detailing what I could and mostly couldn't do for 40 hours a week at 10 cents an hour--take a break, smoke, drink coffee, show up late, be in the room alone with the civilian teacher, etc., any of which would result in immediate job termination and The Hole. "Sign at the bottom."

Her eyes narrowed to slits of black mascara and her voice dripped venom. "You work for me and will report all prisoner code violations to me."

141

This meant I was to snitch on everyone in class, implying of course that they were to snitch on me. Gino had been right—snitches were everywhere; I was supposed to become one.

The treacle solidified to iron. "You do *not* work for the civilian instructor. You do *not* work for Ms. Wynette." She waved a dismissive circular hand, creating a little tornado. "Wardens come and go; I've seen five. You work and report directly to me. Understand?"

"Yes, ma'am," I managed feebly.

"I've heard a lot about you, Mr. Peterson," she said in a voice that indicated none of it was good. "Probably you've heard about me."

"Yes ma'am," I nodded timorously.

She glowed. "It's all true. Go."

I fled.

"Not as bad as I thought," Gino said in surprise when I reported the meeting to him on the weight pile. "Instead of having ten guys ass rape you tonight, she gave you a decent job."

Mario caressed my butt. "If she'd promised me the TA job, I'd rape your ragged old ass myself."

I swatted his hand. "You already have a job and if you taught GED you couldn't watch *The Bold and the Beautiful*. Besides, she can't have that kind of power."

Gino laughed. "Ever seen her on the yard? When she leaves her office at the end of the day, she looks like a shrimp boat sailing to the gate. Fifty guys follow her like seagulls, all begging for a job, happy to take you out like Wade did. And who are you going to complain to? You have no rights. There's no due process. This is their

142

world, Peterson. They make the rules and break the rules and there's nothing you can do."

I took that in quietly, but I knew my high profile status offered some protection. The media was *my* uncle, though a double edged sword--a curse in the enmity it created among guards, administrators, and inmates, but also a blessing in the fear it created: others could be beaten or "disappeared" without notice, but whatever happened to me featured the 6 pm news.

I was a creature of the media. For some inexplicable reason--ok, not so inexplicable: sex, money, and murder—I'd been chosen to tantalize the public, sell newspapers, and boost TV ratings. Anything about me foddered front pages and highlighted newscasts: the Anti-Christ brought to justice; Darth Vader gets his just desserts.

The public didn't want the vile story to end; new negative twists were constantly sought: the sale of my house, declaring bankruptcy, the prison "fight".

Yet that notoriety was my protection. If I screamed Rape, it wouldn't prevent the hosing, but it'd bring unwanted attention: How did Mr. Peterson get ass raped?—not that we're upset, but prison is supposed to be safe from such things.

The authorities understood this, which is why they'd treated me with caution and hadn't sent me to The Hole for the "fighting" incident, possessing gang papers, or hanging out with Mario and Gino. I could do damage. Cost jobs. There was détente, which they had to hate me for—a rogue inmate—but they hated media attention more.

Their clever solution was to punish me in a way that made them look good: teaching GED. But I didn't mind; I was actually pleased—it'd be meaningful work. I could help others.

Moreover, with a job guys couldn't begrudge me a cell now, and with Mario and Gino leaving shortly, it would fill their void. This had not worked out badly at all.

Nevertheless, as their departure neared, I fell into a funk. I felt safe with them. I slept well. I'd even been able to repress misery for all that I'd lost.

On The Street I'd had many friends, but only a few had stuck by me when it really mattered after Kathleen died. All my good Liberal Democrat friends had bailed at the disclosure of my bisexuality while Mario and Gino, as apolitical as they were amoral, didn't give a shit.

In the Marines, we trusted each other because our lives depended on one another, but prison survival was solitary. I had been fortunate to find Mario and Gino. We liked and trusted one another, rare in prison where most guys were loners, socially inept, and rightfully distrustful of others. Gino and Mario had grown up in a family (of sorts) whose survival depended on trust; they had decided to include me in their trust, so I trusted them.

When they left I'd be alone. I began to mope, dropping my head, acting sullen and remote.

Of course Gino tried to cheer me up. One day near the end he said offhandedly, "You know I'm never going to write you."

"Oh fuck you."

"I'll be too busy cunt diving and eating pussy all day. But you'll be all right. You're doing fine. Keep it up. Just remember *omerta*—silence."

144

But getting over their departure was tough. I was losing friends, but also protection. Their aegis had brought reserve and respect in how others treated me. Would that last or would I become vulnerable again? Maybe *more* vulnerable: retaliation; schadenfreude. Would guys who'd been jealous of my association with Gino and Mario turn on me?

I desperately needed to replace their protection. But how? With whom?

Casually trying to mask my concern and fear, I asked Gino a couple days before he left, "Anybody here I can trust?"

"You fickle fuck. Looking to replace me already? *Nobody* can replace me."

"I was thinking maybe Chris the Cocksucker could."

He'd laughed. "Yeah, right. Ok, now think: who do I talk to?"

"Mario and me."

"Who does Mario talk to?"

"You and me."

Then the wonderful shrug affirming the obvious: There it is. "But we're leaving--Uncle Louie's sending a limo. Who's left? Just you. You can't depend on anyone."

Back to square one. I tried to hide my disappointment, but Gino knew. He grinned as he gestured towards a massive guy on the weight-pile who'd recently been allowed to lift weights with them—a unique development. He had to be all right or Gino and Mario would never have associated with him. "Big Tom is solid.

I talked to him about you. Straight up guy. In for murder. He'll help you."

Then he whispered, "But Jesus is he a redneck. He's from Mt. Airy, Mayberry in those old Andy Griffith shows. I can barely understand him."

I grinned. "He kent unnerstan youse needer."

"Huh? Oh. You asshole," and he hammered my head, though not as hard as usual. Maybe with a little fondness? I hoped so, but probably not.

Two days later he and Mario left. As Gino disappeared out the door, he gave the finger to the guards, called them "cocksuckers", and blew me a kiss. "*Ciao bello.*"

I went to my cell and lay on my bunk staring at the walls and ceiling. I'd lost my only friends. In my mind I saw a future as gray and empty as the walls and ceiling. All the sorrow and loss I'd been able to keep at bay began to close in, suffocating me.

I shut my eyes and pulled the shitty thin pillow over my face. Ommmmm.

But it didn't work this time.

END PART I

II

2004-2007

12. A New Fresh Hell

I'd spent most of the week after Gino and Mario left in my cell morosely reading, averaging about a page every five minutes as I'd stop to close my eyes and sigh in self-pity. I'd finished *Lord of The Rings* and had started Philip Roth's *American Pastoral*, still on the library shelf unread. I'd also jotted embarrassingly trite entries in my journal: "Went to chow (soy burger), took a shower. Got a copy of practice GED math test. Flunked it. Now what?"

When thoughts turned to my children, the rest of my life here, and I got sick of chanting Ommmm to little effect, I went outside to escape from my gloom. It was an overcast day perfectly reflecting how I felt, and Big Tom was on the weight pile to make things worse. We were alone under the darkening sky that threatened rain.

"For Christ's sake, stop moping," he said scornfully.

"I liked Gino and Mario. I miss them," I said mournfully.

"Let's not get squishy gay here, Peterson, but yeah, they were all right. For Yankees."

Tom was a hairy bear with a buzz cut, down 15 years. Weightlifting was his obsession and he looked every minute of the 15 years he'd worked out. Fiercely muscled with a persona to match, he had a great sense of humor always expressed with a straight face.

148

"Gino asked me to look after your sappy old ass," he announced, then added, "Since I'm your new daddy, I'm going to give you good advice." He put his arm around my shoulder and said in a comforting voice, "It's how to deal with losing someone you get close to in here."

I looked at him expectantly, then he shouted in my face, "*Don't* get close to anyone."

I jumped back at the blast.

Gentleness gone, he pointed to the bench. "Your lift. If you call 185 pounds weight lifting."

Shock over, I lay on the bench but waited for a Big Tom story that I knew was coming.

"You can't get close to anybody because they're always leaving. When they ship, it hurts. I learned that from Kenny years ago. I cried the day he left. He had a gorgeous ass. I used to fuck him in the shower. Course he hated it, but I sure loved fucking him."

I stared at him until he pushed me off the bench. "Move if you're not going to lift."

I was never sure if Big Tom's stories were true or not because he told even the most outrageous with the same flat delivery and conviction. However, I felt this one was true.

"So when does your GED job start?" Tom asked. Mopping fake tears from his eyes, he whined, "I'm going to *miss* you on the weight pile. Boo hoo, boo hoo."

"As soon as I learn the math, butthole."

"It's GED, for Christ's sake. High school math. Even I almost managed that. Came close, nearly finished seventh grade. But I thought you went to Duke."

149

"I did, but when I looked at some problems--.2x.2, ¼ divided by ½--I couldn't answer them. I flunked the practice GED math test, so how can I teach it?"

He had lost interest and was gazing beyond the fence in reflection. "Did I ever tell you why I left school? I was fucking these dwarf twins. I mean *fucking*." He turned to me. "You know, dwarfs have regular size snatches. Well…"

"I don't want to hear this," I said. Actually I did, so I shut up.

"One would sit on my dick and the other would sit on my face. Then I'd lift them off and swap places—like juggling bowling balls. They had a friend, Betty Sue—she was real size, but her snatch was tighter than the dwarfs'."

"For God's sake, stop." I said, about to roll off the bench from laughter.

"Anyway, Betty Sue got pregnant. She's my baby's mama."

"We were talking about GED, not a Johnny Cash song," I said, moving off the bench.

"*You* were talking about GED. But go on, bore me with the details. I got another 20 years to do. Might as well make them seem like 25."

He loaded the weight bar with two more 45 pound plates and strapped on dumb bells, maxing out the bar with 415 pounds. He was in the middle of a ten rep set when I said, "I'm going to McNeil for help me with math. He's the TA for the college courses."

Big Tom slammed the bar down and jerked forward. "The fuck you are!"

Again I jumped, actually scampered a safe ten feet away. "What's wrong? He seems all right—keeps to himself, real quiet."

Tom shook his head emphatically. "McNeil is why they have prisons. And wacko bins. There are some seriously fucked up people here. McNeil's one."

"What's so bad about him?" I asked, moving back to the bench, but still not sure if he was serious.

Big Tom stood, pissed for real, a scary sight, and I backed away again, but he closed the distance with one giant step and pressed his face into mine. "Do NOT go near Robert McNeil."

"Tom, I need help with math," I said appeasingly. "He teaches it. Can *you* help me?"

"No, but I won't stab you in the back or fuck up your life either. He will."

I knew Tom wasn't going to harm me; he was just woofing to scare me, so I felt I could argue with him—a little. "C'mon, he can't be that bad."

"He killed two people for no reason. One guy's wife was nine months pregnant. He let his brother take the fall—his own brother! Totally innocent. That poor fuck is on Death Row. They made a movie about the murders. When they showed it on TV here, McNeil ate popcorn and laughed through the whole thing. He's a dangerous wacko you can't handle."

McNeil was 32, six feet, thin, had red hair and wore glasses, his demeanor meek and unimposing. He seemed a harmless geek who was TA for the computer and electrical engineering course the community college offered "select" inmates favored by Mrs. Snow. He didn't talk to anyone, seemed to have no friends, and exercised alone, lifting light weights and running laps at a good pace for thirty minutes. He was tautly fit but not threatening—certainly not as imposing or menacing as Big Tom.

When not at the school in a separate building behind yet another razor-wire fence, he tended gardens in front of the unit and at Medical because the bald headed chain gang guard/assistant warden had a flower fetish, akin to Dracula collecting Hummel figurines.

I had planned to approach McNeil when he returned to the unit that afternoon, but Tom was so vehemently opposed that I decided to observe more because I respected his opinion. Nevertheless, I really needed help; I couldn't do 8th grade math.

The next day on the weight pile, Tom asked if I'd talked to McNeill. I shook my head.

"Don't," he said. He might have been woofing, but he was dead serious.

Several others were weight lifting with us, Bloods from their tattoos. Unlike Mario and Gino, Big Tom didn't care who worked out with him. If you could lift weights, you were good. He didn't discriminate and didn't care how much you could lift, even me who slowed exercise down considerably because I had to remove two of the 45 pound plates and the dumb bells when I lifted, which he had to replace when he lifted. He was an easy going guy who had no prejudices. He got along with everybody, partly because no one wanted to fuck with him.

BK, a young black nearly as strong as Tom, but weighing 100 pounds less--about what I did, 160--had gold

152

front teeth that gleamed when he smiled or, more frequently, snarled.

"BK? What does that stand for?" I'd asked when I'd met him. "Burger King?"

He rushed me with such quick fury that I didn't have time to move away but Tom jumped between us as BK's gold teeth flashed furiously and he screamed in a thick New York accent, "It stands for Brooklyn. Brooklyn-- BK, get it?"

Tom asked him in a deep southern drawl, "Bruk Land? Whars that? You a Yankee?"

The two faced off a few seconds, then Tom winked and said, "Leave the old man alone."

I hadn't been too afraid. I'd gained confidence from Gino and Mario--so what if I got in a fight? Or beat up. This was prison; get used to it--but it wasn't all bravery on my part: I knew Big Tom had my back.

Seeing Tom there for me, BK stopped scowling. He waited a moment. I thought I heard rocks grinding, then he broke into a wide grin, gold teeth gleaming. "You were just funning with me weren't you? Burger King. BK. Good one. I like that." He laughed, pounded me on the back and told everyone about Burger King. "You know what Mr. Peterson said?"

He was proud of it and from then on I never had a problem with a Black on the weight pile. They yearned for jokes and laughter. We all did. I'd learned from Gino the value of humor as a weapon, as long as the behemoths got the joke—or had someone explain it to them.

That afternoon I approached McNeill in the day room when he returned from teaching. As soon as I got

153

close, he backed away. When I held out my hand he seemed confused. He stared at it a few seconds and finally took it with a weak grip. I smiled, but he wouldn't meet my gaze. Ok, there was something wrong with him, but normal behavior in prison was rare because the men weren't normal. Whatever that is.

I told him I'd been offered the GED TA job and needed help with math. I also needed tips for how to deal with student inmates who didn't want to be inmates *or* students.

To my surprise, McNeil knew I'd been offered the job. Ms. Snow must have told him—he was a guard/staff favorite, obviously a snitch—how else did he get a prize TA job? That should have alerted me to danger, but I missed the warning, as I ignored Tom's.

"Let's talk," he said nervously, pointing to a table in the day room.

Yet the only thing he wanted to talk about was me-- my trial, the books and columns I'd written, my military service, my kids. He knew all about me.

I stiffened as warning bells and flashing lights went off in my mind. I had never spoken about any of this to anyone. How did he know? *Why* did he know? Most of all, he wanted to know about my media access. He'd seen me on TV during the trial, knew a news crew had followed me into prison and that every network had featured my "fight" with Larry Wade.

"Let's cut a deal," he said. "I'll help you with math if you help me get my story out."

"What story?" I asked suspiciously.

Glancing about to make sure we weren't overheard, he whispered, "Tomorrow. We'll take a walk outside." Then he went to his cell and shut the door.

Tom was right, something was amiss or missing with McNeil, but I didn't see anything *dangerous* in his behavior, just strange, like with most men here.

The next day he brought math books from the college so I could brush up. I put them in my cell to study later, then we went outside. He said that for helping me, he wanted my help to tell the true story of his murders for the first time. It would prove his brother's innocence and get him off Death Row.

"Your brother is innocent?"

"Yeah," he said off handedly, not as if an injustice had been committed, but as an inconsequential fact. "I'll tell you the story, you write it up, and we'll send it off to the media."

Ok, I thought—if that's all he wanted. Good guy; he's doing the right thing, so we bumped fists for a contract. Later, after I was nearly killed by the nutbag, I wondered: What was I thinking! Write up a man's confession to two murders for public dissemination? How stupid could I be? But it *wasn't* stupidity; it was hubris, almost lethally misplaced confidence in my ability to handle myself in prison.

On reflection, it's a wonder I wasn't killed or seriously hurt, and when I recall events, I shudder at my close call.

We worked on his story for two weeks, usually walking around the track as he emotionlessly told me his tale of double murder. At first I was so shocked I had to

155

suppress a desire to physically distance myself from him, push him away in revulsion, but I never let on and in time grew numb to his bloody litany.

I've known many men who killed other men—I did myself, got a Silver Star and a promotion for it—but we rationalized our killings with duty, honor, country; we were sanctioned—trained, armed, and paid to do it. For many it was easy and came without remorse; no doubt some enjoyed it, but none did it rotely without emotion like McNeill.

It wasn't his crime I found so disturbing, but his demeanor. Yet I still didn't see danger. I made no connection to what he had done to who he was now. Instead, I steeled myself to listen because I wanted to help his innocent brother. And out of fascination, like covering your eyes in a scary move, but peeking between your fingers. It was a study in horror—up close next to a monster. Walking beside him. Pals!

Soon however I began to feel that *my* hands were bloody, that I was complicit. I caught myself rubbing them like Lady Macbeth, and afterwards I showered to cleanse myself.

Many guys had committed terrible crimes. Child molestation! I couldn't understand the crimes or relate to whatever drove the criminal, but in every man, I saw sorrow, grief, pain, and need. All had a semblance of humanity. Except for McNeill.

He seemed a human imposter with programmed responses that he couldn't get right, like HAL in *2001 A Space Odyssey*. Everything was off: his smiles were forced, his laugh faked; he didn't understand humor, for when he did laugh, it was not at the punch line of a joke, but somewhere in the middle.

I found myself inadvertently moving away from him as though he was contagious, yet I'd force myself back to his side and seek eye contact. Looking into his dead eyes was so unnerving that I'd often fake a yawn to hide a shudder.

After several weeks, McNeill said he'd grown closer to me than anyone in his ten years' incarceration, but I could not connect with him on any level.

Big Tom watched with mounting silent disapproval, dynamite with a burning fuse. Finally he detonated. One afternoon he suddenly raised a fist and yelled, "I *told* you about McNeill. He's a bug. A fucking psycho. You asshole!"

"Relax," I said. "I'm watching him carefully. Everything will be fine."

"It will not be fine. He's a killer, a backstabbing motherfucker. When I save your ass from him, I'm going to beat the shit out of you too." Then he tossed down the weights in disgust and went inside.

I knew Tom meant well, but I felt he was wrong about McNeill. I simply didn't see what he saw. I've known many violent men--they're often drawn to the USMC, but I didn't sense danger in McNeill, so I continued to ignore his warnings.

Pride, ego, and hubris blinded me. McNeill's story became *my* story, my good deed, my contribution: helping Elmer Ray McNeill, an innocent man get off Death Row would get me credit and praise. How sick was that?

I became so absorbed in writing the story that I seldom thought about my children or my appeal. Sublimation of course. Instead, I buried myself studying math books until I finally passed the practice GED test.

I imagined Kathleen laughing, but I was happy and proud.

I could do 8th grade math!.

13. GED

It is one thing to understand 8th grade math; teaching it to young prison gangbangers is another. I wanted to help, but could I? My only other teaching experience was long ago tutoring young Marines in patrolling, machine guns, and hand to hand combat, but they were eager to learn any mayhem that might result in more proficient killing; they listened attentively.

Young GED felons didn't, and I spent many anxious hours thrashing on my bunk, pacing the rec yard, steeling up courage before going to class in a small room with barred windows, blackboard, and 14 small desks to begin my dollar a day job as assistant to the community college instructor teaching them math, science, social studies, and English.

Mr. Painter was mid-thirties, fit, with sandy hair and an aura of decency that hung above him like a halo, appropriately so since his real vocation was the ministry.

His manner inspired trust and he dispelled my nervousness with a warm welcome.

"It's nice to meet you, Mr. Peterson," he said despite that Ms. Snow had no doubt told him I was a psychopathic serial killer. To him I was just another sinner like the ten black and four white inmates in his class; he was not there to judge or proselyte, just teach, and he seemed genuinely pleased to have my help because he told me that he really wasn't a teacher.

He was a Charismatic Christian Pentecostal minister who'd taken the job only until he got his own church. DOC had hired him to replace a woman whose brief tenure had sent her fleeing the classroom. Young and attractive, she'd lasted two days. On the third, a burly inmate approached her desk, whipped out his dick and started to masturbate in front of her. She screamed and ran to the front gate, never to return.

"Anyone try that on you?" I asked.

"Thank you Jesus, not yet," he said.

I liked him immediately and saw that he deeply cared for those in his class, manifesting incredible patience with guys who were, at best, recalcitrant to learn. Ignoring him, they talked among themselves, slept at their desks, and otherwise showed no interest in learning.

The blacks, mostly muscular young Bloods from their tattoos--dog paws, the number 5, and GKB (Gangsta Killa Blood)—weren't hostile to me at first: I was invisible. An old white man did not exist in their world; they simply ignored my offers to help.

Every morning I'd say, "I'm here for a big buck a day, that's my pay. Make me earn it. There's no racism in math."

Nope, racism was in everything; somehow 7x8=56 was white bigotry. My effort to learn math had been wasted. Nothing I did made a difference.

"Why won't they let me help?" I asked Mr. Painter after a discouraging week sitting shunned at my little desk up front.

"They don't care about a GED," he'd answered. "All they want is a private cell. They get one for being in

160

class. That's why they're here. And they get gain time whether they learn or not. It's easier not to learn."

It was depressing to enter the window barred guard guarded schoolroom at 8 knowing that a whole day of being ignored lay ahead. I'd put on a pleasant face to greet the miscreants, hoping this wasn't the day I'd be stabbed by some murderer or doped up perv who didn't know and didn't *want* to know that B was the answer to a question he didn't give a shit about. Sometimes I'd want to bury my head on the desk or flee in frustration.

Big Tom had no sympathy when I complained on the weight pile. "Fuck 'em," he'd say. "Let 'em be dumb. Stupid hasn't hurt me none."

"You're in *prison* for being stupid!"

"So are you and you went to Duke."

"A gross miscarriage of justice. The Court of Appeals will straighten it out."

"Yeah, right. You're gonna die in here, Peterson."

I inhaled sharply and involuntarily raised a hand to ward off the terror, worse than a physical blow. No. NO. The appeal would succeed. It was my only hope to be free, to see and touch those I loved. I was so desperate that I never dwelled on it because if the appeal failed, I *would* spend the rest of my life in prison. I would die here.

Tom had thrown the nightmare in my face. "No!" I shouted at him

Gradually the young blacks accepted me, or maybe they just got used to me hanging around—we were together all day—because one afternoon a Blood asked a question. Apparently after a 4 hour nap in class, he'd awakened rested and was bored.

I was so surprised, I looked up from my desk. "What?"

He asked again; I answered without elaboration. Then another asked a question. I gave a quick answer—no explanation, no lecture. Then others wanted help.

I felt like pounding my little kiddie desk in triumph. Yes! I could help them.

At first, they didn't come to my desk, but called out, "Hey Mr. Peterson, I need an answer," and I'd go to them. Shortly, a few wanted to know *why* that was the answer. These were not stupid guys, just uneducated; curiosity and wanting to learn quickly took over for many.

It was an extraordinary experience—an old white man helping young blacks who *asked* an old white man for help. I was so pleased, not in self-satisfaction, but genuinely happy to help. I stopped going to their desks and had them come to mine. From there we'd go to the blackboard to work out problems. Joking and laughter followed.

Though fronting a tough exterior, they were young and playful--Doberman puppies--and within a month several got their GED's despite a lapse in certain science areas: Mr. Painter did not believe in evolution so we skipped the fossil section.

We didn't discuss science. Or religion. And never politics--he was a Republican: George Bush ranked just behind Jesus in his pantheon; Dubya could have been at the Last Supper.

Gino, scorning my liberal politics, had once said, "Peterson, after you've been here awhile, you'll end up a racist like the rest of us."

"Nope," I'd answered, "My only fear is that I'll end up a Republican."

But a Republican like Mr. Painter? That might be ok. He *cared*.

Though reluctant to show appreciation, the Bloods were proud to get their GEDs. I was happy helping them and working with McNeill after class and on weekends to save his brother. I was constantly busy, loneliness and sorrow buried with thoughts of my appeal.

One morning after a 15 minute break lifting weights with Big Tom, a massive black with Blood tattoos blocked the path on my way back to class. Whoa, I thought, drawing up short, stomach tightening. I'd never seen this monster, but numerous guards were on the yard, so I was more wary than frightened.

He scrutinized me a moment, face immobile, then he spoke with a gravelly yet gracious voice. "Mr. Peterson, you need anything? Can I help you?"

I saw Tom tensing on the weight pile prepped to jump in. Relieved by Tom's presence and the monster's non-threatening manner, I said cautiously, "Thanks, but I'm good, don't need a thing."

Everyone knew that favors often came with an unacceptable catch, an offer you absolutely should refuse: "Remember that honey bun I gave you? It's payback time. Bend over." Better to go sugarless.

Sexual predation was so prevalent that DOC showed us a movie about it. Real actors demonstrated the perils of accepting the kindness of strangers which—and we all laughed at this—began with candy left on a new inmate's pillow just like at a Hyatt.

"I wish somebody'd leave candy on my pillow," a guy shouted. "I'd eat it, *then* kill the cocksucker."

"No, he might leave more the next night," Big Tom had said with practicality. "Kill the motherfucker when he stops leaving candy," though I doubted anyone would have put a mint on *his* pillow. Tom wouldn't have bent over any more than Gino and Mario would have.

It turned out I had nothing to worry about from the Big Bad Blood. The monster nodded at my refusal and said, "You need anything, let me know. It's yours."

Turning to go, he added, "Appreciate what you're doing for the brothers." Then he was gone.

As I let out a deep breath, not a bullet but a bazooka dodged, Big Tom ran up. "What'd he say? What'd he want? That was CJ, Claymore—like the mine that blows up in your face. He's the head Blood. He never talks to white guys."

"It was nothing, everything's good," I said and went back to class, especially grateful to Tom who'd been ready to come to my defense against a guy I doubt even he could have handled.

When I entered the room, the young Bloods smiled. So I knew: word had been passed that I wasn't a racist and would help blacks get their GED's. I'd been watched and appraised for two months, every word, look and action judged for sign of racism. I had passed the test.

Happy? Yes. Proud? Yes. As Gino had predicted, Claymore's benediction signaled they'd decided to trust me. I didn't know what for, but at least now I had my ally--Claymore and the Bloods. I couldn't have found a more powerful one.

When in Hell, it helps to befriend the Devil.

From that moment teaching became easier, enjoyable even. I looked forward to class every morning: the guys wanted to learn, I wanted to help; there was camaraderie.

For many this was the first time anyone had helped them. Now and then when a guy solved a complicated math problem or passed a test, his delight made it all worthwhile. I felt pleasure. Pride. Joy. In prison!

But there was sorrow too: Squirrel, my favorite student, utterly beyond control.

Thin, wiry, handsome, he was the most sullen obstinate guy I'd ever encountered. The only way I got information about him was in an essay he *very* reluctantly wrote about himself. I said I'd help: I'd ask questions, he'd write the answers.

How old are you? He scribbled, *24*.

How many years have you been down? *9*.

What are you in for? *Merder*.

Who'd you kill? *Cunt*.

I guess he felt that needed explanation, so he told me he found his girlfriend—they were both 14—in bed with another guy, so of course he shot her. It really wasn't his fault, he explained, she deserved it.

Write that down, I said.

I felt we'd made a major breakthrough, but the next day he was gone.

"What happened to Squirrel," I asked another Blood.

"He's in The Hole. Someone called him a bitch, so he shanked him. He'll be out in a couple days."

A couple days in The Hole for *shanking*? Stabbing someone? That offense usually brought six months solitary confinement, but I was told Squirrel had spent 7 *years* in solitary—hence his nickname. Of course he was a bug after that and why authorities had given up extended stays—they didn't work, and they didn't want him buggier, if that was even possible.

Sure enough, he was back in class several days later.

Teaching him was joy and trial often interrupted with trips to The Hole for fighting. Other Bloods told me that when he entered prison, he'd fought innumerable times to protect his ass, literally his ass, so now he interpreted any aggressive action or remark as a sexual assault.

He was a tough little bastard who'd have made a great Marine. I did everything to help him—encouraged, coaxed, yelled, but he was too damaged. He really wanted his GED, but he needed mental help more.

When he returned to class from The Hole after the shanking, he begged me to help him catch up on what he'd missed. He had passed four of five required tests for GED. Only math remained. He desperately wanted to learn but would not accept criticism, which in his mind was telling him that he was wrong, as he invariably was. He could not stand to be corrected.

"Two and two are not five no matter how many locks you hit me with," I'd say. Locks or rocks stuffed in a sock and slung bolo style into a skull were the equalizers in prison. Even if you could bench press a Buick, a sock would bring you down.

"OK," he'd say finally, teeth grinding.

I could tell him he was wrong; *I* could correct him because I was old—could have been his grandfather--and in the Mariana Trench of his psyche he knew I wanted to help him, but no one else could, not even his Blood brothers. It got so he would only talk to me in class and sought me out on the rec yard just to be near. He felt comfortable with me and under the scar tissue of his being, I found him sweet and endearing, but it was like hanging out with Caliban.

"Get rid of your pet," Big Tom would whisper whenever Squirrel came around. He didn't want to lift weights, just have someone safe to be with.

Alas, Squirrel did not make it through GED. A guy said something he took the wrong way which led to overturned chairs, broken windows, a trip to emergency for the guy, The Hole for Squirrel, and finally transfer to another prison.

This happened often. I'd work with a guy, help him, and then...he wouldn't show up one morning. Sometimes it'd be for a disciplinary violation, but sometimes I never knew why. Often I was relieved— another asshole gone--but with some like Squirrel, I felt loss. I had become involved. I cared.

I don't know Squirrel's root problem--bipolarity, schizophrenia, ADHD, sexual abuse, genetics--but all would have been aggravated by years in solitary.

Squirrel will never be right in his head. GED won't help him. Neither would a Ph.D.

Yet as nuts as Squirrel was, he paled in insanity and danger to McNeill.

After Larry Wade's attack, Gino's tutoring, and Big Tom's warnings, I should have been prepared for McNeill madness, but I wasn't.

When I was a young and foolish teenager, I loved horror movies. British Hammer Films scared the shit out of me, especially *The Horror of Dracula*.

One foggy night in San Francisco, my mother told me to take out the garbage. I knew, absolutely knew Dracula was waiting outside. I protested, delayed, did everything I could to avoid going out except tell my mother that Dracula was in the backyard, but my brother Bill who knew I was terrified of vampires, snuck outside to hide by the garbage can.

I crept out—I might even have brought a crucifix—and made my way through the mist to the can. Just as I got there, Bill leapt out, screamed, and jumped at me.

I hit him in the face with the metal garbage pail, breaking his front teeth.

Oh Christ, the uproar. When my mother rushed down, saw Bill's bloody face, broken teeth, and heard my excuse—I thought it was Dracula—it would have been better for me if it had been him.

Fifty years later, I encountered someone even more frightening than Dracula—Robert McNeill. And he was real.

14. The Sociopath

December was cold and miserable. A tacky little plastic tree in the day room with tinsel and pathetic strings of lights twinkled at night in semi-darkness next to the guard's desk, more Twilight Zone than joy and celebration. Guys studiously ignored the tree because Christmas underscored their isolation and sorrow, their failures as sons, husbands, fathers, and lovers.

Depression was palpable; even Big Tom, not a morose guy or one given to introspection grew sullen, but I consoled myself with lovely memories of past happy Christmases and listened to Christmas music all day on my radio.

As a child, Dad loaded us in the car every Christmas Eve to view the lights from all the homes where we lived, stopping now and then to scan the sky for Santa's sleigh. It was a happy tradition I repeated with my sons.

Masses, carols, such lovely memories, but I kept my pleasure to myself and tried not to dwell on the sorrow of separation from those I loved.

The season highlight was a Christmas "Party" overseen by Mrs. Snow and guards with concentration camp mirth. Summoned from cells and bunks, we waited in line for an hour to get a paper plate of chips, cookies, and a soft drink donated by a generous Christian group.

Later we learned that cakes had been donated also, but Mrs. Snow's favorites who'd been chosen to distribute the goods stole them. What they didn't eat, they sold.

Profits from canteen sales bought everyone a two-piece box of Hardee's chicken and a biscuit. For men who had nothing and never Street food, it was a welcome gift.

Of course many bartered it for cigarettes and a Noel blow job. I ate the chicken.

When class ended for a two week Christmas break, McNeill and I walked long hours in dreary weather made gloomier with McNeill's gruesome emotionless tale of two murders. Never raising his voice, he simply and dully recited the horror.

It seemed so macabre that sometimes I'd stop on the track, shake my head to clear my thoughts and remind myself—this is *Real*: I'm with a cold blooded killer describing his murders. Nevertheless, I never felt fear. Warned by Tom, I was on guard for any sudden movement or bizarre behavior, but McNeill never manifested anything unusual, so I walked beside him—horrified at his tale, but not afraid.

In an insane asylum, crazy becomes normal. Prison operates the same way. After a while, you think--yeah, he committed murder, but he's ok. Rape? Oh sure, everybody does it. Child molester? Awful, but he's a good ball player; we need him at third base.

The bar for normal becomes very low; even so, Robert McNeill didn't clear it, and that was evident from our first day on the track. He was hyper-active, constantly looking about, whispering, "Don't talk so loud," though no one was around. His paranoia was so unnerving that I too began looking about to see if someone was listening.

Though there were many dangerous violent men around me, I usually found something in each to relate to or like: BK with his gold teeth was an evil bastard who would drop someone in a heartbeat, but he loved to joke and we'd tease each other; God knows Big Tom was difficult—a murderer!—but he was funny, and I'd witnessed loyalty deep within. Bloods were fearsome, but loyal to one another.

There were more murderers in Unit 2 than in my platoon in Vietnam. Those Marines killed willingly—eagerly—yet none were as unsympathetic or disturbed as McNeill with his lifeless eyes and cold recitation of carnage, even my radio operator Martin with the severed ear.

Nineteen, a blond surfer from Florida strong enough to lug the twenty pound radio and batteries along with his rifle, bandoliers, helmet, and back pack without breaking a sweat, Martin was a sweet kid. And quick. He loved to catch snakes and could grab one off a tree or in the grass. Then he'd press it into my face. I told him each time that I'd shoot him if he did it again, but that didn't stop him and of course I never shot him.

One night after mail call, he came to my bunker in tears—crying—not a common sight among Marines. Holding a letter despairingly in his hand, I thought he'd received news of a death in his family, but no—the girl he was going to marry when he returned to the States had broken off the engagement, a frequent tragedy for men overseas.

"Did she find another guy?" I'd asked.

He handed me the tear soaked letter, which as I recall read something like, "It's over. I never want to hear from you again. I didn't know you were so fucked up."

"What did you do?" I asked.

"Nothing. I just sent her an ear."

"Excuse me?"

"It was my good luck piece, the only thing I had to give her, Lieutenant."

"Where did you get an ear?" It wasn't his; I saw he still had two.

"From a gook. After an ambush, he was dead, so I cut off his ear. I mean, if he'd killed me, he'd probably have cut off my dick, so I thought it was ok."

"Jesus! If I'd known you cut off an ear, I'd have court martialed you."

"Lots of guys do it, Lieutenant. I mean, they're dead. Who gives a fuck?"

"I do! It's a war crime."

But of course I knew guys took souvenirs from the dead. After one firefight, I came across a PFC prying a tooth from a dead enemy soldier. He said it was for his necklace, and he showed me a string of betel stained teeth.

I took it away and said I'd court martial him if I caught him doing that again. I can't remember what I did with the damn thing. I certainly didn't keep it, can't imagine I threw it in the shitter, but I don't recall burying it either. What *does* one do with a necklace of human teeth?

"Martin, you've been here too long. You can't send an ear to someone in the States. They don't understand war and what we go through. Write her and tell her you're sorry. She'll read the letter. Just don't send her any other body part."

I knew *I'd* been there too long because when he left I couldn't stop laughing. I kept visualizing the poor girl expectantly, lovingly opening a letter from her betrothed and a human ear falls out—an engagement ear.

But I sympathized with Martin. I understood—war can fuck you up.

However, I could not sympathize with or understand McNeill.

He gave me a scrapbook containing news clippings of his murders and trial--a souvenir like serial killers keep photos, clothing, and body parts of their victims (Martin with his ear; PFC Sutphin with those teeth). I read every word.

On September 20, 1993 around 10:30 pm, Robert McNeill, then 26, entered the Six Forks Food Lion grocery store in Raleigh and murdered John Ray, 27, and Michael Truelove, 19.

McNeill worked there part-time while attending N.C. State as a junior in engineering.

When McNeill knocked on the locked front door after closing, Truelove, a clerk counting money in the safe, let him in; he thought McNeill had forgotten something until he pointed a pistol at him. Believing this a holdup, Truelove reached in the safe for a sack that contained $2,300 and held it out. As he did, the phone lit up, signaling a call from the storeroom. McNeill knew it was John Ray, the store manager he had come to kill.

"Why did you want to kill him?" I asked. I'd read the articles but still didn't understand.

"I'll get to that," he said smugly. "You'll understand."

When McNeill gestured with his pistol towards the storeroom, Truelove started down the aisle clutching the sack. Suddenly John Ray came around the corner. Seeing McNeill with the pistol, he ran towards the storeroom. Truelove ran too.

Ray pushed through the swinging double doors, Truelove right behind him, pursued by McNeill who saw Ray run into the dairy cabinet that had no lock; he was trapped.

Truelove, desperately clawing through grocery carts and pallets, stumbled and fell. McNeill fired two bullets into the back of his head, then walked into the dairy cabinet and shot Ray once in the face and again in the side of his head as he lay on the concrete floor.

Grabbing the sack of money, he went out the back exit to his truck and drove off.

Minutes later, John Ray's eight and a half months pregnant wife arrived. When she got no answer at the front door, she peered in the window, saw the open safe and called 911.

Police suspected a robbery gone wrong because $17,000 was left in plain view. When they got a list of store employees, a detective recognized McNeill's name as the grocery manager of the nearby Tower Food Lion that had been robbed a few months earlier. That crime had not been solved, but police suspected an inside job.

When questioned, McNeill denied he'd had anything to do with either robbery and said he'd been with his younger brother Elmer Ray the night of the shootings.

Elmer confirmed Robert's alibi, but during questioning, police learned Elmer owned a Ruger Blackhawk .357, the type gun used in the murders. Noting that Elmer smoked Alpine cigarettes in the interrogation room and an empty Alpine pack had been recovered in back of the store, police arrested Elmer and Robert.

"Why did you leave $17,000?" was my first question.

"I didn't care about the money."

"Then what was it about?"

We were bundled in heavy jackets, but I didn't feel cold as we walked the track. McNeill's matter-of-fact tale of murdering innocent men had deadened my feelings.

And my good sense. No alarms went off as a man who'd murdered two others in cold blood confessed. For the first time. Only to me.

After the unsolved Tower robbery and a woman's harassment charge, McNeill had been transferred to Six Forks with the same salary, but demoted to clerk under John Ray. Both had the same wedding anniversary. McNeill felt he should get the weekend off because he had seniority with Food Lion, but Ray took it because he was store manager and his wife was eight and a half months pregnant.

McNeill looked at me triumphantly. *That* was his reason.

"You killed them because you wanted the weekend off and Ray took it?"

He nodded. He'd murdered a man, widowed his pregnant wife, left the child fatherless, and killed another man for a weekend off. My jaw dropped in incredulity.

His eyes narrowed, then fury flared in them and his body began to shake.

"Elmer had nothing to do with the killings?" I asked quickly trying to diffuse the tension, backing a step away.

"No" he said coldly, still glaring. "It was his gun. I stole it from him, but I made him swear we'd been together the entire time and never mention I had the gun."

An ex-felon who had worked at the Tower store called the police hot line to confess being part of that robbery and fingered McNeill as the mastermind. A jury later convicted McNeill and sentenced him to twenty years for armed robbery.

Elmer remained in jail for the Six Forks' killings.

The case languished two years until the DA announced a stunning breakthrough in December 1995: a third brother, the oldest, Michael said both brothers had confessed to him.

Vehemently denying this, Elmer and Robert were arraigned for murder and given separate trials. It came out that Michael had been sleeping with Robert's wife, but the judge in Elmer's trial refused to allow testimony about the affair which defense attorneys said had motivated his false allegations.

To prove his innocence, Elmer had to tell the jury that Robert took the gun. He never did; he would not betray his brother. For Robert to exonerate Elmer, he had to tell Elmer's jury that he alone murdered Ray and Truelove, but he didn't; he let his brother be convicted.

The jury sentenced Elmer to death. A lone hold-out on the jury in Robert's trial resulted in two life terms without parole.

I finished the first draft of the story the week after Christmas. He proofed it, made suggestions, and agreed to send the revised story to one of my attorneys and a journalist friend.

I felt good. I had accomplished something that might get an innocent man off Death Row, but on January 1, 2004 just after morning Count at 5:30, McNeill banged on my cell.

"I've been up all night tossing and turning. I didn't get any sleep," he said as though reciting from a script. "I have this gut feeling. You know how they are? You have to go with them. I need your notes and the first draft."

"Rob, what's wrong?" I asked in surprise, but sensing danger in his robotic speech and dead eyes, I moved away to sit tensely watchful on my bunk.

He repeated, "I have this gut feeling; I need everything you wrote."

"Rob, those are *my* notes." They could help Elmer.

His eyes suddenly caught fire; hatred and fury shot across the orbs and I saw the frenzied feral look that must have been in them the instant he murdered Ray and Truesdale.

Feeling the terror they must have felt, I recoiled in shock at his fury.

"Now you're feeding my paranoia," he said in a low possessed voice out of *The Exorcist*.

I'd never seen an expression on a human face as wild or frightening. The only similar looks had been on

177

dogs ready to attack, hackles raised, teeth bared, eyes demonic. Goya's painting *Saturn Devouring His Children* captures that expression of rapturous violence.

He gazed frantically about the cell, seized two folders on a chair by the door which he knew contained my notes, then he ran up the stairs to his cell and slammed the door.

I jumped up to shut mine then sank shaking on my bunk. My God, he could have killed me! He *would* have to get those notes.

Wade had attacked me to get moved; I should have anticipated that, but even with Tom's warnings, I couldn't have anticipated this; I had been taken completely by surprise. Again. In less than three months, I could have been killed twice. Tom had been right—I didn't understand these men. I *couldn't*. I was among madmen— for the rest of my life, living with Robert McNeill's, locked in with murderers. I slumped over in dread at the awful realization.

When I saw Tom a few hours later, I told him what had happened. "You were right, he's crazy. He might have killed me."

Tom was more angry than sympathetic. "You gonna listen to me from now on? *All* the animals here are wild, but some are just fucking nuts and you can't predict what they'll do."

I sat on the bench too drained to lift weights. "How am I going to make it, Tom?"

"First off, mind your fucking business. Drop this helping people horseshit. They're too fucked up. No one can help them."

We stared silently at one another, then he almost smiled. "Happy New Year."

I nodded dully. "Oh. Yeah. I'd forgotten. Happy New Year to you too."

Dropping down beside me as close to touchy feely as he ever got, he said, "Don't worry about McNeill. He knows we're tight; he isn't going to fuck with me. I'll bang into him a couple times to send a message.

"But that won't solve your problem. You need protection from everyone. You'll never make it past 2004 at this rate. You might not even get to February. You're a target—rich, famous. And old. You need someone to watch your back all the time."

"Great idea," I said sarcastically. "Who?"

He pointed to several Bloods huddled on the yard laughing and high fiving. Rubbing his fingers together, he said, "Talk money to them. Get your GED Blood dummies to help."

I looked at him in surprise. After a moment letting that sink in, I said, "At last, a good idea from you." Now all I had to do was figure out a way to get their help because Tom was right: threats were everywhere and I'd proved woefully—almost fatally—inept at seeing them.

Prison is a world of predators and prey; strength rules. Rae Carruth constantly had to ward off guys who wanted to earn a name by taking him down like gunfighters in the old west, but he was 29, a professional athlete, an NFL football player more than capable of handling himself. Rae didn't need help; I did; I was 60. A writer.

As I wrestled with my problem—my life!—I never spoke with McNeill again, but I rewrote the story and sent it to one of my attorneys and a journalist friend. My attorney gave it to Elmer's lawyers and the journalist said he'd write about Robert and Elmer.

Everything looked good for helping Elmer, but then McNeill wrote my attorney and threatened her if she interfered in his affairs, though he didn't specify how.

Alarmed—he was a convicted murderer—she called the warden: "I understand threats from my clients, but I don't even know Robert McNeill."

The warden summoned me to her office. Ms. Wynette had no interest in Elmer's innocence, only concern that my writings could trigger publicity about an innocent man on Death Row. She said that if I helped another inmate in any way she'd send me to solitary.

I listened in silent disgust. When she dismissed me, I had an ominous feeling I'd hear more about this, so when called back to her office the following week, I was worried.

It happened the day Count didn't clear for five hours. Had an inmate escaped? I hoped so for I'd lost all respect for authority: I no longer considered myself an *inmate*; I was a convict: Cool Hand Luke who wouldn't cooperate and couldn't be broken.

Yet I still had faith in the judicial system: I was innocent; the Court of Appeals would soon overturn my conviction. In a few more months I'd get out. All I had to do was survive until then.

When count finally cleared that day, I was ordered to Operations, the admin building within the wire where I overheard the assistant warden tell someone that Ms. Wynette was out of her head—this was her worst day since two inmates escaped in 2001.

Today she'd had to explain to DOC headquarters why it took five hours to account for all inmates. Couldn't she control the place? Did they need to replace her?

When I entered her office, Ms. Wynette sat behind her desk drumming a pencil, obviously stressed; two snapped ones lay next to her left hand. Nevertheless, she was pleasant as she explained that a French film crew wanted to interview me for a documentary. Their request had been approved by DOC. Did I want to talk to them?

Relieved that this wasn't about McNeill and excited at the prospect of seeing the filmmakers, I eagerly said yes. Jean-Xavier de Lestrade had spent a year filming my case and trial. This prison interview would be for the last of eight episodes in *The Staircase,* later shown throughout the world.

She gave me a date in February and asked if it would work for me. I said yes—as if I had any control of my days. "I plan be here. I don't want to mess up your count."

Recoiling, she snapped the third pencil. "Good," she seethed and pointed to the door.

The next day in class, I was summoned by loudspeaker to see Ms. Drew, the prison psychologist, considered the most attractive woman at Nash. Guys would slobber, plead insanity, threaten suicide, and say anything to see her, but even if they got an appointment, they usually waited weeks or months.

Hearing my name called, students glared at me with jealousy.

Now what? I wondered as I walked to her office not particularly worried but curious: why did the psychologist want to see me? And just how attractive was she?

When I got to her office in another unit, a guard stood outside her door eyeing me suspiciously. She must be gorgeous, I thought. After I knocked and was told to come in, a small black haired pleasant looking woman in her late thirties, a definite 6 on a 10 point beauty scale, easily topping all the other females at Nash, greeted me apologetically.

"Ms. Wynette asked me to see you, Mr. Peterson. She feels you're adjusting too well. She said she's never encountered anyone who's adapted to prison so quickly. She wonders if this is a cry for help." She looked at me expectantly. "Is it?"

Jesus, I thought—I'm not the one here who needs help, but I explained politely that I'd adapted so well because it was pointless to cry or beat my head against the walls—no one would listen or care and I'd only hurt myself. I told her I missed Kathleen and my children desperately, but dwelling on my loss and pain would only make me more miserable.

"I am not crying for help. I'm struggling to remain sane."

She said she understood and would tell Ms. Wynette that I was fine; I believed the matter closed. A few weeks later, the French filmmakers arrived to interview me. They spent an entire afternoon filming: How did I feel about my conviction? How was I adapting to prison? Did I have hope for release? The 8 part, 6 hour documentary would air later in the year.

The day after the French left, I was called to the office of the Unit Manager--The Fat Man, 300 pounds on a 5 foot frame, so out of shape he could barely waddle to the unit in the morning. Two stone silent officers were with him. As soon as I walked in, The Fat Man pointed at me. "Take him to The Hole."

"For what?" I asked incredulously as they cuffed and frog marched me out.

The Hole--solitary confinement! The most dreaded place in prison. The Abyss. Guards did whatever they wanted there. There were no cameras. Beatings were common. Men died.

As guards dragged me across the yard to the infamous Hole, a small concrete bunker behind two more rows of razor wire, I tried to look brave, but I wasn't.

I was definitely afraid. And pissed. The warden had waited until the filmmakers were gone to lock me up. DOC had not wanted me filmed in The Hole--that would have raised embarrassing questions about Elmer Ray's conviction and the judicial system--so they'd waited until the film crew was out the gate to drag me to The Hole.

But why? What had I done?

Led past Medical, I saw McNeill tending flowers. He smiled obsequiously at the guards, then he looked at me and grinned triumphantly.

Suddenly I understood. This was the bastard's doing. I had lost my job, cell, and visitation privileges because of the insane--guilty!--brother of the innocent man on Death Row I'd been trying to help.

Big Tom had warned me that McNeill would fuck up my life, and he just had.

Once again I'd been a fool. It was *my* fault. Furious at my stupidity, I twisted and struggled against the cuffs, but the two guards restrained me, one smacking me on the back of my head.

Then anger evaporated, replaced by fear, for just beyond another razor wire fence loomed The Hole.

I'd hit bottom—the lowest ring in Hell.

15. The Hole

Pushed roughly into a barren cell with wash basin, toilet, metal table, and a concrete slab for a bunk, guards strip searched me and took my belt and shoe laces--standard suicide prevention. I was wild, a caged feral cat, eyes wide, hair on end. Crazed.

That motherfucker McNeill! God damn him!

When they left slamming the iron door behind them, I wanted to throw myself against it, beat my fists against the wall, the concrete bunk, my chest–anything!

But instead I dropped down on the bunk. Raising my gaze to the ceiling, I drew deep breaths to calm myself, yet when I lowered it, I saw the iron door and barred window and got pissed all over again.

To divert my anger, I studied graffiti scrawled on the concrete walls by a hundred Kilroy's before me: gang symbols I recognized courtesy of Gino--Blood dog paws, Crip pitchforks, Latin King crowns, Aryan Nation swastikas; obscenities, lots of sucks and fucks—tits, dicks, vaginas, with crude drawings. And names, none of which I recognized.

It was too depressing, so I returned to *my* crisis--The Hole! How could this have happened? *Why* did it happen? How long would I be here? What would happen to me in here?

All I knew was that I was in one of two wings of The Hole, a heavily secured concrete bunker behind two extra strands of razor wire, each wing with 10 cells and a shower cage.

The nine inmates on my side who had watched me dragged in began clamoring as soon as the guards left the unit: "What are you in for?" "What'd you do?" "What's the charge?"

"Homie!" a familiar redneck voice yelled.

Of course Underwood would be here. But it was good to have someone I knew in this new deep shitter—misery loves company kind of thing, so I dropped to my knees and shouted through the door slot where food was shoved, "I don't know why I'm here, but I'm innocent."

"Yeah, right," nine voices derisively yelled back.

"I got a fighting charge," Underwood shouted unnecessarily, but with great pride.

"I got dirty urine," yelled One Eyed Reber who'd been in Unit 2 with me. He'd jammed an arrow in his eye when he was 13 and used that as an unsuccessful alibi for why he couldn't tell the child he molested was 11—"I couldn't see her." She was his cousin.

"I'm in for jacking," screamed the notorious transgendered Psycho, aptly named and frequently drugged senseless on psychotropics. That he managed to masturbate even while comatose impressed us all.

"Jacking what?" Underwood yelled. "You haven't got anything, you tranny fuck."

"That's cause you sucked it off. Remember? You loved it, you faggot motherfucker."

"I'll kill you, cocksucker," bellowed Underwood, banging a metal food tray on the bars.

It turned out I knew most everyone: my student Jay Bird (in for two murders)—I'd wondered where he went when he didn't show up for class; Little Bubba (one murder), another of Big Tom's work out partners; and Chief (one murder), a Lumbee from my unit with whom I'd exchanged no more than ten words in four months, the quintessential silent Native American.

The three (Folk Nation) were in for fighting. They got in a drunken (Chateau Tomato Paste—non vintage and not sold in stores) brawl with monster gang brother Big Bubba in an eye gouging ear biting teeth broken dispute over a stolen radio they destroyed in the fight.

Smokey, with a lovely lilting voice--he claimed relationship to Smokey Robinson--yet another student was in for stabbing, a Street vocation he was perfecting with more success than he was having with GED math.

I returned to my bunk feeling better; I could manage this; it might even be fun. Besides, The Hole was a badge of honor, proof you weren't beaten down--institutionalized.

Supposedly, the Hole was where bad boys went when they were badder, but really it was whenever authority wanted you there. With a hundred rules, inmates couldn't help breaking one, whether a major violation—escape, fighting, drugs--or a minor one like walking out of the chow hall with an apple, masturbating, having an extra pair of skivvies, or violating a rule called "other", which meant anything authority wanted it to mean.

I learned this first-hand when a guard told me that afternoon he was investigating officer in my case—Misuse of Legal Mail—an "Other" charge authorities had made up to fit my "crime", DOC's Catch-22: you're guilty of

187

whatever we want you to be guilty of even if you didn't do whatever it was that we haven't labeled yet.

Mystified, I asked, "How did I misuse legal mail?"

"That's what I'm investigating," the hulking buzz haired officer said smugly. Asshole.

"Misuse of Legal Mail," I yelled through the door slot when the officer left.

"What does that mean?" Psycho screamed.

"It means he's fucked," Underwood shouted.

Indeed I was, for the investigation went on 33 days.

For some, two days in solitary would be cruel, inhumane, and unable to bear, while for me, forced to listen to rap music or watch Adam Sandler movies for 24 hours would be more than I could handle; mercifully I was spared those atrocities.

But 33 days in Solitary? No problem, especially since I was allowed books and my radio because I was in for "investigation" not disciplinary action (yet). Once convicted of an offense, inevitable in every case, you lost those privileges, but until then, I had writing materials and books friends had sent that I'd always wanted to read but had never found time: the Greek tragedies, Proust, Coetzee, *Doctor Faustus*. My Philip Roth book had been confiscated and returned to the library; I could go to the Hole but Philip Roth couldn't.

I listened to classical music on a 24 hour classical, took a daily shower, set up an exercise program of push-ups, sit-ups, running in place, answered letters, made diary entries, and started rewriting *Operation Broken Reed*, a non-fiction thriller Harper Collins had bought the previous year for $250,000, but cancelled when an editorial director learned I'd been charged with murder: you can't be a writer *and* a murderer. Pick one or the other. So much for art. And the First Amendment, and for innocence until proven guilty.

I kept my radio ear buds in most of the time because screaming rarely ceased--obscene taunts or just noise, but I soon adapted and even managed to sleep through the bedlam, not surprising since I once slept through a mortar attack in Vietnam. Exhausted from an all-night enemy assault during Tet, I told my gunnery sergeant, "Wake me at 2 if I'm still alive."

Hole Rules were simple: you were allowed to go into a wire cage resembling a large dog kennel, 10'x10'x10' once a day for 15 minutes or take a 5 minute morning shower in an exposed cage, shave once week, and get a haircut once a month. And of course lights were never turned off, only dimmed from 10pm until morning count at 6:30.

Routine keeps infants, animals, and men sane; it's the unexpected—chaos—that fucks up minds. Prison scrambled routine with unexpected cell searches and lock downs, but Hole routine never varied. That was comforting; boring is ok.

There's nothing more boring than meditation, so I spent a lot of time meditating, sitting on the bunk with eyes open. I'd stare at something until it blurred and my mind would blur of thoughts. For me, Buddhism was not a religion so much as a coping device.

But how did I, Catholic raised and Marine trained, become a Buddhist?

When I was seven years old living in Japan, a maid brought me (kidnapped, according to my mother who was probably playing bridge at the Officers Club) to a Buddhist temple where a mystical seed was planted. Over the years, as Catholic Christianity became cacophonous, condemning, and damning, Buddhism germinated into serenity, comfort, and acceptance.

But the Catholic god lingered with bells, incense, and rituals, reinforced by Sister Virginia whacking my knuckles in catechism at the Church of the Little Flower in Reno when I was 10. I don't remember why. Perhaps she just liked corporal punishment.

Doubting God's existence, the first crack in the wall of my Italian Catholicism also started when I was 10. My four year old cousin Terry swallowed Drano—a glass containing its residue was left on the kitchen sink. The acid ate through his esophagus and stomach. He lingered near death for months. His struggle to live became a family crisis because he had not been baptized. My mother's brother, Uncle Jimmy had eloped with Aunt Ruth when they were 17, she pregnant with Terry. They didn't have a church wedding and Terry wasn't baptized.

Nonna was out of her head. If Terry died, he would go to Limbo; he would never be in the presence of God. I was horrified. Terry would go Limbo because he wasn't baptized? Punished for something not his fault? What kind of a God would do that?

The end of Catholicism for me came a few years later as an altar boy in Japan where my father was stationed. Army priests were lenient about certain sins—a whorehouse was just outside the gate, so sex didn't come up in the confessional: Don't ask, Don't tell in original form.

Too young to go to whores, I flogged away fantasizing about Melanie (and sometimes the shortstop, sometimes all three of us). This wasn't asked or told in Confession either.

When I returned to the states, I seldom served mass, but once at 14, I was asked to fill in for a sick altar boy. Before mass, I had to go to confession. I related my usual sins, a hefty catalogue of transgressions, and then asked forgiveness of God and the priest.

"Is that all?" the priest inquired when I finished.

All? I searched my mind: I thought I'd exhausted human failing, so I said, "Yes, Father."

"You never abused yourself?"

Abused myself? I envisioned flagellation, cutting myself, burning myself with cigarettes (which I had stolen, but dutifully confessed), but couldn't come up with anything.

"No, Father," I said.

As I did an extended penance at the altar, I kept wondering about abuse. What did he think I was doing? What sin had I missed? Leaving the church, I noticed a rack of pamphlets in the vestibule. And there was **SELF-ABUSE;** I grabbed it.

OH MY GOD! The priest meant beating off. I had no idea this vocation of mine was a sin. God cared about hand jobs? And I had lied to the priest about it! Should I run back and tell him? It was bad enough great-grandmother Porch was up there watching Mikey whack

191

away—I was told the ever vigilant dead saw everything—but God was watching too?

Later in my bedroom, I decided that no sensible God cared about this, and if He did—too bad, I couldn't stop. Grandma! Close your eyes.

Catholic doctrine changed over the years, but too late for me. I became, or at least tried to become, a Buddhist. Nothing seemed to matter to the Buddha. On the other hand, everything mattered to the Pope—eating meat on Fridays, masturbation, the shortstop on my team, rubbers!

Sex was definitely wrong, but the Sixth Commandment against killing was ok if it was war and they were gooks. The older I got, the less right that seemed.

Catholicism crystallized for me in 1980 at St. Mark's in Venice: four stolen bronze horses on the loggia façade, an incredible jeweled mosaic behind its marble altar, and a rifle on a pillar amongst the pews. Theft, Greed, and Violence. I compared that to the simplicity of a Buddhist temple in a grove of trees in Japan with priests murmuring Ommmm.

Ommmmm, the echo of the universe, resounded in me; "Hail Holy Queen, Mother of God," seemed ridiculous. Besides, Ommmm was easier than memorizing prayers.

I kept constantly busy in my cell, but after a few days, claustrophobia and stink set in, so I went "outside". Cuffed, I was brought to one of eight connected wire cages.

When led to mine, a young, short, scarred, tattooed Crip (pitchfork, crown) in the next cage staring forlornly into the distance, shouted eagerly, "Mr. Peterson! Help me."

I gestured around my cage. "I don't think there's much I can do for you."

"No, no, I just want advice."

No! Helping McNeil was why I was here—"Misuse of Legal Mail" turned out to be sending one of my attorneys the article I'd written to save Elmer McNeill.

Yet of course I offered help. "What's up?"

"I'm leaving tomorrow. First thing in the morning. Going back to The Street."

"That's great," I said. "Congratulations."

"No!" he cried desperately. "I don't have any place to go. And no money. I can't go back to the hood. I'll get in trouble. But that's not the worst. In here I get meds. I won't on the Street. I'm Bi-polar. Without meds I go crazy. What should I do? Help me, Mr. Peterson."

Don't! I told myself, but how could I not?

"When you get to Raleigh, find a church and ask for shelter or ask them to direct you to one. Then go to Social Services. Fall on the floor, start rolling around and tell them you need medication or you might go crazy."

He nodded thoughtfully. "That's a great idea. They'll take care of me, won't they?"

"Somebody should help," I said, though without confidence. Most guys were in here because no one had helped them.

I never saw him again, but I stopped going outside; it was too depressing. I stuck with a daily shower, though that too was an ordeal. For the *ten* step walk from cell to the shower cage, I was painfully cuffed through the slot with hands behind my back, uncuffed in the shower, recuffed to leave, and uncuffed when I got back to my cell; lots of guys didn't shower.

The trick to staying sane was not to let guards get to me. I would not allow them or anyone in my mind, so I stayed busy meditating, reading, writing--letters, my diary and book--exercising, listening to music, and masturbating. It's incredible what isolation does to the libido, though I may have been the first and only inmate to do it to *Lysistrata*.

Others found less erudite outlet. Psycho would suddenly—and frequently--yell, "I'm jacking. Wanna watch?"

"You seen that new guard?" Underwood screamed once. "That's what I'm jacking on."

That led to lots of obscene banter; I'd seen her— hard to miss; she looked like a rhinoceros.

"I'd love some of that, wouldn't you?" he yelled.

I thought, No, not even if I was another rhinoceros; my masturbatory imagination far exceeded reality.

One morning there was loud scuffling outside my door.

"I need to talk to Mr. Peterson," someone plaintively called.

I peered through the slot. It was The Retard—Big Tom's appellation.

When a young black started following me on the yard, I asked Tom, "Who is he?"

"That's The Retard."

"He's stalking me. Why?"

"He can't understand why you're here."

194

"Neither can I!"

"No, he sees you on TV and doesn't understand how you can be on TV and here at the same time. And he sees you talking to everyone. He wants you to talk to him. He's lonely."

Now he was at my door. Contact among Hole inmates was strictly forbidden, but guards would allow talk *if* the inmates didn't cause trouble. "How's it going?" I asked.

He shook his head sadly. Trying to make conversation, I asked, "Where are you from?"

"Unit 2."

"No, I mean, where were you born?"

He looked puzzled. "I don't remember being born."

I suppressed a sigh and asked, "What can I do for you?"

"Oh Mr. Peterson, I need help. I need a Bible. A real one."

On the yard, he carried a Bible as he followed me— I was afraid he might start proselytizing--and Bibles were allowed in The Hole, so I asked, "Don't you have a Bible?"

"No," he said mournfully. "Not a real one. All I have is a Gideon Bible."

"That's a good Bible."

He shook his head. "Oh no, Mr. Peterson. Gideons are a tribe that lives in motels."

"That's it!" the guard yelled. "I can't take any more of this," and he dragged him away.

Big Bubba in the next cell drawled in the most southern accent I'd ever heard, "God *daammmnnn*, and I thought I was stupid."

Underwood shouted, "You are Bubba, you are. You're the dumbest motherfucker in here, including Smokey who doesn't even have an IQ."

"Fuck you," Smokey sang.

"Yeah, fuck you," Bubba yelled back. Fa—uh—kk. Three syllables.

Big Bubba, Raymond Goforth, said he desperately needed to talk to me and asked if I'd go outside the next day. He told me through our adjoining wall that he had a wife and four children, not all by her. He was facing a murder charge and in The Hole for fighting Jay Bird, Chief, and Little Bubba over the stolen radio. It had taken all three to bring him down.

I hadn't been outside since my last encounter, so I said yes, eager for some—any—diversion, and curious to see what my "neighbor" looked like. He didn't disappoint.

Big Bubba, 29 with a seventh grade education, shaved head, jagged teeth and twisted nose was 6'6", 320 pounds, straight out of WWE.

In cages the next day, Bubba said he needed to tell me about the guy he killed.

"How did you kill him?" I asked.

"I hit him."

"With what?" He held up his fist. It could have knocked over a Redwood. "Yep, that would have done it."

Bubba hit a guy in a dispute over money. The guy died. Bubba was arrested for murder. That took ten minutes to relate. He had frontal lobe problems resulting from a work accident when a steel beam fell, fracturing his skull. He was 100% disabled, receiving $755 a month, not enough to support his wife and four kids, so naturally he sold drugs.

He said he hadn't meant to kill the guy and didn't understand the murder charge. He felt his public defender wasn't helping and asked if I'd read his casework and explain it to him.

Sending kites, weighted notes on a string tossed cell to cell was how we communicated, but there was so much material to Bubba's case that he asked a guard to give it to me. Guards liked Bubba, we all did, and no one wanted to piss off a guy who had killed someone with his bare hands, actually just one hand, so the guard brought his casework to me.

I read the police notes and witness statements, then the Medical Examiner's report. Victim's cause of death was "Acute alcohol poisoning" with a lethal blood alcohol level of .45. In addition, he had 80% blocked arteries and scarring on his heart.

Christ! How could police, DA, and his own attorney have missed the ME's report?

I wrote a letter for him to explain it to his attorney. The next morning Bubba was gone.

I feared I'd be next to disappear because I'd helped him. I packed my belongings. Everything I owned fit in one small plastic bag. Though expecting to be "disappeared" at night to Pumpkinville, my term for a remote prison in North Carolina's mountains, nothing happened.

I listened to the Metropolitan Opera Saturday broadcasts of Wagner's Ring Cycle for what seemed 300 hours. I read 120 pages about a dinner party in Proust's

Germante's Way, but I found no lessons in Proust, just lovely observations, no love except for his mother, Odette and Albertine--all unhealthy obsessions, and no children anywhere.

I wrote new scenes for *Operation Broken Reed*, exercised and masturbated. I kept busy all the time. Burying sorrow, pity, or even anger had become natural reflex.

Then it was Easter. We got a little turkey with collard greens and a small cup of ice cream. Yet that Easter meal was better than most meals, the worst--cold catfish nuggets that I couldn't eat. There were many hungry days in The Hole.

Breakfast was usually oatmeal gruel or powdered eggs, Lunch a slice of bologna and instant tasteless potatoes, Dinner bologna again or a hamburger with more soy than meat.

A lot of soy was served. Underwood worried he'd grow tits; he'd heard soy did that.

I told him he had enough testosterone so that he needn't worry. That pacified him though he had no idea what testosterone was. I told him it was in his balls.

"Great! I got big balls," he shouted. I said I was happy for him—and not surprised.

Every week, the officer investigating my "Misuse of Legal Mail" charge came to tell me that he was still working on it and would add darkly, "It doesn't look good for you."

By the third week, I didn't care; I had adapted to The Hole.

Two things besides meditation kept me sane: my appeal and visits from family and friends. Three months was the usual time for the Court of Appeals to render a decision--it had been four. Any day now injustice would be righted and I'd be released. In the meantime I was allowed visits because I hadn't been convicted yet of Misuse of Legal Mail.

One week, my son and his fiancée Becky visited for one hour, non-contact through Plexiglas. They were to be married in a few months. Clayton's pain on seeing his father in handcuffs was palpable, but I told him not to worry. I was fine.

I wished them a happy wedding and long life, but my heart hurt so badly that I could barely breathe. The grief was *physical*, crushing. My heart ached as if someone were squeezing my chest. I couldn't make it stop. Then the pain travelled to my head, bore into my mind, twisting and turning, gouging like a blade. And there was no anesthesia.

Visits were always like this--life sustaining, but when left alone, the pain was unbearable. I'd rush to the window for a last look as those I loved departed, watch them disappear from my life again, then I'd turn away and try not to cry.

Yet I'd look forward to another visit. Joy again. Agony again.

The Hole was like a roach motel where inmate roaches checked in and out constantly--The Bates Motel with *lots* of Norman's, but I knew that for me the end of it was near when I was brought to the Warden's office. With her were my lawyers and several DOC officials. The investigation was finished! All charges would be dropped if I agreed not to write any more stories about inmates unless I changed the names; I couldn't use real ones. I agreed.

An unresolved issue was nicknames. I asked--if I write about someone nicknamed Squirrel, do I have to change it to Chipmunk?

My attorneys rolled their eyes and Ms. Wynette just stared at me.

Finally after 33 days, the charges were dismissed. To save an innocent man on Death Row, I'd spent 33 days in Solitary, lost my job and my cell.

I was happy to get out of The Hole but not happy when I returned to the unit to find I would be on one of 16 bunks in the middle of the Day Room that we called the Trailer Park, sharing two cum and piss splattered toilets. Gino had been right.

To my further disgust, McNeill was still in the unit; nothing had happened to him. We kept wary distance from one another, but I watched him carefully. And gleefully saw him taunt the eight Muslims in our unit who met several times a day in a corner of the day room.

They would face east, drop to their knees and pray. When they stood and turned, they stared into McNeill's open cell across from them. He had taped a huge portrait of Jesus on the inside door.

You're going to pay for that, motherfucker, I thought. You've picked the wrong enemy this time. Muslims *will* retaliate for disrespect.

Indeed. A short while later guards burst into his cell and found a shank.

No one knew if it was his shank or if it'd been planted, but he was taken to The Hole then shipped.

I only regretted that I hadn't been able to get back at him. Bad Buddhist.

Later authorities discovered he'd hacked every student's school computer. They were forbidden to do anything on them except assignments. McNeill had collected a trove of violations—letters they'd written and games they'd played—to report to guards. Snitch points.

He also had white supremacist materials and Internet articles about me. That explained how he knew the details of my life.

I no longer cared because something wonderful had happened.

16. Sophie

My life changed forever in December 1969 with a tragedy that prepared me for all subsequent sorrows and travails; it enabled me to survive prison.

After Vietnam, the Marines sent me to the security guard detachment at Atsugi Naval Air Station in Japan, 25 miles south of Tokyo.

One night just before Christmas when returning to base with one of my platoon sergeants, a Japanese truck trying to beat a train at a railroad crossing slammed into our vehicle. Pinned to the wheel, my chest crushed, a lung collapsed, I couldn't breathe and was unable to move as Sergeant Ken Beverly beside me cried, Help me, Lieutenant, Help me.

I didn't remember anything else until taken from an ambulance and carried on a stretcher into Zama Hospital when I overheard a corpsman say, "This one isn't going to make it either."

That's how I knew Ken died, and I passed out thinking I would die too--no white light, no dreams, no memories, no pain, no Jesus, no Devil, just nothingness.

It was as I hope death will be.

But it was Hell when I regained consciousness several days later in agony that morphine couldn't relieve, nor could it erase the horror of Ken's death.

He was the sweetest guy—in a gung ho Marine sense: brave, honest, decent, loyal, an extraordinarily

handsome muscular middle weight boxing champion with short dark hair, bright
and eager, shy, always smiling, a 21 year old Vietnam dog handler who'd joined the Corps to get away from Blackshear, Georgia where his father tenant farmed and raised pit bulls.

One of the most miserable days in my life was visiting his parents a year later after I'd been medically retired from the Marines, sitting on a dilapidated sofa in their wooden shack viewing a photo album of Ken. The first picture was of him in a crib, the last in a coffin in his dress blue uniform. They were so proud. I was bereft.

I drove out to the cemetery with his father in the new purple Plymouth Roadrunner he'd bought with Ken's $10,000 Death Benefit. The old man—overweight, toothless, bearded, in overalls with only one strap--spat tobacco juice in a can on the floorboard and brought me inside the Hard Shell Baptist Church where women sat on one side and men the other. There was no electricity in the unpainted wood church, but there were holes in the floor for spitting tobacco.

When I drove out later by myself and sat in the weeds beside Ken's grave letting sand fall through my fingers, I wept. Vietnam was three years behind me, but its tragedies were there again with Ken in his grave. They have never gone away.

During my trial, the DA inquired with the Marine Corps about Ken's death, wondering if I'd killed him. Christ, the lengths they went to.

After two weeks in the Intensive Care Unit, I was moved to the orthopedic ward among patients like Vic with no arms, Red with no legs or dick—so many mutilated guys. Other wards had burn victims, those with brain damage, blind, but no ward had PTSD victims; those wounds hadn't been diagnosed yet.

I don't know what happened to any of the men on that ward, but I know every guy there facing the rest of his life maimed wondered, "Why me?" There was no explanation other than you got in the way of a bullet or a mine; or in my case, a truck. Even if there was someone to blame—government or God—we still had the rest of our lives to live maimed, glad we weren't dead like buddies taken to Graves Registration. Or Sergeant Beverly in the Zama morgue.

Was I supposed to thank God for my survival? What about Ken? Why'd you kill him? Why are the dead dead and we aren't? After that, I could never praise God. But I never blamed him either. You lived or died on whim, fate or chance; prayer and goodness had nothing to do with it. Life wasn't mystery so much as meaningless since we all would end up in the morgue. Sure, better him than me, and better tomorrow than today, but tomorrow *will* come.

Of course when those guys went back to "The World" as maimed freaks ravaged with PTSD and were called baby killers, they probably felt sorry for themselves and blamed God or government. But I was alive; I had two arms and both legs. How could I feel sorry for myself? That ward made prison bearable.

Ken Beverly, dead 34 years in 2004 would have given anything for one of my prison days, so would those Marines in Vietnam dead nearly forty years. They wouldn't have liked prison, but they'd have gladly changed places with me.

Except I didn't want *their* place. Prison was awful, but it wasn't the morgue, and The Hole wasn't as bad as that orthopedic ward, so after Zama Hospital I could handle anything.

Even Kathleen's death. I thought love had died with her. But then....

Boy meets girl in school or college. Man meets woman at work. Or in a bar—grocery store, gym, child care, airport terminal, swimming pool, even a hospital visiting dying spouses, anyplace where men and women interact.

But in prison? What are the chances of finding love there? Auden didn't mention prison in *O Tell Me The Truth About Love*, but I doubt he would have been surprised I found it there, though not as he might have envisioned or desired. Yet it did "come without warning."

A month after my conviction in October 2003, I received a letter from Paris.

Sophie Brunet edited *The Staircase*. She had not come to America—the rushes were sent to her in France. I knew nothing about her until she sent a letter offering friendship.

Then she sent Proust's *In Search of Lost Time*. More letters came. More books.

Since she knew everything about me (300 hours of film), she told me about herself. Born in Reims, she moved to Paris to study film, edited many movies, and won several awards at Cannes; she was a socialist, married with a 10 year old son.

I wrote that what I remembered best about Reims besides champagne was the smiling angel on the Cathedral's north portal façade. Her next letter included a postcard of the angel.

In the beginning, I was flattered with her interest but viewed her letters as nothing more than friendship: I was in a North Carolina prison for the rest of my life, she was in Paris. What else could it be? It was enough to get her letters. More than enough. Wonderful. At mail call I would take her small scripted letter with French stamps to my room and caress the envelope in happy recollections of France.

Once Sergeant Hardy, a particularly unpleasant officer who of course rose higher in the system, called me to her office. Concealing a packet in her hands, she told me that I'd received dirty postcards from France, but I couldn't have them.

Dirty French Postcards! "Can I see them?" I asked eagerly.

She flashed them quickly, more to torment than to accommodate me, I'm sure: Rembrandt, da Vinci, Rubens, Delacroix postcards. Tits and dicks from the Louvre!

I laughed and said, "It's called Art. We're allowed to receive 'art'."

After she checked and had that verified, I was allowed to keep the filth. I pasted them on my wall until ordered to take them down: they marred state property.

All Sophie's postcards were carefully selected, some very old ones purchased from kiosks along the Seine that evoked fabulous memories of past visits to Paris which lifted me from grim prison into her world, such a better one, yet so far away, and unattainable.

After several months of exchanging letters, when she didn't receive an answer to one of hers, delayed or destroyed, she sent me an angry hurt one. I was surprised and perplexed; she'd become more personally involved than I'd realized, yet what possible future could there be for us beyond letters?

She was seventeen years younger, married with a child, and she had a successful career. She lived in Paris. I was sentenced to die in a North Carolina prison. All she knew of me was what had been filmed. Was she Pygmalion, the artist, and I Galatea, her film creation?

Of course not, she wrote when I suggested this: she had spent twenty years and thousands of hours in dark rooms editing hundreds of individuals, but after watching my case, she knew I was innocent and was drawn to me for my obvious love for Kathleen and my children, and her belief that a great injustice had been committed. She wanted to visit.

Whoa! Fly from Paris? Meet face to face? A flight plus hotel and renting a car would cost thousands. For a two hour visit? It didn't make sense. I was old. Poor. Incarcerated. It was too strange to believe; there had to be something wrong with her. What if she was crazy?

But I wrote back nervously, "I'll put you on my visitors list."

As I puzzled Sophie's desire to visit, my programmer summoned me to her office one morning. A programmer "guided" an inmate through his

207

incarceration—in my case unnecessarily; nothing could reduce or increase my sentence.

My only previous experiences with this pleasant middle aged woman had consisted of signing a form declaring I'd received a magazine that I couldn't have.

Numerous copies of *The New Yorker*, *Vanity Fair*, *Rolling Stone*, *Interview*, *GQ*, *and Sports Illustrated* had been banned because of a woman's nipple in a photo shoot or ad. "Frontal Nudity"—one aureole!—got a magazine censored. Someone at DOC went through every issue of every magazine to insure inmates never saw a female nipple, though little boys' nipples for Chesters who cut out and saved little boys' underwear ads were fine.

The only female tit exceptions were National Geographic and "Art"--African tribeswomen's and 400 year old "full sized" Rubens's. Guys could go into cells and bathrooms to fuck each other, but a woman's bare tit was verboten.

Of course this drove up the price of porn books and skin mags brought in and sold by guards for $50 each. They rented for 2 stamps an hour, 5 stamps overnight. A "penetration" magazine paid for itself in a couple weeks; some were years old still in good condition because the only rule was to bring them back "unsticky"; otherwise you had to buy them for 250 stamps.

Expecting to be told I couldn't get a magazine— another tit!--I was surprised when my programmer said I would be getting my GED TA job back.

No! I liked having no job with days free to read, write, and exercise. It was like being retired, only in the world's worst rest home.

I politely demurred; she shook her head. "Ms. Wynette, *the warden,* wants you to teach."

Fucked! If I said no, I'd be shipped to Pumpkinville too far away for family and friends to visit. Losing visits was the Damoclean Sword held over my head: two hour weekly visits seeing those I loved, holding their hands were what I looked forward to most. Why go on if I could never again see those I loved? And Sophie would never find Pumpkinville.

So of course I said I would teach; I'd do anything to keep visits, but I dreaded going back to school—all day with a bunch of sullen sometimes violent men who didn't want to be there any more than I did, but at least this time I knew what to expect. I also knew my reputation for helping Bloods along with CJ's support would precede me; the young gangbangers would be respectful.

But I had immediate problems with Mr. Johnson, the new community college teacher who had replaced Mr. Painter who'd gotten his church ministry while I was in The Hole.

Mr. Johnson, a pleasant doughy mid-thirties black initially welcomed my help, but on the first day when I went to the cabinet to get supplies for a student who'd run out of paper, he yelled, "I'll get it," and he hot footed it to the cabinet near the door.

This happened twice more that day. Every time I approached the supply cabinet he threw himself in front of it. When class ended, I confronted him. "Mr J., what's up with the cabinet?"

He looked embarrassed. "I can't let you go in the supply cabinet." He fidgeted, gazed at the floor, then said

209

to the ceiling, "Mrs. Snow told me that you lost your job because you stole things from the cabinet. She said not to let you go in there anymore."

"What! That bitch!"

He jumped back three feet. In fairness, I was, after all, in prison for 1st degree murder.

"Mr. J., I did not lose my job because I stole supplies. The warden will tell you it had nothing to do with GED. Check with Ms. Wynette."

Then I headed for the door. "Never mind, I'll fix this myself," and I bolted to the Unit Manager's office in the main wing, realizing on the way how warped my life had become: I could live with everyone believing I had murdered two women, but not that I was a thief.

Of course the Fat Man immediately resolved the problem and the following day I retrieved supplies from the cabinet without difficulty.

Unfortunately Mr. Johnson proved a troubled man who brought his problems (he hinted they had to do with his mother; he still lived with her) into the classroom, problems which had to pale to those of his students—and me!—in *prison*, some—me!—for the rest of our lives.

Who cared about his fucking mother? At least he had one and got to see her. The rest of us were drowning in this shitter—motherless, wifeless, womanless, children less.

First thing some mornings after difficulty with "Mama", he'd put impossible math problems on the blackboard: "3A + 5A= 14A. What's the value of A?", then he'd place his head on his desk to moan for hours.

When perplexed students came for help, I'd wave them away, whispering, "It can't be done." Then I'd go back to writing Sophie.

Our correspondence had become feverish, but I still couldn't figure out why a successful French woman with husband and son in Paris had focused her attention on a sixty year old American bisexual convicted murderer in prison for the rest of his life. Not a prize in anyone's Happy Meal, but time was running out to solve the Why Me mystery; she was coming in a week.

Meanwhile, English class became a nightmare when Mr. Johnson told the students to write an essay on "The Best Booty I Ever Had."

"You mean…." a student ventured hesitantly.

"Booty," he repeated.

"You mean…" the guy queried again.

"Pussy! Ass!"

That brought everybody alive, even the doped up ones, and of course they set to work immediately except for one poor fat white guy who probably had never had booty, or had been the booty himself.

I buried myself in letters, not wanting to participate in this exercise and dreading having to read and correct prison porn essays. I didn't have to; he took them home.

His next assignment was worse: When I looked Under Her Dress I saw…. "Write what you saw," Mr. J told the class. Oh my God, I thought and covered my eyes with my hands.

One student was so pleased with his work that he begged me to read it. The essay began in a Waffle House where he dropped a spoon on the floor when the panty-less waitress approached. He described in detail what he saw in the utensil's reflection.

"Well?" he asked when I finished.

"Absolutely an A paper," I said, handing it back. "Good thing it was a clean spoon."

Fortunately these literary endeavors ended when Ms. Snow's spies brought the subjects to her attention. Severely reprimanded, Mr. Johnson fell into hours of moaning depression. He'd turn on the classroom TV to Maury Povich, Jerry Springer, or some other idiot show, and I would bail, going out to the rec yard weight pile announcing, "You don't need me for this."

Regardless of his porn fixation, Mr. Johnson was dedicated to helping his students, but he was a font of misinformation. In history class he'd talk about Louis XIV who had beheaded all his wives, and the current Queen of England, Elizabeth XII.

I never said a word. White inmate correcting black teacher? Not a good idea. Still, I'd set them straight after class. "No," I told them when Mr. J said insurance companies charged more to insure black cars than white cars, another example of racism in America, "There's no racism in their rates. They charge according to the value of the car and your driving record."

Since Mr. Johnson didn't believe in evolution, science was tricky: What about the dinosaurs? a student asked. Why didn't the Bible mention them? Surely someone—Moses?--would have noticed them tromping about. Couldn't they fit on Noah's Ark. Did they drown?

Genetics was a touchy subject too: Just who was made in God's image--Neanderthals?

212

"My uncle's got six fingers on one hand," a student offered. "How did that happen?"

No one had an answer, but it led to a fascinating discussion of which digit Uncle Festus would use to give someone the finger. Maybe the *two* middle ones?

Mr. J wouldn't have made it in a Street school, but for prison GED? The number of teachers willing to be locked in with murderers, rapists, drug dealers, and perverts for a shit salary with a serial killer assistant had to be limited and the bar severely lowered.

Twice weekly I taught a night class for those with day jobs, many ABE--Adult Basic Education, those scoring below 3rd grade or who couldn't read or write at all.

Community college teachers wouldn't test ABE students for placement—it was too depressing, so I tested grown men who could not even identify vowel sounds. I'd sit at a small table across from a guy, point to a picture of letters, mouth ahh, ahhh... and get a blank look. "A" I'd say and try not to sigh, though I was accustomed to this, for since arrival, guys carrying a rolled up newspaper under their arm or toting a book in pretense would approach me at the bulletin board to ask what had just been posted—they'd "forgotten their glasses."

Sugar asked me every week to read his gambling tickets so he could choose which team to bet on. He was 50, a big amiable rapist, but so illiterate he couldn't figure out NY and PHI (his team!) abbreviations, and of course the plus/minus point spread was trigonometry to him.

Sugar was raised in rural North Carolina during segregation, so I understood why some older blacks couldn't read, but there were many young guys too--black and white. In 2005!

When Durham experimented with a "magnet" high school for "problem" students, principals sent their worst ones there. It was a short lived experiment with predictably disastrous results—open warfare in the classrooms and hand to hand combat in the halls.

Of course many ended up in prison. In my class! Like Blunt and Smooth, stunning young monster Bloods who looked out of an MTV rapper video.

One day, the two were in the canteen line behind me. "Mr. Peterson," Blunt asked, "London and Germany, that's the same thing, isn't it?"

"No," I said, ever the teacher. "London is a city in England. Germany is a country. In fact, they were big enemies in the war."

"What war?" Smooth asked.

"World War II. The war with Hitler."

"Who?"

I searched their faces to see if they were joking. They weren't. Hitler was in the white world; he had no relevance in theirs. Of course neither did math or science.

Jay Bird was the most troublesome of the several hundred students I taught. He'd robbed and murdered two elderly women when 22, wild on dope and he stayed wild for thirteen years incarcerated. Fierce, with a pony tail to the middle of his back, Jay Bird was hard core Folk Nation who'd fight in a nano second. And yet—I really liked him and enjoyed his company.

One warm night on break outside when we took off our shirts, I noticed his scarred chest. "Jesus," I said.

"How many bullet holes have you got?" He'd been in a shoot-out with the police after the murders.

"Five," he said, pointing to four wounds on his chest. I waited. "I shot myself in the balls when I was 12; I dropped the pistol and it went off. Want to see the scar?"

I knew then (Ok, I knew earlier) he was nuts—what kind of lunatic shoots himself in the balls? Even worse, what kind of lunatic admits it? But Lord did he want to learn. He tried harder than anyone, but he could not take tests: he'd panic, then lose control completely, a frightening event which took two guards to quash. Storming out, he'd swear he was never coming back—"Fuck it. Fuck all you motherfuckers"—but he'd be back the next night. He really wanted his GED, and when he finally passed, he was so proud. He wept.

"This is the only thing I've ever done in my life that I could be proud of," he said.

With two murdered women and his nuts shot off, I knew this was true.

Nevertheless his GED won't matter—he'll never get out of prison. That's a good thing; none of us would want to run into Jay Bird on The Street.

Or Perry, 34, immensely fat with diabetes and high blood pressure, slow and childlike. His first conviction came at 16 for child molestation. Sentenced to 12 years, he served 4; ten years later he got 23 years for raping a minor. He came to night class and played with his dick the entire time. Barely able to read, he was incapable of simple math. Using fingers not around his dick to count, he still got the answers wrong.

Every Monday I taught him subtraction; borrowing 10's from another column posed enormous difficulties even when I told him to pretend he was stealing 10's from that column, yet by the end of the class, he had it, though on Wednesday—everything forgotten—we started again. This cycle lasted for two years and I am sure Perry still can't subtract. Or ever will.

Of course Perry's problem was genetic and incurable. Knowing that, knowing that many of the guys suffered problems beyond their control—born in poverty to crack addled whores, growing up without a father, sexually abused, travesty upon travesty, I'd go back to the block after class, run into my cell and throw myself on the bunk overcome with futility.

What's the point? They won't get jobs on The Street; they'll end up back here. And I'm never leaving! I'd pound the pillow raging at Perry who'd never learn subtraction or stop playing with his dick; at guards— sadistic fucks; the judicial system—corrupt! And God— worthless or evil. But I'd keep reminding myself: Sophie is coming, and all my anxieties would transfer to her visit. Then I'd murmur OMMMMM and in the morning trudge back to class.

The day she arrived—after an unsuccessful wild eyed attempt before the metal mirror to make myself presentable in prison garb and shit haircut—I headed to Visitation like the four-eyed fat tuba player in the high school band on a blind date with the head cheerleader.

When I entered the visitation room, I spotted her immediately: petite, fashionably dressed with a scarf looped casually around her neck, hair stylishly gray perfectly coiffed, a confident superior look on her playfully amused face. No prisoner's Old Lady or Baby's Mama.

Attractive, intelligent, funny, fluent in English with the most charming accent, she put me at ease immediately with an amusing description of the Red Roof Motel in Rocky Mount where she was staying, while she ignored with élan a nearby woman giving a welcoming hand job under the table to the inmate she was visiting.

I wanted to say, "It's customary," but felt it too soon.

We joked and laughed for two hours. There was no awkwardness. We barely touched on my case or plight, instead we discussed books and films and places we'd been. She made everything easy and natural. It had been two years since I had spent any time with a woman, and after the visit, I lay for hours on my bunk thinking of Sophie and remembering Kathleen, comparing their similarities, contrasting their differences.

Both strong intelligent women, they would have liked one another and gotten along great; their differences would have made them compatible.

Sophie's smile was soft and mild with gentle irony reflecting layers of subtlety, while Kathleen's smile was open and frequently raucous, as direct as her speech-- straight forward with little subtlety; you knew exactly what she thought, meant, and wanted.

Sophie hinted at mystery. Kathleen didn't because that might bring misunderstanding; if she was happy she wanted you to know; if she was pissed, she didn't want you to miss it.

Sophie's eyes were gentle, understanding, and sympathetic. Kathleen's were more lively, sharp, and penetrating. They had different voices also. Sophie's was caressing with a lovely lilt; Kathleen's was more energetic, rapid, concise, and blunt.

I decided the differences between them had a lot to do with their professions. Sophie was an artist, serene and accepting, while Kathleen, an engineer, was more challenging and emphatic. There was almost an Old World/New World difference between them. I loved both.

Sophie was so soothing and kind, so removed from my gruesome prison world that I was beguiled and captivated. She was exactly like her letters: intelligent, funny, warm. Alas, I remained old, poor, and had no prospects.

When the visit ended, we'd had such a wonderful time that I knew this would continue, but I couldn't make it happen. *She* had to find time to visit, make the trip, and pay for it.

For me, this was impossible to believe: a soft, loving, funny, intelligent beautiful woman had reached out to me from France. It seemed fantasy. It *was* fantasy, so much so that I could not believe it even as it was happening.

I felt like a life preserver had been cast into the dark tumultuous sea swirling about me. I clutched it. Suddenly, I had a life within life in prison.

Yet I was conflicted: what would my children think? What would Kathleen think?

But most importantly, when would Sophie come again

17. GED Redux

I knew men could kill: willingly, eagerly, gleefully. I'd seen it on the battlefield; I'd done it myself. The Marines taught me how and gave me medals for it. It's called war. I hadn't been surprised; I'd read history. Men killed for country, religion--*anything*, murdering in defense, anger, lust, beliefs, or just thrill. They raped and tortured too.

Now I lived among men who bragged about such things. In GED class, a petri dish of horrors, I taught them reading, writing, math, science, and social studies. There were many grim days when for reasons of chemistry, genetics, or whim, one of them would decide that 9:48 a.m. was the perfect time to go batshit: tossing books, another student, yelling at the top of his lungs, collapsing on the floor, or threatening mayhem, frequently against me.

I HAVE GOT TO GET OUT OF HERE! I'd scream silently and back away as the guy exploded/ imploded. But with no escape, I'd take a deep breath and calm myself with my coping device—Buddhism in two words: It's Ok. Move on. And the core tenet--Fuck it.

However, the Buddha himself, dragged from under his banyan tree into our classroom might have lapsed teaching murderers, thieves, rapists, child molesters, druggies, and perverts. No contemplating your navel here

Siddhartha. Better not turn your back on them either. Or even close your eyes. Meditation could be lethal.

Still, his teachings of stoicism helped me help 76 guys get their GED's from 2004-2006, rewarding work well worth that dollar a day.

In my third year, Mr. Johnson disappeared—just didn't show up one day. I'd long suspected something amiss when against regulations several students often stayed after class, but it wasn't my business: See no evil, Hear no evil, Speak no evil is difficult in the Kingdom of Evil. So was Don't Ask, Don't Tell, Don't Know. Alzheimer's was my alibi when asked about something I didn't want to discuss or disclose. "I'm old; I can't remember."

Ms. Joyner, white, fifty, attractive, replaced Mr. Johnson, but her first day might have sent the Buddha home screaming; it sent her fleeing the classroom. She wanted a computer set up on her desk, so I moved the supply cabinet to access the wall plug. Behind it, I found a paper bag. Thinking it contained supplies, I handed it to Ms. J who put it in the cabinet. Then I plugged in the computer and left.

Later, Ms. Joyner opened the bag to find cocaine and a cell phone. Horrified, she streaked to the Fat Man. Cocaine in the GED classroom! LOCK DOWN LOCK DOWN LOCK DOWN! The Rocky Mount police were summoned, but the crime was never solved. Why bother?—the perp was already in prison.

For me, the most heartbreaking part of GED was the Father Read program, sadder even than testing ABE students who couldn't identify vowel sounds.

We had a small selection of children's books from public library discards which a guy could check out to read to his child at visitation *if* he demonstrated that he could read the book himself—not always the case.

I spent many hours coaching big burly men how to read *The Little Engine That Could, Goldilocks,* and *The Three Billy Goats Gruff.* At visitation I'd see the felon fathers reading the stories to children perched on their laps; they'd smile proudly, but the sight filled me with sorrow: poor men; poor children. What were their futures?

But there so many happy, funny, and rewarding times that I looked forward to class every morning, eager to get out of my B Block cell to help others. To laugh and joke.

Doc was 40, short and slight with delicate features, a good artist whose hustle was making greeting cards--of course with paper he'd stolen from the print plant where he worked.

Card making was lucrative. Buying cards was so much easier than writing letters with words and sentences, elusive complicated formations that failed to express even more elusive complicated feelings, but a card--four stamps--was done for you with a well scripted and usually correctly spelled generic inscription decorated with a heart or flower.

Doc came every night to learn math, only math because he couldn't read or write, just his card greetings: I Love You; Happy Birthday; Merry Christmas. Like many, Doc focused on math because there were no mystifying multiple choice questions to read or answer. While words confused them, they knew numbers, though two plus two frequently equaled five.

I used stamps for addition and subtraction, and cocaine for decimals, division, and multiplication. How many grams in a kilo? At $20,000 a brick (kilo), how much are two grams? How many grams can you buy with $50,000? If you cut it by half with baking soda, what's your profit per gram?

I'd joke, "If you want to run a business instead of hustling nickel bags on a street corner, you need math." This worked for most guys because they wanted their own business. I was offered numerous lucrative (25% of drug profits) consigliere jobs for my expertise—*when* they got out of prison, and *if* I did.

Doc, however, was not interested in cocaine; he fixated on algebra when he observed me helping another student. The x's fascinated him, and he begged me to teach him algebra. He was so eager that I got him started, but the concept of "x" baffled him.

"The x can be anything—it's the unknown," I said. "So if 7 x's are 21, what is one x?"

"But what is x," he persisted; the x had to be something. He would not let it go.

"Make x a honey bun," I said. Frosted honey buns were the favorite item in the canteen.

"If one x, one honey bun, costs a dollar, how much do 7 honey buns, 7 x's, cost?"

No problem—7 dollars. He could do honey buns. After two hours, he understood x. He was so pleased and excited that he asked me to give him homework for practice. Exhausted with a severe headache, I wrote quick problems on a sheet of paper: $7y=42$; what is y?

Doc looked at me in horror. "What's y?" he asked.

"Y is the unknown. Make it anything. Make it a honey bun."

His horror deepened. "Oh no, Mr. Peterson, x's are honey buns."

Of course not all students lacked skills. Many got their GED's without my help; they were intelligent guys whose high school careers had been interrupted by hold ups, shoot outs, rapes, rehab, and other legal complications, but successfully resumed in the slammer.

However, a few gave me the creeps.

The "yuk" factor is a good life guide. Children don't need details about certain behavior; it's enough to say, "If it feels yucky, it's wrong." Six and seven year olds joining the Cub Scouts don't need details about sodomy and fellatio--"yucky" will suffice. Likewise, little girls don't need gory details about strange men offering candy to help them look for their lost puppies.

"Don't violate a corpse" is something else that doesn't need public addressing. "Leave grandma alone in the coffin," should not have to be taught.

On The Street, Allen drove for a funeral home and was returning with an 80 year old female corpse when police investigated a hearse bouncing up and down off the side of the road. They found Allen and the corpse in intimate (on his part) and inanimate (on her part) coitus.

He did not want my help in class though he scored 5th grade level. He wanted female help, not for instruction, just proximity, but Ms. Joyner wouldn't go near him because he literally slobbered over her, eyes fixed on her breasts and ass, so she had me deal with him.

He was disgusting and never learned a thing. Young, athletic, handsome enough to score sugar daddies, he got hurt in a basketball game on the rec yard. Sent for physical therapy to Nash County Hospital, he made the female nurses and patients so uncomfortable he was forbidden to go back.

"He grossed them out," a guard told us.

"Good thing they didn't see him in the morgue," Big Tom said.

Andre, unbearably arrogant, smug and egocentric, was another inmate I couldn't stand. Twenty-five, handsome, intelligent and articulate, he radiated such dangerous vibes that I never trusted him. Just sitting next to him with a pencil twitching in his hand made me nervous.

Shortly after his release, while watching local TV news one night, I saw his picture flashed on the screen; Wanted: For murder, rape, arson, and mutilation. A sixty year old woman's charred remains had been found in her burned house; she'd been raped, murdered, her hands cut off to prevent identification, and the house set on fire. So much for rehabilitation.

"You teach those skills in GED?" Big Tom asked me.

When I said yes, Tom said he was going to sign up for class in the morning.

Two other inmates made me so uncomfortable I dreaded helping them, but we were all cast offs in the same doomed lifeboat, so I did what I could.

Rick had tried to commit suicide with a shotgun after he'd accidentally killed his mother, but at the last

224

second he jerked the gun blowing off the lower part of his face, including his mouth. It was grotesque.

His mother had been hanging up clothes in the backyard when he, drunk, mistook her for a deer and blew her away. Horrified and truly loving his mother, he turned the weapon on himself--and missed. Partially. He was convicted of 2d degree murder and sentenced to prison.

He felt a bond with me because he'd also been a Marine. Rick was a gentle guy off the sauce and truly remorseful for killing his mother. I wanted to help— Semper Fi and all that—but I couldn't bear his slobbering; drool dripped on the desk, his assignments, and my hands. Doctors said they could graft skin from his ass to make him look better, but he refused.

"They can graft my ass," Big Tom said. "He's disgusting."

Ronnie, with Graves' opthamopathy, had huge protruding unfocused eyes like the English comedian Marty Feldman. It was disconcerting to sit across the table trying to explain algebra; I never knew where to look or where he was looking.

Ronnie was pathetic, a short fat child molester, dreadful snitch, and religious fanatic who proselyted in class and complained whenever the F bomb was dropped, which was constantly, a literal carpet bombing. He also stood at his cell window that faced the rec yard to masturbate on shirtless guys working out on the weight pile.

"Your boy is jacking on us," Big Tom would say. "Doesn't he see enough of you in class?" I'd just shudder. Ronnie had no friends, no social skills, and I *did* feel sorry for him. He got his GED, but I wondered what use it would be.

One morning before class I was unexpectedly called to Visitation. Thinking it might be my lawyer with news of the appeal—my release!—I rushed to the visitor's building, but when I entered the room, Clayton stood waiting for me.

My heart froze and I could not breathe. Someone had died. Oh my God, I thought in terror--please don't let it be one of my children. Seeing horror on my face, Clayton hugged me immediately, knowing of course what was going through my mind. "It's your Dad," he said quickly. "Granddad died yesterday." Relief swept me as I eased into a chair.

My son stared at me, then I broke down: I was a son too. My father was dead. I cried.

All Clayton could do was rest his hand on my shoulder, and he cried too, knowing that someday it would be him hearing this news about me.

"It's ok," I said at last. Then we talked about my dad, our relationship, and my relief that it was him, not one of my children. It was in the order of things. Dad was 87. He had led a good life. He'd had four children, landed at Normandy in WWII, had a 30 year military career, and been married to my mother 60 years (maybe worse than Normandy)--she had died three years earlier. He had been a good man and I loved him.

"How did he die?" I asked.

"Uncle Bill (my brother with whom Dad lived after Mom died) said they had been watching TV when Granddad suddenly said, 'I'm afraid.' "

My father had never been afraid. He'd faced death and my mother many times. He was a fatalist--everything in life had been determined, even when it would end, so there was no need for worry or fear; it had been written. "Dad was afraid?" I asked incredulously.

"Uncle Bill was surprised too. He said he asked Granddad if he wanted to see a priest. Granddad thought a moment, then said, 'Hell, no.' Then he went to bed and died in his sleep."

I laughed. Yeah, that was Dad. I went back to the unit and told the guard that my father had died and I wasn't going to class.

I didn't leave my cell for two days. I thought of all the deaths in my life--Kathleen's, George's, Liz's, my mother's, so many relatives, Ken Beverly's, so many from Vietnam, but mostly I thought of my father and how much he had meant to me.

I hadn't realized that until I was grown with children of my own. He was understanding, supportive, rarely critical, and always seemed proud of me. I never felt in competition with him or that I had to prove anything to him. He didn't set a bar I had to overcome; he let me be me.

So Dad joined my other dead in shuttered memory along with lost love: Kathleen.

But love was not completely lost. There were my children, my brothers, Patricia (I could never not love my former wife, mother of my sons), and now there was Sophie.

She had returned several months after her first visit and continued to come three and four times every year for

227

two hour visits under the watchful eyes of guards insuring there was no contact beyond a simple kiss on arrival and one on departure.

We exchanged hundreds of letters—Abelard and Heloise. She was a life raft I clutched out of desperation, my escape from prison to warmth, touch, love and hope, yet I never got over my amazement that she was coming to see me, nor could I imagine what she suffered from friends and colleagues: You're *what*? In love with an *American*? In *prison*? For *murder*? What is *wrong* with you?

What did her husband think? Her thirteen year old son?

I told my own children about Sophie and they were happy for me, but they didn't understand the depth and complexity of the relationship. Neither did I, for everything since Kathleen's death made no sense; Sophie was just one more inexplicable aspect of the story. My wonderful wife had died; I was in prison for the rest of my life; I'd lost everything I owned. Why not have a French woman join the nightmare? Write her in! Send her over.

I would get so excited about an upcoming visit, fantasize about it for weeks, and the visit would be even better than I imagined. We'd laugh, hold hands, stare into one another's eyes, kiss, but then it would be over, yet the desire for another visit grew more intense.

Sophie got a mobile US telephone number which I called collect most evenings; all calls had to be collect and were recorded. Those 15 minutes calls cost her thousands. But oh, what they did for me. What *she* did me: Breath; Hope; Life.

Whenever down, I'd reach under my bunk for one of her letters or I'd call her in Paris to tell her about Perry playing with his dick or whatever else bothered me. She'd listen, comfort me, and make me laugh. She restored me and made me stronger.

We talked of a future after the Court of Appeals freed me, for surely justice would prevail. Any day now. But one September 2006 morning before class, I was at a table reading the *News and Observer* when a guy slid into a seat across from me.

"I'm really sorry, Mr. Peterson."

I looked up curiously. "For what?"

"I just heard on the radio that your appeal was denied."

Shock Jock radio was popular and I a favorite topic. That morning they had gleefully announced that the Court of Appeals had denied my appeal; I would remain in prison until I died.

I thanked the guy for the news and pretended it didn't bother me, but when he moved on, I brought my hand to my mouth to stifle a scream. Oh God, no. No! I gripped the table so hard my hands went numb, then I jumped up and went outside to be alone. At the fence I leaned my head against the wire in despair; tears blurred my vision. This was the rest of my life.

My stomach hurt so much I almost fell to my knees. No! This can't be. I wanted to run away, hide; I didn't want to go on. I felt completely defeated. Sick.

The next day my attorney came with details. The decision had been 2-1 against me; the dissenting opinion sent the case automatically to the state Supreme Court.

The dissenting judge said trial errors were so egregious and unconstitutional that I deserved a new trial, but while the other judges agreed there had been unconstitutional errors, they considered them "harmless". So now the Supreme Court would decide.

"How long will it take?" I asked.

"Could be another year."

A year, I murmured over and over trudging miserably back to my cell. I lay on my bunk for an hour, eyes open on the ceiling, hands folded across my chest. Ommmmm.

The mantra helped, but I knew Sophie would help more so I called her. She had heard the news and though devastated, she comforted me and said this was just a setback. We *would* live together in Paris.

Big Tom was more worried about how I would survive Nash. "Ok, the court fucked you. You're here for the rest of your life. Man up! And get protection." He pointed to a group of blacks across the yard. Bloods. He rubbed his fingers together. "Give them money."

"There isn't any money here. It's a cashless prison."

He dropped his head in disgust. "Jesus, Peterson! Your Yankee gangster buddies would whack your dumb ass for being so stupid. Think! What do we use instead of money?"

"Stamps." Stamps, then 37 cents in the canteen were the currency for all transactions: Cigarettes cost 3 stamps each ($1.11). A pack, 50 stamps ($18.50). Weed was 20 stamps a blunt (7.40); Methadone, 50 a pill. A cell phone, 500. A punk or female guard? Like the market

230

price for fish on The Street, it changed daily and depended on the catch. Everything was for sale and had a price--in stamps. You were rich if you had them.

After cigarettes were banned, prices skyrocketed—$5 *per* cigarette, $100 a pack. Guards would buy a carton on The Street for $35 and sell them to inmates for $250.

"Who has stamps? Lots of them?" Tom asked.

"Bloods," I answered. "They own the dope. And gambling." Though prohibited, gambling went on from wake up until lock down because guards considered it harmless activity that kept inmates occupied. Bloods "owned" the poker tables; anyone who set up their own would be shanked unless they paid "tribute". They also owned "Pools" and "Parlays" on NFL, NBA, college games, and NASCAR races. "Tickets" to bet cost 2 stamps. Thousands were bet weekly. Just as lucrative was the "vig" or interest on loaned stamps--100%: usury to shame Gino and his Uncles.

"What do Bloods do with the thousands of stamps they collect?"

When I looked at him blankly, he exploded. "They sell them for money to pay guards to bring in more contraband! Guards double their salaries that way. They want cash or a money order, not stamps, so Bloods need money to pay them. You have money. Buy their stamps! Send them a money order. Then they'll protect you because they'll need you."

Of course. Bloods sold their stamps to get them back on the market--trickle them down. They were as Republican as Reagan. But because possessing more than 25 was a write up and excess stamps confiscated, Bloods sold them wholesale, 40% to 50% off. It was like buying money half price from the Treasury Department: 37 cent stamps for 20 cents.

Bloods had what I needed--stamps and protection; I had what they needed—money. Yet another match made in Hell.

I needed stamps because after *The Staircase* was televised in 2004, I corresponded with more than one hundred people overseas and in the U.S who had seen the documentary. My weekly $40 click would have gone for stamps if I'd paid regular price in the canteen.

I also needed stamps for bribes: better chow from the kitchen, prescription glasses from the Optical Plant, a new mattress from the warehouse, medication from Medical, a new radio, a new watch, cards, pens, legal pads. Everything was for sale. Most importantly—protection.

Excited at the possibility of solving my problem—survival--I went to gold toothed BK. "Know anyone who'll take a money order for stamps?" He did. If I sent a $100 money order to a Street address I'd get 500 stamps; $200 to a certain guard's PO Box would bring 1000.

So began my fiduciary partnership with Bloods. I had an ally, they had a bank.

Flaunting regulations was dangerous, but I've always had a problem with authority. Perhaps it's the Italian in me, a gene seemingly immune to regimentation that thrives in festive chaos. Resistance is in my nature; I even did it in the Marines.

At OCS in Quantico, one of my drill instructors would yell himself apoplectic at my lack of marching proficiency, or rather at my unwillingness to march lock step with everyone else. It drove DI's crazy, but it was my only means of self-expression.

I was on my way to Vietnam soon, like immediately—the plane was on the runway, the enemy waiting in ambush on the banks of the Cua Viet River. Marching in formation was not my priority. It was, however, for Drill Instructor Stewart who ranked marching in formation with cleanliness and godliness, and who'd run up to me on the drill field and scream, "Peterson, you'll never learn how to march."

Purposely out of step, I'd say, "I certainly hope not, Drill Instructor." Nevertheless, I was a good Marine despite Chief Drill Instructor Parrot's reservations: I didn't think "Irish Pennants," dangling threads on uniforms, deserved the attention he and the USMC demanded.

"Peterson, you're such a shitbird, you'll never get out of Vietnam alive. Your own men will shoot you to save themselves," he'd yell at me in satisfaction and hope.

A year later, I encountered Sgt. Parrot after the 1969 Tet Offensive that killed two of my men. I'd escorted their mangled bodies (my radio operator's head had been blown off) from the DMZ to Graves Registration in Danang. He'd saluted and asked in wonder, "Still alive?"

Despite the horror and my grief, I laughed.

"Who would have guessed it," he said. "Lt. Davidson killed, and here you are…so far."

I couldn't laugh at that. A year earlier at Quantico, Ron Davidson—"Plant Life"—had almost killed me. Ron, with a Master's degree in Phys. Ed., was the strongest guy at OCS. He could do push-ups and pull-ups until DI's got tired counting them. Because I so annoyed the DI's (that

233

marching thing and Irish pennants), they matched me against Ron in a pugil stick fight. Pugil sticks were four feet long, heavy, and we wore little protective gear.

Ron and I were placed in a circle and told to go after each other; it was not a fair fight. He was much bigger and stronger, but so muscle bound that I easily parried and dodged his thrusts. Finally in fury he grabbed the pugil stick like a baseball bat and clubbed me over the head. I lay unconsciousness for fifteen minutes. He was so concerned and contrite.

Ron went to Force Recon, sort of a Marine SEAL, and was killed his first week in combat, a sniper bullet in the brain. His body—Human Remains, Davidson, Ronald F on the cargo manifest—was returned to the States the day I left for Vietnam. Not a good omen on my way to war: if Ron couldn't make it, how could I? But I did.

The Court of Appeals decision was not a good omen either, but I *would* make it in here. Fuck rules and regimentation. No more marching in prison formation.

So I went to The Dark Side for survival.

18. THE DARK SIDE: BLOODS

There is no bright side to prison. No comfortable spot in hell. Prison is dark, darker, darkest, and pitch black. Prisoners aren't meant to be comfortable any more than are the Damned. It's supposed to be miserable: punishment not reward.

But I didn't want to be miserable, so I decided to do whatever necessary to make it less hellish--*except* become a "model" prisoner cowering before guards, kissing ass, and snitching. My models were Gino and Mario who rebelled against authority. Of course breaking laws and rebelling had brought Gino and Mario to prison in the first place, but it was also what made them—us—men *in* prison.

I yearned to be Cool Hand Luke, but I was too old. Besides, that was a movie; this was real. Without Uncles like Mario and Gino had, I secured protection with Bloods, a relationship cemented with money: I had it, they wanted it. What good was my Marine disability retirement if I couldn't spend it? So, following the adage that *Money Talks and Bullshit Walks*, I decided to ride. Bad Buddhist perhaps, but even the Dalai Lama has a chauffeur.

After Gold Toothed BK set me up buying Blood stamps with money orders, I became their bank. They provided protection.

235

When I arrived, guys warned me that dangers lurked everywhere: Never shower without a shank, Never have your back turned from a door, but with Blood protection, I thought my only problem might be a student meltdown in class.

I worried about that when an older black wearing a fez stared intently at me for days. About 40 years old, well-groomed with a trim gray beard, his harsh gaze so unnerved me that I seldom took my eyes off him. One day he finally asked, "Mr. Peterson, "Do you know who the first President was?"

Though suspecting this a trick question, I answered anyway. "George Washington."

He started to protest, but another black warned him off. "Don't. Let it go."

I was puzzled, but pretty sure my answer was right. A little later a bulletin board notice announced an upcoming religious celebration—the birthday of Noble Drew Ali to be observed by the Moorish Science Temple. I had never heard of Noble Drew or the Moorish Science Temple, so I looked them up in the library's encyclopedia *Africana*.

Noble Drew Ali didn't go beyond the fifth grade, worked in a circus, was mentor for Wallace Fard Muhammad who founded the Nation of Islam in Chicago; he died in prison. The student who questioned George Washington as the first President was a follower of Noble Drew.

Moorish members wore Fez's and had unorthodox views: George Washington not being the first President; blacks were the original inhabitants of America—

"sovereign citizens"—not subject to tax or criminal laws. I got along well with them all; we just didn't discuss history.

I had less success with Muslims and Christians.

My initial encounter with Muslims came when I went for my first haircut. The barber was Muslim with a big picture of Osama Bin Laden in his cell. I considered letting my hair grow longer—a lot longer, but when I finally risked the haircut, Ali and I got along fine. Raised Christian in the Bronx, he converted to Islam after incarceration and seemed relieved that I wasn't a Bible banger, but he had no idea what a Buddhist was, and I didn't bother to explain since I wasn't sure myself.

Ali was devout, a genuine follower of the Prophet, but many others had little understanding of Islam; for them it was an anti-white gang.

Jabbar in my GED class ranked second among the 50 Muslims at Nash, a tightly knit group which scorned "infidels". Of course, the infidels thought Muslims were heathen terrorists and avoided them too. As a Buddhist, I didn't care one way or the other. Not giving a shit seemed to me one of the main tenets of Buddhism, though cloaked in lovely high minded koans which usually baffled me.

Maybe if I had stayed at Harvard I would have understood them, but had I remained, I probably wouldn't have become a Buddhist.

When the VA offered to send me back to college on the Vocational Rehabilitation Program in 1971 after my Marine disability discharge (there weren't many job opportunities for tank commanders or guys who could call in air strikes), only Duke and Harvard accepted me because I already had a BA, but didn't want a Master's degree.

237

Everywhere else I applied demanded I enter a Master's program. Only Harvard and Duke thought it novel to study and learn without being in a restricted field. So I went to Harvard. For two days.

There on a bench in Harvard Yard I began my conversion to Buddhism.

Recently released from Bethesda Naval Hospital no doubt suffering PTSD, I arrived at Harvard to a frenzy of anti-war protests. The war was raw in memory: I knew many guys who had died in Vietnam and some still there— Marines with rifles, not Harvard students at peace booths badgering me to sign anti-war petitions.

I wanted to study quietly and forget Vietnam, but I felt that might be impossible in Cambridge. On my third day, weighing whether or not I could do it, a guy with long hair and lots of jewelry interrupted my bench thoughts: he wanted to introduce me to Sheila.

I looked about but didn't see anyone. He pointed to the ground at what I thought was a wig on a leash. Sheila was his angora guinea pig. That's when I decided I wasn't ready for Harvard. So I went back to Duke and became a Buddhist.

Jabbar, thirty, tall, muscular, with a trim goatee, a dignified elegant man, seemed to accept me and my Buddhism, but maybe only because I was helping him with his GED.

The Imam, Hakkim, a little older, tall with full beard, did *not* accept me. Whenever we were close to one another such as in the canteen line, he'd move five feet away. Unacceptable disrespect, so of course I tried to move away first. It is *so* hard to be a good Buddhist.

Hakkim and Jabbar were in for murder, not men to be taken lightly despite their "devout" manners. Indeed, a Holy War developed between us and a Jihad was issued against me.

I was unaware that Muslims draped prayer rugs over the unit phones at evening Count Time so that when Count cleared they had immediate access to the phones because no infidel dared touch their prayer rugs; that would bring immediate physical retaliation.

One evening after Count, I went to a phone and began punching in Sophie's numbers when Jabbar started screaming, "That phone is reserved." Other screaming Muslims joined him.

The Muslims had neglected to place their rugs on the phone that evening. I told them phones couldn't be reserved and continued my call. They were wild. When I hung up, I asked other infidels what the yelling had been about. They explained the prayer rugs. The next night and every night thereafter, prayer rugs were placed on the phones with great ceremony.

A week later, my attorney sent word to call him that evening. Not being a complete fool—or martyr—I notified Captain Lucita at Visitation that I would be going to the hospital that night. Captain Lucita was the new head of STG. An attractive trim Puerto Rican fireball—think Rita Moreno in black leather with whip, handcuffs, and pistol— she made Ms. Snow look like Little Bo Peep. I called her Frau Himmler. We had a contentious relationship with many run-ins over the years, some I won, some she did, and some ending in a draw.

Unperturbed, she asked why would I be going to the hospital. I explained the phone/rug policy. By the time I got back to the unit, guards had been ordered to prevent prayer rugs put on phones and to announce that phones could not be reserved. I knew Frau Himmler wasn't particularly concerned about my safety, but I also knew she didn't want it on the news that I'd been clubbed to death by Muslims over a prayer rug on a telephone.

I made my call without incident, but the Muslims felt (correctly) that I was responsible for the no rug policy. I sensed a jihad developing. It arrived Mother's Day 2005.

Hakkim took community college courses. First thing every morning, he came from his second floor cell to place books on one of the six metal tables guys used for playing cards, writing letters, or socializing. He also put books on the seats so no infidel could sit there. The table was a few feet from my cell.

Hakkim was in class all day and only sat at the table at night to watch TV. Alone. I couldn't believe the infidels put up with this disrespect. A good Buddhist wouldn't have cared, but it bothered me. My mother had not raised a coward and the Marines hadn't trained me to be one, so one mornig as soon as count cleared, I walked out of my cell and put books on three seats at Hakkim's table and sat on the fourth.

When Hakkim came down, he was out of his head, but even if he swept my books off the other seats, he couldn't sit at the table with an infidel; all he could do was pace and fume.

I blistered my ass sitting at the table without moving all day. No one, Muslim or infidel came near me.

At lock down, I collected my books and went back to my cell. Hakkim immediately rushed down with a spray bottle to disinfect the table and seats.

Next morning, I stayed in my cell as Hakkim raced downstairs with his books in such a hurry that he fell, scattering his books everywhere. I didn't go out because I'd proved my point—I could get the table anytime. But tension with Muslims escalated.

While forty of us watched the season finale of *Lost*, Hakkim and Jabbar were called to the sergeant's office. When they came back they pointed at me, "That faggot motherfucker just had us shipped." They screamed at me for hours. Everyone fled the TV area, leaving me to watch the show by myself; I just ramped up my ear phones. In the morning they were gone.

It turned out that Frau Himmler had decided Muslims were too powerful, so when their problem with me developed, they were shipped to other prisons using me as the pretext. When the other Muslims finally realized what had happened, they apologized and I never had another problem with them.

After Hakkim and Jabbar left, the six remaining Muslims in our unit knelt to pray several times a day at one end of the Day Room. Christians got together to pray at the opposite end.

It was a sight: blacks facing East praying to Allah, whites holding hands praying to Jesus. But the Christian cabal was short-lived. When one guy, a murderer, wanted to confess and testify, another said murder broke a commandment and he shouldn't be in the group at all.

Then someone accused that guy of being a child molester who shouldn't be in the group, then someone said *he* shouldn't be in it because he had a punk. And so it went, each pointing a finger at another, *all* having broken at least one commandment (this was, after all, prison) and the group broke up. The Muslims kept praying.

Ken, an oversized black Evangelical Christian in the cell next to me could not stand that I was a Buddhist--or as I told him, *trying* to be one. "It's like with most Christians: you aren't really Christians, you're just trying to be, failing daily at Christ's teachings."

Ken said to me once, "I finally know why I'm in prison."

I thought of offering, "Could it have anything to do with the rape you were convicted of?" but I said nothing.

"I'm here to save you," he said. Well, that was too much even for the Buddha, so I said, "Ken, if your salvation depends on saving me, *you* are going to Hell."

Another time, almost apoplectic he yelled, "It's nothing. Buddhism is NOTHING!"

I assumed a pious pose. "You're right. Buddhism is nothingness. Nothing is Everything in Buddhism." Every day when I'd pop off with some asshole remark, I'd admonish myself, Bad Buddhist, bad Buddhist.

That's certainly what the Chaplain thought, for a little later the mail clerk told me that I'd received a package that I couldn't have—the Chaplain had forbidden it.

"What does the Chaplain have to do with my mail?" I asked.

"Somebody in Switzerland sent you Buddhist Mala beads. They look like Catholic rosary beads or Muslim worry beads. The Chaplain said you can't have them because they came from an individual not an official church. He's sending them back at his expense."

I went to the Chaplain to explain that Buddhism didn't have regular churches, that there was no such thing as a Trinity Avenue Buddhist Temple in Rocky Mount.

A smug self-satisfied man more guard than minister, he said NO. Regulations were regulations; I couldn't have the beads.

I told him that as a good Buddhist, it would be fine to get the beads, but it would also be fine not to get them, and I walked out thinking that was a satisfactory Buddhist Fuck You.

Two days later however, the mail clerk called me to the warehouse and said the Chaplain had changed his mind; I could choose one set of beads and donate the other to the Chapel.

"Why did he change his mind?" I asked.

The Chaplain had discovered it would cost his office $25 to send the beads back to Switzerland, so now I could have a set.

The next day the Chaplain called me to the Chapel and invited me to join a meditation group, but I declined. "Meditation is like masturbation," I said, better practiced alone in the privacy of one's cell. To do it in a group is called a circle jerk and I didn't want to participate.

I thought he was going to pepper spray me, but it ended well--I didn't have to see him or go to the chapel again for five years.

I was comfortable—cell, job, visitors every week, and Sophie. Rich too because I had enough stamps for a

243

new watch, spare radio, extra ear buds, medicine and vitamins from Medical that I couldn't get, in particular fish oil capsules, Omega 3. Only guys with bad cholesterol got them. Mine was too good, so I gave guys with bad cholesterol 10 stamps ($2.50) for their month's supply. They would fight to sell me their fish oil—"I'll take 8 stamps!" Of course they immediately bought candy and honey buns with my stamps, skyrocketing their cholesterol.

Getting stamps was easy because of Bloods, but it led down a slippery slope to what Frau Himmler considered The Dark Side where "dangerous" inmates undermined order and authority; she considered me one of them. We had to be stopped.

I understood, and sometimes thought—I'm not being a good inmate, but then I'd regain my senses: I shouldn't be an inmate at all. Fuck 'em.

At first, this Dark Side was merely gray—a $100 money order got me 500 stamps—but the price of stamps kept rising. Like The Street: inflation. Then greed increased: why go to the chow hall for shit food when I could buy sandwiches and chicken from the canteen? Soon I was buying 1,000 stamps.

Frau Himmler vigorously fought The Dark Side: Bloods who bribed guards and me who funded Bloods buying her guards. We were major threats; she could smell the weed.

She thought she had me when she found discrepancies in my $40 weekly canteen allowance. I rarely went to the canteen, spent almost nothing, yet my locker was filled with sandwiches and other canteen items that others bought for me with stamps I sold them.

She called me to her Admin building office. "Last week you mailed 68 letters. You used 147 stamps, but you only bought two in the canteen. Explain that."

"I bought two stamps?" I asked in surprise. With 1000 coming in, I couldn't imagine why I'd bought *any*. Then I remembered. "Oh, right. I was in canteen line and a guy begged me to get him a couple, so I did."

That drove her crazy. She knew I was buying Blood stamps, but she couldn't prove it.

My downfall came from hubris and pride. I liked getting over on guards and thwarting Captain Lucita; I reveled in breaking rules. Worst of all was pride in associating with Bloods—a white guy with access. What an ego boost— a "Player" like Gino. White among blacks: Prison Chic. I thought I was cool, but I was only rich.

The Blood association brought me down. I deserved it.

Just outside my cell was a Blood poker table. Guys played from wake up until Lock Down. Quick ran the table. In his late twenties, lean and mean with lightening hands (hence Quick), he could handle any problem which arose, frequently with the turn of a card.

Of course the game was crooked with marked cards and shills. To gamble, merchandise—toothpaste, soap, shampoo, *anything*--was converted to stamps valued at 25 cents each: $2 toothpaste from the canteen brought 8 stamps, a $20 watch or radio got 80. The cashier's cage was like Costco.

When the table closed at night, winners could choose merchandise or stamps; most chose stamps because it was the currency everyone used. Occasionally the table lost. When Quick couldn't cover losses, he came to me for stamps. I'd give them to him to pay the winners and next morning he'd pay me back from the Blood treasury. I didn't charge interest because I was getting their protection. I had partnered with the Devil.

The slippery slope to the Dark Side turned into an avalanche. I blame it on Walmart.

Money orders were slow, cumbersome, and risky—they could be traced, lost, or cashed by anyone. The Street provided an ingenious solution, untraceable instantaneous money transfers--fast, easy, and safe: Green Dots. Available at Walmart. A guard could purchase a peel off 16 number "account" known only to him for $4.95, no identification required.

Fourteen number "Refills" or "Re-loads" from $20-$1000 sold for $4.95. When those numbers were given to the account holder, the funds were transferred immediately, available like a debit card. Switzerland at every mall!

One day soap and deodorant were missing from my cell. I felt sure Skip, a pasty mealy young white had done it because he'd begun to gamble heavily at the table though his only stamps came from his hustle cleaning cells--two to sweep and mop. He came to mine twice a week. That's how bad things had become; I had a "housekeeper".

When I confronted Skip about the theft, he denied it of course. I fumed for three days. If I let him get away with it, I'd become an easy mark subject to more theft, so I told Quick the bank was closed: items stolen from me had been gambled at his table.

Like all well run organizations, Bloods kept records. Sure enough, Skip had exchanged Dove soap, $2 in the canteen, for 8 stamps; my deodorant brought 10.

"We'll take care of the problem," Quick said, returning the stolen items, but I worried Quick might go too far so I went to Duck, head Blood after Claymore had been shipped. Duck was big, muscular, articulate, and smart. When we first met, I'd asked how he got his name--he didn't look like a "Duck", he looked more like "Rex"; a Tyrannosaurus. He'd laughed. "On The Street, when people saw me, they'd yell 'Duck,' here he comes.'"

Of course. I explained that I didn't want Skip hurt badly or the *Po*-leese all over it.

"Got you covered," Duck said. "I'll get D Lord on it."

D Lord, his main lieutenant--early twenties, sleek, more Raptor than Tyrannosaurus--was in for robbery, B&E, and drug trafficking. Not interested in giving up his life of crime, he wanted to augment it by writing. He'd given me several stories to look at--"Hip hop shoot-em ups" with lots of drugs, sex, and violence. Nikki Turner and the rapper Fifty Cents found a huge market for this genre.

After reading one story, I said, "D Lord, sooner or later your hero (himself of course) has to reload—no gun has that many bullets. And no one can fuck that many times in one afternoon between six shoot outs with fourteen dead Crips in his crib."

"Yeah, I can," he said. That was the most I ever got out of him. At first I thought it was just me—old and white—but he rarely spoke even to his bros. A glare meant no; a blank expression was yes. I never saw a smile.

Like many young gangbangers, D Lord wanted out of Nash—too sedate with too many old guys. He wanted to go to the Foothills, the prison for gangbangers with constant action and friends who spoke his non-verbal language: fists, knives, guns.

Duck said D Lord needed to be "taken care of", so I transferred $100 to his account--twenty times what I'd lost with that damn soap and deodorant.

Duck tipped me off about the hit. "It's going down on the rec yard after chow," so I settled that evening against the fence to watch what I had bought. At exactly 6, D Lord ran up to Skip on the volleyball court and hit him with a blow as hard as I'd ever seen, definitely a $100 hit. Floyd Mayweather would have gotten a million for it.

Only when I saw Skip splayed in the dirt did I realize that I'd set myself up for "Contract for Hire" that could send me back to Street court. TV and newspapers would have a field day. How could I have been so stupid?

Please don't die, I begged Skip silently when guards screaming LOCK DOWN rushed to the motionless thief. He didn't die, but I fretted in my cell, gnawing my fingernails, staring out my cell window every few minutes until he returned from the hospital bandaged like a mummy.

When he was able to talk, he said he'd accidentally run into the volleyball pole: fingering a Blood could be lethal--you wouldn't survive the second attack.

But witnesses to the assault fell over each other to snitch: "I'll tell, I'll tell. Me first." So with threats from

Captain Lucita and a promise for transfer to protective custody, Skip identified D Lord as his assailant and claimed that I had paid him to do it.

D Lord and I were taken to The Hole—my second trip.

There was no hope for D Lord—all those witnesses. My fate rested on D Lord's silence.

Did Omerta apply to Bloods for an old white guy? I must have paced 50 miles in that 9x12 cell.   Fuck fuck fuck! Stupid! Arrogant fool!

But Omerta held! I was released! Duck told me what had happened. When Frau Himmler promised D Lord she'd drop all charges if he identified me--"We don't want you, we want Peterson"--he said, "Fuck you."

She threatened that if he didn't identify me, she'd ship him to the Foothills.

He said, "Fuck you" again, so she sent him to the Foothills where he'd wanted to go all along. I wasn't so lucky. 1,000 letters from people all over the world including Sophie's postcards were trashed. I was allowed to keep 25.

300 books were confiscated; I could keep 10. I offered to donate the rest to the library--literature and art books worth $5,000 that Sophie and friends had sent—but I was ordered to mail them out because Frau Himmler was afraid I might go to the library and read them. It cost $60. Fortunately I had enough stamps. But no longer a job or cell.

Worst of all Captain Lucita transferred me to Unit 3 to live on a bunk sharing a toilet with 15 guys. She was determined to make my life miserable, so she put sharpshooters on me, some really good snipers—guards and snitches.

The Dark Side got much darker.

III

2008-2011

19. EVEN DARKER

I expected to encounter murderers, rapists, thieves, and drug dealers in prison, and I did. I knew there were pedophiles too—strange creepy guys who haunted playgrounds and priests who preyed on altar boys—but I thought pedophilia was rare, yet when I got to Unit 3, guards told me that a third of the guys there were child molesters. Not just creepy guys and priests, but fathers and grandfathers, jocks, and others seemingly normal.

"Welcome to Chesterville," they said.

Unit 3 Block B was only slightly less notorious than The Hole, but worse than Hieronymus Bosch's depictions of Hell; he never painted children being molested. Nothing was in the Bible about it either. Why had God overlooked child molesting in all those Shalt Nots? Dante didn't even have a special ring in Hell for them. Was it too horrible to contemplate?

My only encounter with a pedophile had occurred when I was 15. I was an occasional altar boy at Fort Monroe, Virginia where my dad was stationed and his 85 year old mother, my Grandmother Dell, lived with us. Riddled with cancer, she suffered worse than the amputees at Zama Hospital, screaming and begging to die like Greg Schmidt, but there was no relief for her pain.

252

The night before she died, my parents left me to babysit my siblings and take care of my grandmother.

Oh Christ it was awful. She screamed unrelentingly, Let Me Die, God Let me die. The lamp in her bedroom cast macabre shadows over her tortured face as I lifted her onto a bedpan and cleaned her afterwards. She was skeletal, weighing less than 60 pounds, yet lucid enough to beseech me to help her die. Please, please, she begged.

She died the next morning while I was in high school. That afternoon I went to the rectory at St. Mary's Star of the Sea to see the priest, the one who had asked me about self-abuse.

When the housekeeper invited me in, I saw Father Belton tripping down the stairs in a dress and high heels, reeking of perfume. He seemed nonplussed at my presence and when I told him my grandmother had died, he suggested we go to the church to say mass for her. He said he'd change and meet me there in five minutes.

After slipping into something more comfortable-- like a cassock? I wondered. Five minutes later he offered a mass for the repose of her soul and I rang the bells, crying throughout the service. He was in his forties, soft and effeminate, but I was grateful for his kindness.

Those forgiving feelings disappeared later when I learned about atrocities other priests and child molesters committed. Now I was *surrounded* by such men with no cell, no job, and no Blood protection.

Every morning when I woke to guards screaming COUNT TIME COUNT TIME COUNT TIME, my eyes flew open, my body lunched forward, and I'd panic. This can't be! Fury would overwhelm me—for the jurors who convicted me, police who'd lied, the judicial system, but immediately anger gave way to sorrow: Kathleen is dead, love is lost, my children are gone forever, then I'd settle on the worn thin mattress. Ommmmm.

When count cleared, the Chesters gathered at a table to wait for chow near the guard. They needed protection, and as pariahs they had only themselves for company.

The notorious Scout Master RC seemed their leader. He'd molested the Cub Scouts in his charge and looked like the *Star Wars* character Admiral Ackbar with eyes on the side of his head. When Big Tom first saw RC, he said, "What kind of parent would let their kid go camping with him? He'd have a better chance with Big Foot."

The men at the table were as unsettling as praying mantises, soft like overripe fruit with ingratiating Uriah Heep manners, hands clasped close to their chests, eyes that never met yours. Creepy. Of course I quickly learned other pedophiles in the unit were not at the table. They appeared normal; one, a terrific athlete, looked like a young Brad Pitt.

It was easy to avoid obvious pedophiles, but what about normal looking ones? There was another problem: maybe they were innocent, wrongly convicted like I had been. I solved the dilemma Hollywood style—on looks: Creepy was out; normal looking ok: profiling. Admiral Ackbar was out, Brad Pitt was in.

I turned to the problem of protection, but that also resolved itself in Hollywood fashion—a bromance.

As I headed to the rec yard to exercise on the third morning, several guys yelled, "Don't go out there! JS is on the bench. No whites allowed."

Surely he couldn't be worse or scarier than Gino, I thought, but when I peered out a bathroom window to check, I saw King Kong on the weight pile--arms the size of my thighs, thighs like my chest, his chest a Volkswagen. Ok, no fresh air or exercise today.

His reputation matched his looks; he was a very big very bad boy.

Convicted of murder at eighteen, JS had spent 15 years in high security with over 50 infractions involving violence. On his first night at Nash, a female guard seeing him naked in his cell doing push-ups accused him of gunning her down. Berserk, he threw himself against the iron door. She screamed and ran. Three male guards rushed to his cell but were afraid to go in, and more afraid he'd get out. Finally he was calmed and the female guard transferred.

"Never fuck with him," I was warned, but after two days stewing inside, I decided to risk the weight pile. If worst came to worst, I felt I could outrun him--he looked too muscle bound to even walk. Nevertheless, I ventured out with trepidation, ready to bolt instantly.

On the bench, his bare billboard sized back facing me, 455 pounds on the bar, the most I'd seen, he didn't move until I got 10 feet running distance from him and said, "Everybody warned me not to come out here. They said a Silverback Gorilla was on the weight pile."

He turned *very* slowly, eyed me carefully--no threat at all--then he laughed.

255

Apparently he'd been waiting for me for his first words were, "I heard you were a bank. And a post office. Want 500 flags (stamps)?"

King Kong wanted to do business? Partner? Restraining myself from an embarrassing display of relief, I said nonchalantly, "Sure."

We bumped fists, protection problem solved. He pulled a piece of paper with an address from his pocket. "Memorize this and eat the paper." Then he slipped me a bundle of 500 stamps. "$100."

I think he was serious about eating the paper. "This isn't Mission Impossible, JS. Don't worry; I have Alzheimer's when I talk to *Po*-leese."

JS did a thriving business in contraband—tobacco, drugs, cell phones—with extensive guard contacts who worked with him, not just for the money (if they didn't take it, another guard would) but because they wanted him on their side if things jumped off (turned bad). Better friend than foe. My sentiments exactly.

Under JS's Pterodactyl wings, I felt as secure as I had with Gino and Mario. More protection came with JS's homie, the monumentally nutty and even more dangerous Johnny Blood. His coiled ferocity kept anyone from even thinking of crossing him.

JS was 300 pounds muscle, Johnny a sleek 6' 2", 220 pounds. Also in for murder, Johnny would go to the mat for *anything*: his contraband sunglasses and even the cap he wore sideways in the unit, strictly forbidden. His prison record was long and violent. Guards never harassed him because like a cobra, he'd attack *anyone* who moved against him.

JS smoldered volcanic intimidation, a ticking bomb; Johnny was a live grenade. The two had known each other since teenagers at Polk Youth Camp where they'd first been sent. Now mid-thirties, they had not survived prison, they had thrived in it.

My first encounter with Johnny came when he shouted across the rec yard one morning, "Peterson, come here." Following Gino's advice to never back down, I just stared at him.

"I said come here," he yelled again. When I didn't move, he rushed up and furiously thrust his snarling face into mine, eyes bulging, teeth bared, but I stood my ground (JS was nearby) and said calmly, "You need to get a dog. Maybe *he'll* mind when you call him."

Absolutely crazed, his eyes widened even more and his lips drew back ferociously. I thought I'd made a lethal mistake calling his bluff, but Johnny abruptly turned and stormed back to the unit. I almost sank to the ground in relief, yet a minute later he stomped back. I drew in my breath sharply, but this time he said as if nothing had happened, "Let's talk."

Because he rarely laughed or even smiled—dead serious always and completely paranoid—Johnny was fun to tease: I'd short him stamps, make up outrageous stories (he always believed them), and warn him about impending doom—an approaching asteroid, a cell shake down, but only up to his twitching point, just before he turned into Jimi Hendrix electrocuted.

JS and I laughed after every incident, though never to Johnny's face. "He's gonna get you one of the days," JS warned. "You know how he got his name—Johnny Blood?

Not about the gang. About *blood*. Once a young banger called him a punk. Johnny was going to kill him. I said I'd handle it, so I called the brother to my cell and told him to apologize. While we talked, Johnny came in. 'Well?' When I said I was still working on it, Johnny yelled 'Fuck that,' and sliced him. Blood everywhere—floor, ceiling, walls, me. Ever since he's been Johnny Blood.

"He got an assault charge, went to Street court then was sent to Max Lock Down for two years. Came out a bug, stabbed an officer and went back for two more years. Total whack job when he got out. You seen that Cuckoo Nest movie? That's Johnny. They drug him like those guys, but like a mosquito, the bug juice don't work anymore."

After that, whenever I encountered Johnny, I'd ask, "You had your meds today?"

"Not all of them," he'd growl, "so don't fuck with me, Peterson."

The first time we did business, he said he needed a money order to cover "merchandise" (a cell phone) that a guard was bringing in. He'd get me the stamps after he sold it.

"You want a loan?" I asked.

He did not like that word or the idea that he was getting something upfront without paying. "Your stamps are guaranteed," he said fiercely, face pressed into mine.

Speech was a physical act for him. We bumped fists to seal the deal and Johnny became my go-to guy for problems—for a price; everything was business: eliminating (beating down) a threat cost 100 stamps, but once I had The Terminator on payroll, there was just one.

258

JS's guard connections earned me stamps; Johnny's muscle cost me stamps. Yet despite being the thug stereotype, Johnny was a voracious reader—five or six books a week. He'd go to other unit libraries (forbidden), take (not check out) all the books he wanted (forbidden—a *librarian* was going to stop him?) and read every moment that he wasn't engaged in mayhem.

Every morning I'd get a book report—the stories and characters were real to him.

"You know what that motherfucker Reacher said?" Lee Childs didn't exist, but Jack Reacher was in the unit with us. I'd listen with rapt, but well concealed amusement.

The Fat Man called me in three times to warn me about Johnny. "He's the most dangerous man on state."

Johnny swelled when I told him. "Believe it."

I laughed. "The Fat Man is wrong; I'm the most dangerous."

"You just got the most stamps."

I smiled. "Like I said."

With Johnny and JS for compadres, life was safe; another Blood made it comfortable.

Slim, 23, 6 foot four and an excellent basketball player, was one of six Honor Grade inmates, the lowest security, men soon to be released. Their jobs were to clean the admin building as well as mow and weed whack beyond the razor wire. They wore special green uniforms and were the only guys allowed out the gate.

Slim was a Duke fan--his mother had been cured of cancer at Duke Hospital. We were the only Duke supporters in an Inferno of UNC fans. He often brought me the warden's secretary's Yoplait yogurt which he stole from the admin refrigerator.

Before and after work, Slim visited the Chester JH, "Princess Di," for blow jobs.

I gave JH the nickname after he begged me for articles and pictures of the real Princess Diana. He was obsessed with her; the 10th anniversary of her death was approaching. I had subscriptions to many magazines, plus *USA Today* and *The Wall Street Journal* with pictures and stories. He papered his cell with the photos I gave him, hence the nickname.

JH was 48, white, fat, and effeminate with a Life sentence for *many* Crimes against Nature. His victims were young boys.

I couldn't bear to be around him; I'd just hand him the articles and photos and turn away.

We come into the world tabula rasa, yet some are flawed marble Michelangelo couldn't have worked with. Even with tragic childhoods for JH, RC with the Cub Scouts, Alan with the corpse, and Robert McNeill-- probably for Vlad the Impaler, Hitler, and Stalin too-- mitigating circumstances aren't excuses. I couldn't separate their crimes from the criminals.

While prison is macho, gays and homosexual activity tolerated—not so much a Pope Francis "Who am I to judge?" philosophy, but a Buddhistic "Who gives a fuck?"--Chesters aren't tolerated; many guys had been molested when young and many feared for their children.

Slim however, young and horny, didn't care, thus two trips daily to Princess Di whose success, besides oral skills, was based on $40 a week that his mother sent--until

260

she died, a royal crisis for the Princess: reduced income limited the dick he could buy.

Besides yogurt, Slim and the other Honor Grade inmates ingenuously smuggled in dope. When they returned from work every day, guys on bunks sprang up like meerkats waiting to get the signal—a nod meant dope, a head shake meant no delivery.

I eagerly watched too: dope meant business--stamps to sell! I had become part of the cartel; I was financing drugs.

In 2007, dope traffic was centered in the warden's office--without his knowledge.

Dope was dropped on prison property outside the wire by Street contacts of Honor Grade inmates who'd drive by at night to toss packages onto the property. Next morning, the Honor Grade detail would pick up the contraband when mowing and pass it to Slim in the admin building. Slim stowed it in the warden's office where he worked cleaning up.

Later, he'd bring it into the warden's bathroom where he'd hidden a scale and baggies, then the dope would be smuggled to the unit, usually "suitcased" up someone's ass.

Nash was often underwater in a sea of dope—sold for stamps, a bonanza for me. This enterprise lasted until Slim's time was up and he was released.

Slim told his Honor Grade replacement about the scale and baggies, but the inmate went to the wrong bathroom. However guards observed him searching, which tipped them off that something was up, so they looked in the warden's bathroom and found the drug paraphernalia.

Drugs in the warden's office! LOCK DOWN LOCK DOWN LOCK DOWN.

A SWAT team and drug dog rushed in. Frau Himmler, the chain gang assistant warden, captains, lieutenants, and sergeants arrived. Every inmate on a bunk was brought into the corridor past the drug dog which sniffed us, then we were lined up and the dog sniffed us again.

On the bunk beside me was a young muscular Blood named Street who had fallen into gangs in the projects, but he had a good nature, also his GED, and he liked to read Nikki Turner hip hop shoot 'em and fuck 'em ups, several of which I gave him.

When Street and I went into the corridor and were placed in a line up, the dog sat behind us *twice*, the signal we had drugs; the dog went particularly nuts over me; he kept jumping at my leg. I heard the assistant warden on his radio to the warden: "It's Peterson. The dog has Peterson." I was sweating profusely.

Had someone planted dope on me? A set up? I didn't smoke dope because I feared the frequent random piss tests. Drug Possession would get me returned to court with criminal charges, massive publicity, and the final nail in the coffin of any hope to get out.

However, while they wanted me, the rogue inmate, for any violation, officials doubted I was dealing dope—stamps to buy dope, but not dope itself, yet the dog had fingered (actually nosed) me, but if they hauled me to The Hole, reporters would want to know why. Drugs!

"Where did Peterson get drugs?" would be their first question.

"The warden's office."

That was *not* going to be on the news, so they had a major dilemma: the dog signaled I had drugs, but they didn't want to find them on me.

Street and I were given a complete body cavity search. They found a chocolate granola bar in my pants' pocket where the dog had been jumping. Then the dog was led to every cell and bunk. At mine, he clawed at my coffee thermos which was taken to the front desk. Every guy in his cell was glued to his little slit window and I heard on the radio—"It's Peterson!"

Had someone planted drugs in the thermos? My stomach churned as guards dismantled it, but all they found was residue chocolate that I frequently mixed with my coffee.

It turned out that the drug dog was a chocoholic.

Nothing came of the shake down; no drugs were found. JS, Johnny, and I laughed about it next day. We spent hours together talking, joking, just passing time to keep our minds off our fates—life sentences. They were better, more interesting, stronger, and more amusing than friends I'd had on the Street. More loyal too; Street friends bailed on me with the news of my bi-sexuality. Never heard from them again. Doctors. Lawyers. University professors.

JS let me work out with him, Johnny didn't have patience for anyone not as strong: taking off weight plates and putting them back on the bar was more time consuming and detail than he could handle. He'd start twitching.

Then one morning JS was gone, shipped during the night, out of my life like Gino and Mario had disappeared from it. I sat at a table deeply depressed, but Johnny was used to it. "They got rid of him because they couldn't catch him with contraband. And he scared guards."

"So do you, but you're still here."

"That's cause no other prison will take me. You either, Crooklyn."

Crooklyn, that's the name he gave me; I treasured it.

"We're too much trouble. We're stuck here."

That actually made me feel better: the devil you know rather than the one you didn't. I knew this hell. And I still had Johnny.

He gazed at me levelly. "I need another one of those...what do you call them?"

"Loans."

"Yeah. One of those." We bumped fists.

Life went on. Another day down, another little grey tile pressed into the dull mosaic of my life. Days, weeks, months, then years of tiles forming grey nothingness.

Once I'd travelled the world, seen the Pyramids and the Pope, went to war, raised my children, wrote books and columns, ran for mayor, gone to ballets, operas, and Duke games. Now I was content to work out in prison on a dirt rec yard, buy and sell stamps, and listen to tittle tattle about...nothing really, but I jotted it all down in my journal.

I read constantly-- Roth, Bellow, Proust, Virginia Woolf, Stefan Zweig, Thomas Mann, then I'd take a break with lighter fare—Agatha Christie and *The Hitchhiker's Guide to the Galaxy*. It was like watching Bergman films; after a few, I needed The Three Stooges.

Fortunately there was relief from grim Bergman prison days. Chicken Day was one.

Every six weeks or so, we got a leg and thigh of chicken. God only knows where they found those pathetic tough stringy creatures, probably diseased, mad, or road kill, but it was the only real meat served in the chow hall.

Guys without income or those simply needing stamps sold their chicken for 3 stamps to buy gambling tickets, a honey bun, candy, or cokes. The trick was to get the chicken to the units from the chow hall; the challenge for guards was to prevent it. There was an understanding in the game—no write up if you got caught, and you could keep the chicken if you got it back to your unit—sort of Chicken Tag.

More guards were in the chow hall, kitchen and yard except during a riot to ensure kitchen workers didn't steal pieces, and inmates didn't go through the line more than once.

Concentration camp security existed for the chicken. Guards posted at the only gate leading from the chow hall back to the units patted down inmates; more guards at the units patted them down again. A prisoner had a better chance of escape that day than a chicken leg.

NO FOOD ALLOWED TAKEN FROM THE CHOW HALL was a simple rule with a simple explanation--spoilage, insects, rats. Yet a man whose last meal was 4 pm with no food until next morning might risk a Disobeying an Order charge to take out an apple or crackers.

Chicken was the greatest prize and a source of income—3 stamps

Despite the security, a barnyard of chicken went out the front and back doors; it did everything except fly out, and flocks of chicken was stuffed into crotches, down boots, up sleeves, and under hats ended up back in the units and into my locker. Sometimes I bought 10 pieces.

Tattooing was another diversion in our tedious Bergman days.

One afternoon a couple of us on the weight pile saw Red heave an adding machine onto the roof. He'd stolen it from the sergeant's office--the sergeant's office! Red wanted the motor for a tattoo gun. The sergeant went ballistic. LOCK DOWN LOCK DOWN LOCK DOWN.

"No one's leaving here--Ever!--until I get my adding machine back," she screamed. A four hour search of every cell, locker, and bunk turned up nothing--they didn't look on the roof.

Prisoners loved tattoos: gang tattoos, Confederate flags, Nazi swastikas, Christian crosses, hearts, names (mothers, girlfriends, wives, children), everything except a peace symbol. Some work was good, some awful--with misspellings! Stumpy, a dedicated weightlifter with a bad leg had a gigantic dragon across his back, but it had long eyelashes and little hands held up in the swishiest way--a gay dragon. We harassed him unmercifully.

Tattoos were photographed when you entered. Those added after brought disciplinary action: for health reasons, sanitation, STG, and damaging state property, the inmate—we were chattel. Nevertheless, tattooing was a major hustle.

Red was our Rembrandt. The stereotypical red-headed crazy guy, he could not control his temper. Sent to

266

Anger Management Class, he was expelled the first day for throwing a chair at the instructor.

My Blood buddy Street and Jason, a young redneck on the bunk on the other side of me who just wanted to be like everybody else—nice guy with wife and child, simple as a stick—decided to get tattoos from Red.

"No, No, No," I cautioned. "They're watching him." My elderly sage advice went for naught. Street got his Dog Paw tattoo in the bathroom while look-outs were posted. The next night, Jason went in--for so long guards got suspicious.

The sergeant was summoned, unlocked the bathroom and went in. Oh shit, we thought.

Suddenly a Code--Emergency, Emergency--was called over the radio. The sergeant ran out of the bathroom and into the next block. Everyone went to the window to see what was going on. Jason wandered out of the bathroom, his back dripping blood from what looked like The Last Supper tattooed on his back--the canvas was huge; he was a *big* boy.

"You think Sarge will forget about this?" he asked me.

"Doubtful."

He looked towards the window. "What's going on?"

One of our workout partners had had a seizure. A strong guy in his early forties, he wore a special boot. He always asked for a spot (someone to watch him) even though he never needed assistance, explaining that he had diabetes and was subject to seizures. His special boot was prosthesis--his foot had been amputated because of the diabetes.

This seizure was severe, the Code called, and officers rushed to help. Medical was notified and a nurse arrived with a wheeled stretcher. Officers lifted him onto it. The nurse took hold of his foot. It came off in her hand. She screamed, dropped the foot, and fainted.

After they revived her, they brought the poor guy to the hospital.

The next day, Street and Jason were hauled to The Hole for tattoos.

The biggest diversion, *lifeblood* was visitors: loved ones, friends, proof we still existed in their lives. Yet most men didn't get visits. No more than 20% did. They went years, decades without anyone coming. Some would go the rest of their lives that way.

A visitor's list was posted every week. Most men avoided it; they knew no one was coming. But others ran in hope to check. Then shoulders sagged, heads bowed in disappointment and humiliation—no one cared; they were not loved. They had ceased to exist.

Seeing my name filled me with inexpressible joy. A child or friend or Sophie was coming! Nothing compared to that. I would go back to my cell bursting with happiness to savor until the day came. Visits were oxygen, water, nourishment.

Sophie visited three and four times a year. We exchanged hundreds of letters, my escape from prison to warmth, touch, love and hope. The life raft I clutched in desperation. My future.

We made plans to live in Paris. I'd shop at patisseries near her home, we'd eat at neighborhood bistros; we would laugh and love. I escaped prison in mind and heart with Sophie, soared beyond the wire in a dream future, but my body remained trapped in a concrete world of guards and prisoners, *real* and forever.   Reality was Nash: Frau Himmler, murderers, rapists, gang bangers, and The Hole.

After each visit she went back to Paris; I'd be strip searched then plod past concertina wire to my bunk. I would think loving thoughts, write a letter, drop it in the unit mailbox, but turning, there would be the Day Room, other inmates, my miserable life. I would hang up the phone after a wonderful call or I'd return from a joyous two hour visit and it would all come back. She was my alternate universe, not barbed wire and concrete. Dreams and fantasy,

Yet dreams and fantasies end when dawn breaks through barred windows.   Love flees when reality's demons wake. The soldier tucks away his love letters when he picks up his rifle, his beloved supplanted by danger, the enemy, and death. So it was with me as a prisoner.

Sophie dedicated herself to freeing me. No one-- family, friends or lawyers--worked harder in my defense. She declined job offers, divorced her husband and moved out of their house. She got a U.S. phone number for me to call which cost her thousands in addition to what she spent visiting me three and four times a year. One summer she lived in Durham to work on my appeal.

She lived for me, but I couldn't live for her; I was fighting the daily demons of survival, a battle for psyche and soul. Prison saps worth and dignity; surviving its degradations requires defiance that reduces man to cornered animal.   He becomes secretive, selfish, manipulative, and paranoid. It makes adjusting to the real world difficult.

Sophie was my only real friend in prison, the only one I confided in and revealed my fears to. I didn't want to burden my children with my troubles or sorrows, but I told them to her. Only she knew how afraid and weak and vulnerable I was.

She listened and comforted and advised me, lifting me up like no one else, softening me with her love. Without Sophie I would have become hard and jaded as I struggled to survive. She rekindled feelings I'd smothered in self-protection. I fell in love with her—not only did she breathe life into my spirit in prison, she became my life after prison, my future, but I couldn't understand why she loved me.

Why? Why? Why? I kept asking her. She wrote:

I really wanted to do something for you. Maybe I felt that as an editor I had been taking care of you, trying to tell your story in a compelling way, trying to build your character so that the viewer would find it as fascinating as I did, trying to make your love for Kathleen noticeable, and hoping that my work would contribute in finding you innocent.

I felt like I had failed when you were convicted. I felt I had to go on taking care of you. I already knew much more about you than people usually know when they fall in love. I had been watching you for months, looking closely at your behavior both in everyday life and dealing with tragic events. I had witnessed your interactions with your children, family, friends, lawyers. I knew what had been your secrets for years, decades, or at least some of them.

It was a blend of feelings, like it always is. But truly, my wanting to help you through your trials only enhanced my feelings towards you. My compassion for you also allowed me to engage in that passion. Being in touch with you, who needed life so much and were making the best of every crumb of it was refreshing to me; it was like a new awakening.

When I read that, I felt so inadequate. She was too good for me. I didn't deserve her.

This can't last, I thought.

Yet who can explain love?

20. THE HOLE REDUX. REDUX

Bad things happen in prison—beatings, stabbings, rapes, but the worst, most apocalyptic event for guys during my incarceration was the 2009 smoking ban. Men who'd smoked their entire lives, some for 50 years, were told that canteens would stop selling tobacco. Anyone caught smoking thereafter would go to The Hole.

No more tobacco! That was all guys talked about. I had seen drug addiction first hand, been a Demerol addict in Zama Hospital, but I'd never encountered anything like this.

Patches were sold to help withdrawal, but they cost more than cigarettes. The indigent, given free patches, either sold them for contraband tobacco or rolled them up to smoke.

Like all prohibitions, the smoking ban created a black market: a $2.50 pack of cigarettes or 70 cents box of roll-up (loose tobacco) jumped to $50-$100. Regular tobacco became more expensive than weed.

Guards brought in contraband cigarettes, buying a carton for $35 on the Street then selling them to Bloods for $250. Some guards doubled their state salaries.

Another result mirrored Twenties Prohibition: criminals (in prison!) got rich. Because a guy who once needed three stamps for a cigarette now needed 12.

A cigarette would be broken into three pieces, each sold for 5 stamps. Guys would go into a bathroom or find a secluded spot on the yard to smoke it furtively, risking write ups, loss of job and cell for a minute of nicotine.

Bloods made a fortune selling cigarettes for $1000 a carton (4000 stamps). I made money too; I became the Al Capone of stamps, buying them for 20cents from Bloods and selling them to smokers for 40cents. Thousands of stamps.

Before the ban, every night at dusk on the rec yard, I smoked a cigar--50 cents in the canteen; a box of five cost $2.40. It was a pleasurable peaceful way to end the day--at the fence staring past the wire contemplating my lost world and my children. The past remained free, a place in memory where I could always go. I could be with Kathleen. I could go to Paris, Rome, Athens, Tokyo; I could visit my children as babies, watch them grow, become adults.

Evenings at the fence coaxing memory and love were my special time; it was quiet and I could close out the awful world behind me on the yard, so when DOC announced that canteens would stop selling tobacco and the smoking ban take effect in two months, I bought the remaining cigars in our canteen and sent a note to Big Tom to buy those in his unit.

That afternoon as I was getting ready to shower, guards rushed into the unit and cuffed me. "We're on to you Peterson."

For once my innocence was unfeigned. "For what? I'm on the way to the shower."

No I wasn't; I was hauled to the Security Threat Group office--I had no idea why. Like going to confession as a teen, I catalogued my sins, but I couldn't come up anything that merited handcuffs and another trip to STG this Saturday, so I was more curious than worried.

Captain Spence, central casting's prototype of a tough redneck guard—75-100 pound overweight buzz cut sneering officer with billy club on his belt—was the Officer in Charge that weekend. Cool Hand Luke would have been intimidated. Standing over me threateningly, he thrust the note in my face. "A guard confiscated this. Do you know what is says?"

"Yes, I just wrote it."

Ignoring that, he shouted, " 'Do it immediately. I'll give you the money afterwards.' " Then he carefully placed the evidence in a folder and glared at me. "What does it mean?"

"It means buy cigars in the canteen and I'll pay you when I get them."

"Horseshit! It's a contract to have someone whacked. Who was this meant for?"

Seeing this spiraling out of hand, I fell back on my Alzheimer's, "I forget."

Waving the folder in front of me, he yelled, "You sent this note to contract a hit like you did on that shithead who stole your soap."

For fuck's sake! But I knew there was no way to convince him that this was an innocuous message, and I didn't want to implicate Big Tom, so I tried to look perplexed. "What are we talking about? I forgot. I'm confused."

Then I held my head in my hands mimicking my father when set upon by my mother: "What drink? What alcohol? Who am I?" But that didn't work any better for me than it had for Dad, so Spence slammed me in a holding cell and called Captain Lucita, apparently at a Nazi conference/rally in New York City: Peterson contracted another whacking.

Frau Himmler ordered me locked in The Hole immediately. From Manhattan!

But I wasn't afraid—there was no contract—I was pissed: I wouldn't get the cigars.

I spent three days in Solitary under investigation until the "contract for hire" charge was dropped for lack of evidence, but I wasn't released. To my amazement, I was now charged with possessing psychotropic medicine: guards had "found" 25 pills for schizophrenia in a box of legal papers under my bunk in the Day Room.

"That is total bullshit," I told the investigating officer. "Anybody could have planted those pills. I'm not schizophrenic."

The officer said knowingly, "Guys take them to alter their minds."

"I'm sure they do, but only those with altered minds to begin with."

"Tough shit. Possession is 10/10th of the law. You're guilty."

So I spent two more weeks in The Hole. Captain Lucita had her revenge, but I didn't care—it wasn't like I was missing anything in General Population, and in The

Hole I had a private cell and toilet. I read books from the library trolley that came every few days, did push-ups and sit-ups, jacked off, and slept. I didn't talk to anyone and didn't go out to the dog cages.

However, I lost visitation privileges, but only for those two weeks; otherwise it was a nice respite. For me, a private room in Bedlam was preferable to being on one of its wards.

The sojourn's highlight was getting to know the prison's most notorious and wacko guard--Carter, a legend and flat out nuts.

She was in her fifties, overweight, wore glasses, apparently combed her unwashed hair with an empty beer bottle, had a puckered little mouth, and could recite the inmate regulation handbook from memory. Every inmate, myself included, despised her because she would write you up for the slightest infraction—stepping on the grass--and she had no sense of humor. None.

Yet despite being nuts, Carter was fair and she took pity on me because she knew my charge was bogus. She was strictly by the regs, but she wouldn't twist regs to get you.

One afternoon when she made rounds, I noticed a little ribbon on her uniform. When I inquired about it, she told me it was for Marksmanship, so I asked about the most famous incident involving her, the time she pointed a rifle at the Time Warner cable guy.

Having been banned from every unit for a variety of insanities such as locking other guards out of the unit because they didn't relieve her for a smoking break--the swat team had had to be called in—and allowing inmates to "gun her down," attention she seemed to enjoy, she was assigned to patrol the outer perimeter in a truck. How could she fuck that up?

No problem. Driving around one day, she saw a guy climbing a pole--*outside* the prison fence. The cable truck was parked below and the guy was in a Time Warner uniform.

She stopped, jumped out with a rifle and pointed it at him.

Inmates on the rec yard started screaming, "Shoot him, Carter, shoot him."

The guy looked down from where he was trapped on a pole to see a crazed woman aiming a rifle at him. I'm sure he's still not right.

"Regulations require an officer to take the rifle when getting out of the truck," she told me. "But I wouldn't have shot him." I did not ask: Did regs require you to aim at the cable guy, and did *he* know you weren't going to shoot him?

Besides being quick on the draw, Carter was known to enter young guys' cells at 2-3 am, waking them to say the number stenciled on their chairs didn't match their cell number, which *no one* cared about. What do think she saw when the young males jumped out of bed from a sound sleep at 3 in the morning? Some guys waited up to flash their hard-ons.

"I'm not going to jack until she comes on duty," they'd say in eager anticipation.

Carter had a lot of seniority but had been passed over for sergeant many times. She took it well; even she knew she was nuts.

She was the only officer I spoke with at length, a lonely sad woman in an abusive marriage with a grown daughter. She'd also just had, which I didn't need to know or want to hear about in the detail she described, a hysterectomy.

Everyone—even guards--had troubles. It didn't matter what color uniform you wore or which side of the fence you were on.

While I never had a problem in The Hole, others did. There were no cameras, so guards could do what they wanted: who were you going to complain to if you didn't like the treatment?

To credit the guards however, they were dealing with the worst of the worst. Restraint was a challenge when inmates threw piss and shit at them.

Nevertheless, Green Eyes, a light skinned rather small black (with green eyes) in his early forties, exceeded their limits of self-control. I'd known him for years. Though an incorrigible thief and liar, he was brave and tough and challenged authority as much as I did. I admired him. He *was* Cool Hand Luke--except black and queer.

Being gay was another reason I admired him because he neither hid nor advertised it. Many guys concealed their homosexuality and bisexuality out of shame or for safety—lots of predators sought victims--while others RuPauled it, swishing and preening—advertising to the point that you wanted to beg them to go back in the closet. I had already been outed.

Green Eyes was just...gay, and everybody was fine with it. No one was going to make an issue of it anyway— he'd stab you in a heartbeat.

Green Eyes spent his time writing grievances about anything from medical treatment (or more often the lack of it), tampered mail, guard abuse, or bad food.

Serious or trivial, all grievances had to be answered by the warden, so naturally those writing them were shipped to a worse place, though "retaliation" for writing grievances was forbidden, but they didn't transfer Green Eyes because he *wanted* to be transferred—that's why he wrote grievances including a grievance for not being shipped because he wrote grievances.

I was his grievance "consultant" for grammar advice and proof reading because while smart and quick, he had little education. I spent a lot of time with him.

A cell phone brought him down. Prison authorities (actually everybody) knew there was a cell phone in Unit 2 (1 and 4 also, and we had several in our unit 3). A snitch—someone he had previously stabbed--told the authorities that the phone had been given to Green Eyes.

He was at a table writing yet another grievance when the Unit 3 manager Mr. Roberts (with a massive Confederate flag tattoo on his arm) ran in hysterically one afternoon. "If that cell phone is not on my desk in one hour, you're going to The Hole." I was at the next table.

"What cell phone?" Green Eyes asked innocently, as if he had just been interrupted while reading his Bible. "I don't know what you're talking about."

"One hour!"

An hour later, Mr. Roberts returned with two guards. They cuffed Green Eyes and hauled him to The Hole. "I haven't finished writing my grievance," Green Eyes said.

"Finish it in Seg. I'm sure you'll be writing another one there," Mr. Roberts said.

Indeed he did because when he got to Segregation, Mr. Roberts and several guards beat the shit out of him while he was still handcuffed. Not one to lie down without a fight, Green Eyes head butted Mr. Roberts and bit him Hannibal Lector style. Then they really beat him.

He didn't get out of The Hole for a month. It took that long for the bruises to heal and to wrap up the "investigation"; investigations were never completed until bruises healed.

The resolution was a wash—no cell phone charge, no guard brutality charge, no assault on an officer charge. Mr. Roberts was tested and cleared for AIDS, and Green Eyes was shipped to where he wanted to go. You had to admire a guy like that.

My two weeks passed quickly, probably because I was not eager to get out of The Hole. Unit 2, Unit 3, The Hole made little difference. The units had a rec yard, weight pile, TV, and visitation privileges, but also a hundred screaming inmates, danger, endless bullshit, and constant harassment. As Milton wrote in *Paradise Lost*, "Solitude sometimes is best society," though I might not have agreed had I spent months or years in solitary.

Would I have gone mad? Become a bug like Johnny Blood and Squirrel? Probably. Thoreau might have too. Walden was *not* solitary confinement. I could manage a couple weeks or even a month, but not an open ended sentence.

As I was led out of The Hole in 2007, Queeny, a tall 30 year old child molester with disheveled long blond hair frequently dyed green with contraband food coloring, begged a favor.

My first encounter with Queeny had been on the main yard soon after I arrived. He'd frequently follow me from the chow hall to Unit 2 after meals. I always ignored him, but after one lunch, he threw himself in front of me. "I watched your trial, I saw your movie. I understand you like blow jobs."

I stared at him incredulously. "What! What are you talking about?"

"Blow jobs." It was noon; two hundred inmates and twenty guards were on the yard.

He looked at me expectantly. "Did you want to audition here?" I asked, stunned but amused. "Oh God no," he said and ran away.

That ended the matter until I moved to Unit 3 when his overtures began again. His first conviction had been for indecent liberties with a minor when he was 16; he got a suspended sentence; two years later he got 14 years for numerous sexual offenses with boys.

With his predilection for kids, I couldn't understand his fixation on me other than some unresolved father/son issue. Now he was in The Hole for, unsurprisingly, a "Sex Act."

Sex Act in prison usually means masturbation, a code violation, easily the most disregarded of the hundreds of regulations: crazed Carter even encouraged it.

How many inmates masturbated? There were then 600 of us (later 900); the Hole held 20, so if 20 jackers were locked up, that left 580 flogging away in their cells or in a bathroom.

Masturbation usually became an offense only in front of a female officer who reported it, but the violation existed for whenever authorities wanted. Queeny, however, was caught *in flagrante*, bent over his bunk in his cell with Brownie behind him. Brownie was not gay, or rather, vocal in denying it. He had a job and was close to honor grade and release.

Queeny went to The Hole--*alone*, even though anal sex usually involves a participating second individual. We all knew what went down—Brownie turned "state's evidence": he snitched out everyone about everything he knew, and he knew a lot because his hustle was selling what he stole from maintenance, tools to super glue.

Queeny yelled as I passed his cell, "When you get back to the unit, tell Brownie to send me some tobacco."

"Brownie says he doesn't know you," I shouted back.

"Oh, he knows me all right," Queeny screamed loudly enough for everyone to hear. "He knows me *real* well. He knows me in the *Biblical* sense. Tell that faggot motherfucker to send the cigarettes he owes for fucking me."

"How many do you want?" a voice yelled from a cell.

"You can't afford it," Queeny screamed back.

"You didn't get any for your last fuck. I can afford that," the voice retorted as I left.

When I got back to the unit, I relayed the message to Brownie. He looked horrified, and two days later, just before Queeny got out of solitary, Brownie shipped to another prison—part of the deal he'd struck with the authorities who always protected their snitches.

Of course nothing had changed since I'd left. I returned to a bunk in the day room with no privacy, incredible noise, constant guard harassment, and a brisk stamp business. Visits from family, Sophie, and friends resumed once a week and I could go out to exercise.

When Johnny Blood saw me on the weight pile, he didn't even pretend to miss me. "Crooklyn, I been looking all over for you."

"I been gone for TWO WEEKS—in The Hole, asshole."

"Oh yeah, I think I heard about it. Bug pills."

Life went on. Reading, writing, weightlifting, socializing, visits, calls to Sophie. My days were acceptably numbing.

Then catastrophe.

One mid-morning in November, 2007 I was summoned by the assistant warden, the notorious former chain gang guard no one had ever seen smile. I knew it was bad news.

Indeed, after I trudged nervously across the yard to the concrete admin building behind two more strands of razor wire, he grinned maliciously when I entered his office. Bald headed, trim and fit, about my age, eyes cold boar mean, his face ebony marble marred by a jagged slash that was his mouth in unnatural mirth, he pointed to the phone on his desk.

I picked it up tenuously, "Yes?"

It was one of my lawyers. "Mike? The Supreme Court just denied your appeal. It was unanimous. 9-0. I'm sorry. "

When I didn't say anything, she asked, "You all right? Can I do anything?"

Not about to show grief or weakness to the man behind me, I said casually, "I'm fine. Let my kids know, please," then I thanked the assistant warden and sauntered out of his office, not a care in the world, but in my cell, I lay on my bunk and stuffed a towel in my mouth to stifle the agonized cry wrenched from my gut. No more hope. Doomed to die here. I had hit bottom.

Then, jumping from my bunk I ran into a bathroom, the only place I could be alone. No! This can't be! I won't let it. There had to be a way out. I looked through the barred window to see row after row of barbed razor wire. A truck with an armed guard circled the perimeter.

There was no escape. To where anyway?

The courts weren't going to help. There was no justice, no mercy, and no hope, so I returned to my bunk in defeat: this was the rest of my life.

I closed my eyes and tried to imagine the future— growing older, feeble, dying alone. I folded my hands across my chest and stared at the ceiling. I felt as if I was in the grave.

That's when I remembered Nonna and The Man in the Coffin, the most legendary tale about my great grandmother, and the reason the family believed she possessed occult powers.

In Italy where she was born in 1866 and lived until she immigrated to America in 1894, she once returned to her home in Torino from a week's trip. A neighbor confronted her hysterically—the woman's husband had died while Teresa was away.

Nonna considered a moment, then said, "No. He's not dead. I see him."

"Teresa! He's dead. We buried him three days ago."

Nonna was emphatic. "No. He's not dead. I see him."

The woman ran screaming to the priest. "Luigi's not dead!"

"Of course he's dead," the priest snapped. "I gave a mass. We buried him."

The woman could not be appeased. "Luigi's alive! Teresa says she saw him in a vision. He's alive in the coffin."

So they went to the cemetery and dug him up. When they pried open the wooden coffin, they saw a horrible grimace on Luigi's face, a clawed coffin lid, and his bloody fingers worn to the bone with wood splinters under his fingernails.

The woman screamed and fainted.

The priest turned to Nonna who merely shrugged. "I told her."

After hearing this story many times and thinking like everyone that Nonna was a witch, it finally hit me: Wait! The only witness to this story is Nonna. She probably made up the story to frighten her children.

But whether the story was true or not, I knew how the undead Luigi felt. I was buried alive like him: the original verdict from the jury was Guilty/Death in prison:

the second opinion from the Court of Appeals was Guilty/Death. Now the third opinion from the Supreme Court: Guilty/Death. There was no fourth opinion.

But I was neither guilty nor dead. I was not on Zama's ICU ward or maimed on that orthopedic; I wasn't at Graves Registration in Danang or in the morgue like Sergeant Beverly.

That evening I called Sophie. I never called my children when I was down; I didn't want to burden them with my sorrow and fear.

When I told her about the Supreme Court decision, she handled it better than I had and bolstered me with strength and resolve: *she* was not going to give up; *we* would get through this.

She knew I hadn't killed Kathleen, so discovering how she died became her all-consuming mission. She was determined to prove me innocent. After reading lab reports of microscopic feathers clutched in Kathleen's hands and seeing laboratory slides of Kathleen's hair that she'd ripped from her head which revealed feathers mixed with blood, Sophie accepted the theory first advanced by an attorney and neighbor, Larry Pollard: Kathleen had been attacked outside by a raptor bird; an owl had swooped down on her.

Larry, an avid hunter had placed owl talons over a photograph of the lacerations on Kathleen's scalp. They matched perfectly. This convinced Sophie. Owls were vicious raptors silent in flight and there were hundreds of documented owl attacks on people, many causing the exact same puncture wounds found on Kathleen's face.

While we had owls in our backyard, it was too bizarre for me to accept that Kathleen had died from an owl attack. Besides, how could it be proved?

In any case, there was nothing I could do, so I didn't put any more stock in the theory than did the District Attorney when it was first brought to his attention.

"Where are the feathers?" he'd asked, ridiculing the theory in the media. It became a joke repeated for years. Posters of an owl were put up in post offices and elsewhere: Wanted for Murder. No one took it seriously. Except Larry and Sophie.

After the Supreme Court's decision with no further appeal possible, thoughts of Luigi buried alive and dug up were no comfort. He *did* die in that coffin.

But instead of despairing—what good was that?--I decided to do something constructive.

What could be more meaningful than coaching sports?

21. THE LONGEST YARD

2008 brought 300 more prisoners so that 60 men were on bunks in the day room sharing 4 toilets, overcrowding that rivaled California's prisons which the U.S. Supreme Court had ruled cruel and unusual punishment.

Long limes for the toilet formed after morning Count, so I programmed myself to wake shortly before Count to run in. Toilets stayed occupied all day with guys taking care of one kind of business or another because it was the only place in the Trailer Park for privacy.

I couldn't live that way for the rest of my life; I needed a cell. But to get one I had to have a job. That meant going to Mrs. Snow. Since I had "seniority" on the bunks, she had to give me one; she "rewarded" me with a job scrubbing and disinfecting one of the four showers twice a day—gross work considering what went on in those showers besides showering, so gross that like Gino, I immediately sub-contracted it, paying someone a dollar—stamps or canteen items—to do what I was paid forty cents a day to do.

With privacy at last--9'x12' all to myself—I was as content as I'd been in my 12,000 square foot "mansion". But I couldn't stay in there all day, so I sought diversion beyond mantras, weight lifting, writing (letters and my journal), reading, buying and selling stamps.

I was too old to play ball—softball, volleyball, basketball, or soccer—yet the right age with the right temperament to coach, so when guys asked me to take on the unit's softball team (there was no baseball—that ball was considered too hard and could hurt someone; of course so could a ping pong ball or marble shoved in someone's eye)—I said yes.

Coaching became as consuming as teaching GED: constant action, fun and funny with shorter hours and fewer assholes to deal with; I loved it.

I'd played baseball in my youth, coached soccer for many years in Germany and the U.S, had been a fraternity president, a Marine officer—surely I could handle a bunch of guys on a softball team—*softball* for god's sake!

No one could have coached those guys.

One season's team made the *The Longest Yard* movie team look like pacifist tree huggers: 1st Base, Murder; catcher, Murder—he spent many years on Death Row, released only because his IQ failed to meet qualifications to be assassinated by the state. I used to joke, "Bedrock, you are too stupid for the state to kill." He'd give me a sly look and say, "Guess I'm not so stupid after all," which was true because if his IQ had been higher than 62, he'd be dead.

The pitcher was in for Drugs—cocaine, heroin, meth; 2d base, Rape; 3rd Base, Murder; shortstop, many charges, topped by AWDWISI (armed with deadly weapon with intent to inflict serious injury), a great player but stoned every inning of every game; left field, Murder; center field, Child Molester; right field, Murder. Our star, the short center was Rae Wiggins, aka Rae Carruth, the former NFL wide receiver in for Conspiracy for murdering his pregnant girlfriend.

Rae, powerfully built and incredibly fast, in his early thirties, funny and intelligent, was a terrific player. As the state's most high profile prisoners sharing the same media problems—too much media—the same lawyer, and both prima donnas with a good sense of humor, we were good friends, but frequently I had to tone him down on the ball field.

"Rae, you were a professional athlete, you made millions playing ball. These guys are not in your league—give them a break."

He couldn't do it. When someone missed the ball or made an error, he was right there to tell them they fucked up. "Stop it," I'd say. "After games, I have to give everybody hugs because you're such an asshole."

I loved the challenge and competition. Making rosters and batting lineups, gathering the team, and going to the field was much more fun than walking into a GED classroom. League games, several a week weren't something to do, but to live for, a diversion from prison while *in* prison.

It was like Sparta with bats and balls, an uber masculine society without women or the promise of them—no groupies waiting outside the locker room. No locker room.

But there was a dwarf, Shorty of course, all head and ass, the meanest bastard I ever encountered; he made Dickens's Quilp look like Little Nell. But he was darling. Vicious too. Pure Evil. He lied, stole, cheated, and barely made it out of Nash alive—many thought him a snitch. Probably, but I missed him when he shipped.

When I first saw him on the yard, I couldn't take my eyes off him. A dwarf! In prison? What crime could he have committed? How did he think he could get away with *any* crime: Did you see the perp? Yes, it was a dwarf! How many of those are running around? What about footprints and fingerprints? Tiny! How many perps wear Size 2 shoes?

After one unit shake down, we didn't see him for two weeks while he was in The Hole. A guard told us they'd easily found his contraband stamps and pills.

"We just searched on our hands and knees because we knew he couldn't hide anything above three feet."

Nevertheless, he was very sensitive about his height; we were not supposed to notice that he was a dwarf.

Once he flipped off the performers for the Black History Month celebration. He'd been trying to see his programmer for weeks; her office was in the gym. He wrote daily that he needed her help. Finally he was called to the gym. He showered, shaved, put on his best bespoke little uniform and went to the gym.

When he walked in, fifty black guys and Ms. Snow were rehearsing dance steps and rap routines for the celebration. They wanted to toss him around in one of the acts.

Shorty was out of his head. He framed a camera with his little hands, yelled "Picture this you motherfuckers," and flipped them the bird. Then he stormed back to the unit.

He was very pleased however when I asked him to be the team stat man, partly to make him feel wanted, but mostly because he was so darling. Strutting proudly in his waddling walk, he'd show up on the ball field and guards would say, "Here comes Peterson's bodyguard."

He had to stand on the bench to see the game, but could he ever trash talk! Other team players and sometimes our own wanted to run off the field to strangle him.

Playing as a team was difficult for these guys; they were obviously not team players on The Street. They did not play well with others, and most had anger management issues.

My first rule was that no player could criticize another because I feared that one murderer would yell at another murderer and hell would break loose with me in the middle. "They know when they strike out. They know when they drop the ball. You don't need to tell them. If you have a problem with someone, tell me." That worked for everyone except Carruth.

When a young in shape guy said he could play any position, I put him on 3rd base before a game to warm up and told the 1st baseman to throw him the ball.

Big Show—6'6'' 300 pounds, *Murder*--threw it. He ducked.

I turned to The Dwarf. "Did I just see that?"

The guy was apologetic. "I'm sorry, I'm sorry. I wasn't ready. Give me another chance." So Big Show threw the ball. The guy ducked again.

The Dwarf went crazy, bouncing up and down on the bench. "Get the fuck out of here, you lame ass, worthless…" on and on until the guy ran off the field.

Then Big Show left the team to form his own—he was not coachable and not a team player; all he wanted to do was hit home runs and all too frequently struck out. When we played his team, I told The Dwarf that I'd give him ten stamps if he could get Show to strike out; all he had to do was trash talk him.

Show was strong enough to hit the ball to Tennessee, but he also had rabbit ears that could hear a slur from Tennessee. He had *serious* anger management issues, and at 6'6'' 300 pounds, he was a bull elephant on 1st base and in the batter's box, so when The Dwarf started trash talking him about his mama and the reverse ratio of height and dick size, Show lost it completely and chased him off the field with a bat, getting them both ejected.

Fortunately Show couldn't run very fast, so he never caught The Dwarf.

Besides fighting and chasing dwarves with bats, swearing was grounds for ejection—if you can imagine: murderers, rapists, drug dealers, thieves, arsonists, child molesters playing ball *in prison* with no swearing allowed. The Buddha himself would have sworn at these guys who tripped on the field because they wore their pants pulled to the bottom of their butts, wouldn't tie their shoelaces, and often showed up completely whacked on weed.

Swearing was the fetish of Officer Bennett who warned me before every game--no swearing. I tried hard. In one game, the ball was hit to my doped up shortstop for an easy out. As the batter started for 1st, my shortstop kept playing around, getting ready to make the toss, holding back, just dicking around until I screamed, "Throw the fucking ball, Asshole!"

Mr. Bennett jumped two feet in the air and I was out of the game.

We could have won a big trophy that year except just before the tournament, the warden walked into our unit and was brought up short by cracked shatterproof glass in the control booth. What happened? Why wasn't this reported? Who did it?

We all knew.

Officer Smitty was a well-liked young black guard who joked and played around, gave breaks to guys whenever he could, never harassed anyone or wrote anyone up--except once when a screaming queen propositioned him: "Have you ever had someone take your dick and balls in his mouth and lick your asshole at the same time?"

We teased Smitty about it relentlessly. "Oh, go ahead, give it a try."

Because Smitty covered for inmates—even letting guys dodge piss tests (allowing The Dwarf with dirty urine to substitute a clean inmate's piss)--we covered for him.

Smitty broke the booth window. Blake, one of my best ball players had thrown a spitball at the booth when Smitty was in it. Smitty, pretending that he was at bat playing ball, swung his baton/club and shattered the glass. No one said a word. Then the warden came.

An investigation began; ever-abiding Captain Lucita was on the case. Frau Himmler looked at the camera monitors and locked up Blake. He had thrown a paper spitball at the booth and she determined the spitball had cracked shatterproof glass. So Blake missed the game because no one would snitch on Officer Smith.

The unit manager said he would drop charges on Blake and let him play ball if I told him who had broken the glass, but I would've had to snitch on Smitty, and snitching was an inviolate taboo deemed worse than being a punk, though the taboo was violated with abandon—more in prison than by third graders: Teacher! Teacher! Guard! Guard! I'll tell, I'll tell. Me first!

Though we lost the tournament, we won most games and were the best team largely because of Carruth. He made catches that could have been ESPN highlights, but not everyone liked Rae: he'd played NFL football! Even guards sucked up to him--asking for his autograph!--and he was Ms. Snow's favorite. He got any job he wanted, including my GED job after I went to The Hole. He *replaced* me. A football player! I was humiliated, but Rae didn't last long; he said it was too much work with too many assholes to deal with daily. He became a barber.

One day, Mr. Football and I met Ms. Snow on our way to the gym. She started to titter and sway as soon as she saw him, bringing to mind a tugboat in a typhoon. Of course she studiously ignored me, almost forcing me off the sidewalk as she buffeted closer.

"Looking good! Ms. Snow," Rae enthused. "Love the outfit," he added about a florescent body hugging jumpsuit that made her look like a grounded dirigible.

She squealed and trawled on.

"For Christ's sake, have you no shame?" I asked after she sailed away.

He grinned. "Nope."

Though a tolerant easy going guy off the field, Rae had a problem when Queeny got out of The Hole and formed a gay team. Are they *all* catchers? Someone asked.

The day we played them, Carruth said, "If they beat us, I'm going to kill myself."

"You won't have to," I said. "I'll kill you first." We won.

But we lost the big game. A woman was to blame.

Female officers ran the gym all 8 years I was there, overseeing sports programs, the Men's Club, and determining when and for how long inmates could work out. There were always five or six inmates on the gym staff—some favored inmates became *real* favorites.

Ms. Struckland had shed 100 pounds to get *down* to 150. In her gym office surround by buff horny guys, what could possibly happen? It did. I knew two of the guys well. When rumors spread that they were fucking her, they were immediately shipped.

But not Moag, a young handsome athlete who had blown his wife away with a shotgun when he caught her *in flagrante* with another guy; he became her primary assistant and constant companion. He ran leagues and set up schedules, an excellent athlete but such a pill head that he owed $2000 to guys whose medicine (anything mind altering) he'd buy.

As his addiction grew, so did his arrogance because Ms. Struckland protected him. Though constantly and flagrantly doped up, he was never piss tested.

He played on his unit's team and refereed other units' games, a conflict we futilely complained about. When our team beat his on the way to the championship, he promised to get even. While refereeing the deciding game, he threw the game to the other team.

Carruth was out of his head, but I told him that as coach I'd take care of the problem, so I went to the gym to lodge a complaint. Ms. Sruckland was in her office with Moag. She would not listen to my grievance and Moag threatened me so loudly that another officer ran into the room. Both he and the Ms. Struckland had to physically restrain Moag from attacking me.

I was beyond pissed—not just because he had cost us the tournament, but because for two days afterwards, Moag told everyone that he would get me. He was 30 years younger, strong, agile, and tough; I was not about to fight him—I'd end up in The Hole with my ass beat badly—but I could not ignore his threats: letting it go would only invite threats from others, so I discussed my dilemma with Johnny Blood.

The next day someone attacked Moag, allegedly over a bad debt. After he was released from the hospital and shipped, Johnny said that I owed him 100 stamps. I paid.

However my coaching career was soon interrupted when I went to The Hole yet again. Officer Abercrombie, a female guard with great ambition until fired for having sex with a married officer, found contraband peanut butter and orange juice in a cell search.

Stovepipe, a particularly disgusting sexual predator—huge, ugly, dirty, lecherous, stupid, and a murderer--was head of the maintenance crew which painted the chow hall. One night he stole a ten pound can of peanut butter and a gallon of concentrated orange juice from the store room. He put them on the dolly with the paint cans and smuggled them back to the unit.

Peanut butter was one of the few nourishing foods available, but only to those on "Special Diet." To get on Special Diet, the doctor had to authorize it because of poor health or dietary needs. One perk was an ounce cup of peanut butter. Prescription peanut butter!

Of course inmates who got the tiny cup sold it for a stamp. I was constantly buying ounce cups of peanut butter, so when Stovepipe offered me a 10 pound can for 20 stamps (a 160 stamp value), I jumped on it. He threw in the orange juice for four more stamps. Now I had protein and vitamin C, along with oats, hard boiled eggs, whole grain bread, chicken, bacon, etc...anything healthy that chow hall workers could smuggle out of the kitchen to sell.

Everybody knew—snitches! Once the huge humorless woman in charge of the chow hall summoned me to her office and screamed, "Stop propositioning my workers."

As if that would stop the pilferage. There were lots of pimps and Johns, but hiding a 10 pound can of peanut butter in my cell was stupid.

Officer Abercrombie found them. Obviously I hadn't walked out of the chow hall with ten pounds of peanut butter and a gallon of orange juice, so how had I got them?

I pleaded Alzheimer's to avoid snitching and spent two weeks in solitary.

I should have hidden it better. Or not been so greedy.

Because of the peanut butter bust, I lost my shower cleaning job, my cell, and consequently spent my final two years in prison without a job on a bunk in day rooms.

In retaliation, I abandoned moderation altogether, becoming an even worse Buddhist.

Carl Moore, the most righteous convict I knew became my best friend. Eleven years younger than me, fighting a losing battle over his weight and hair line with grace and humor, he had spent 20 years of the last 30 years in prison for B&E's, larceny, and safe cracking.

He had maneuvered the shoals of prison and knew all the tricks and traps. He had a saying: "If I tell you it's Easter, go paint your eggs." Indeed, his word was that good.

He called himself a "country liberal," his euphemism for racist redneck, but I didn't care anymore than he cared that I was a "communist nigger lover"--his description of Liberal Democrats. We formed our own tobacco cartel to rival Bloods: I provided the funds to buy cigarettes and he sold them, bringing me a massive amount of stamps which I hid in boxes of legal material stored in his cell because they wouldn't fit under my bunk in the Trailer Park.

I was at Visitation the day guards shook down his cell and found the stamps, but other inmates told me about it before I got back to the Unit. Waiting at the entrance was a sergeant with his club and cuffs. "Should I go in, or are we going directly to The Hole?" I asked.

Carl's already in The Hole," he said.

"You don't want Carl," I answered. "You know what you found was mine."

"Nothing I can do about it, Carl's gone." He turned away and left.

Johnny Blood intercepted me as soon I walked into the cell block. "Carl said to tell you he's taking the fall. He told them everything was his."

"I can't let that happen, Johnny."

"It's got to go down that way. It's the code. He knows you'd do the same for him."

I tried to bargain and plea for Carl, but it did no good. "What did you find?" I asked the investigating officer. "Money and stamps," he said.

"How much money?"

"Two twenty dollar bills."

"Oh for Christ's sake, that's nothing. How many stamps?"

"Quit fucking with me, Peterson. You know exactly how many—2,801. I spent the whole goddamn morning counting them." That was the largest number of stamps ever confiscated.

Carl got 6 *months* solitary confinement and was shipped to another institution. I never saw him again, but we communicated—always will. He owned up later that one (1) of the stamps was his. That's what being a convict is about: falling on a grenade to save a buddy.

Though bereft to see Carl leave, it didn't take long for me to get more stamps because I went back to working with Bloods, proving again that greed trumps loyalty.

But greed brought down lots of guys besides me and even some guards.

Officer Gibbs, a fiftyish guard was a nice man—too nice. Inmates circled him from his first day. As soon as a guard came to the unit, he/she was challenged and wooed to see if they could be used/bought. "Hey, how you doing?" was not an innocent inquiry when an inmate approached a guard. He hoped for a response that might lead to further contact.

A guy would ask for paper and envelope: "I gotta write my kid. He's driving my old lady bug fuck. I gotta straighten him out. How many kids you got?" And they're off.

"That goddamn Heat; Lebron is killing us. Who's your team?" Sports! Great bonding.

"I don't want to cause trouble, but...." A minor snitch to ingratiate the inmate to the guard who now thinks he has a valuable informant.

Bait and hook, over and over, day after day, (the inmate has *nothing* else to do) with the sole purpose of snaring a guard to help the inmate.

"What's gas up to these days?" is a question heading one way--how expensive it is on The Street. If the guard offers the slightest opening, the conversation will turn to money--need some? There are easy ways to make it here. Officer Gibbs fell into the trap the first day; he mentioned that his wife was not well. There were big medical bills.

Observing the seduction of Officer Gibbs, I told buddies that he had no shelf life--he was going down the toilet. I warned the excellent Z, a young monster weightlifter to stay away from Gibbs, but the temptation was too great and the reward too promising.

Z flashed him a $50 bill. "Can you get me a pack of cigarettes?"

Gibbs vacillated, but in front of him was a $50 bill for a pack of cigarettes he could buy at any convenience store for $3. Of course Z would sell the cigarettes for $100.

Gibbs took the money and brought in a pack the next day. A little later, Z approached him with $100 for three packs, a $90 profit for Gibbs and a $200 profit for Z.

Nothing goes unnoticed on a cell block so the run on Gibbs began; he couldn't handle all the business, especially from Bloods who had cash. Mine! Greed overcame caution. When Gibbs arrived every morning, inmates rushed him. He tried to shut down the traffic by cutting off several inmates, but all that did was fuel their jealousy of those he was still providing.

One morning I saw Gibbs put a package under the mattress of my weed whacked shortstop. Officer Abercrombie who'd nailed me for peanut butter watched in the control booth.

I ran out to the rec yard and told Dusty to move his package immediately. He did, but Gibbs was toast. Unsuspecting, he continued to take orders and collect money.

When he came to work next day, he was strip searched, overseen by the inexhaustible and apparently sleepless Captain Lucita. 20 Packs of cigarettes and a pound of weed were taped to his legs, along with pouches of loose tobacco and roll up paper for cigarettes and blunts.

Gibbs clutched his chest and fell to the floor; it was not an act. He was medevac'd in custody to the hospital. His car in the parking lot was searched--an illegal gun and more weed were found. State charges were brought against him and he lost his job, but not before giving up the names of his inmate contacts including Z who was immediately shipped.

Though it sometimes seemed I spent all my time subverting authority, I read over 500 books, wrote several thousand letters and thousands of pages in a journal, spent a thousand hours with visitors, taught and counseled, coached, and lifted weights.

The Supreme Court decision devastated me but not friends, attorneys, and Sophie; they intensified their efforts to free me. The only way now lay in a Motion for Appropriate Relief—new and compelling evidence of innocence that had not been introduced at trial.

Sophie focused on owl attacks that inflicted wounds similar Kathleen's; there were many. She and attorney Larry Pollard compiled extensive documentation. Together with another attorney, Millie Hershner, they worked on an MAR based on the new evidence of an owl attack.

A former US Congressman I'd known for nearly thirty years, Nick Galifinakis, joined them and pushed the N.C. Innocence Commission to take on my appeal.

Then from Australia came Ro Hume, a 60 year old filmmaker and writer. Convinced of my innocence by *The Staircase*, Ro rented an apartment in Durham and set to work; almost immediately she found in prosecution notes that the DA had withheld key evidence.

A neighbor had discovered a tire iron in his garden the morning after Kathleen died. He called police saying this could have been the murder weapon discarded by someone fleeing our house, but police did not investigate until *after* the prosecution rested, and they never disclosed its existence, a violation of Constitutional law. Ro engaged her own lawyer to draw up a Motion for Appropriate Relief based on the tire iron. Now there were two competing Motions.

She and Sophie each spent thousands in my defense, visited me dozens of times, but they did not get along.

I loved Sophie, but I was grateful to Ro for what she was doing. They pressed me to choose sides by endorsing each's Motion, yet both troubled me. I didn't see how a tire iron could have killed Kathleen without fracturing her skull or causing brain damage, neither of which had occurred. At the same time, an owl killing Kathleen seemed too bizarre.

But how could I doubt or question those helping me?

Once again Nonna's Luigi came to mind. I imagined him in the coffin listening to people above arguing as they dug for him, wondering frantically: Will they get here in time?

I wondered the same thing.

22. SEX

One evening at dusk on the rec yard just before dark inked us out, my 1st baseman Big Show and I stood at the fence staring out at what little world we could see. It was the best time of day, quiet, a time to reflect, but not too deeply, not to where dragons of the lost past and empty future lurked.

Most guys had gone inside, marking off the day as one more down. Lonely night followed, then morning arrived with another locked-in day.

Beyond the three strands of razor wire and highway we could see a small pond where Canadian Geese glided in to rest briefly on their way somewhere else. There were some trees and a few houses where we wondered enviously about the lives lived within. What did they do? Were they happy? Would we ever be?

Show was 28, 6'6", 300 pounds. He'd been in prison since 18 and faced another eleven for second degree murder; he'll be nearly 40 when finally released. Smart, funny, an altogether good guy--except for that murder—he was like a kid, a very big kid, and like most kids, he had a temper, but he usually kept it reigned in, fortunately for me because I teased him relentlessly about his size, weight, coordination--anything to rile him.

He could have (and probably wanted to) pound me into the ground many times, but we got along well for he loved to joke though few ventured it because of his size and temper. His anger was often faked, but who wanted to risk pissing off a bull elephant? His method of intimidation was to lean into your face, bearing down until guys crumpled beneath him.

Whenever I'd pick on him on the rec yard or yell at him on the ball field for some bonehead play, he'd run over and start bearing down. I'd stand there until I'd finally say, "Get any closer and we'll be kissing." He'd jump back, smile, pat me on the head and run off. Just a kid, a very big dangerous one.

Show had an incongruous job for his size and demeanor; he tended the flower garden that the bald chain gang guard/assistant warden mandated for every unit--Hell with flora and fauna. I called Show the Martha Stewart of Nash, only with a bigger and broader ass.

"A lot of guys think I'm tough," he said softly that evening on the yard, head resting on the fence, staring sadly into the darkening distance.

"I don't. I think you're a big pussy."

He smiled, then shook his head. "Maybe I am. You know, sometimes I go in my cell and cry. I cry and cry."

That broke my heart because I could see this huge man/child curled up on his bunk crying for everything that he had lost, all irretrievable--the life he'd taken, his youth, all those years, and years more to come, his mother and father, girls, friends: life.

I held my arms open. "Come here, big guy. I'll give you a hug."

He laughed. "Fuck you, Peterson," and he headed inside, looking at his watch. "I gotta go jack. It's been four hours."

I remained at the fence. The sorrow was overwhelming, especially when exposed so blatantly and unexpectedly because guys fronted a tough façade at all times; weakness was carefully concealed because it led to ridicule and exploitation.

I had never witnessed vulnerability in Big Show-- but of course it was there, as it was for us all. We were afraid of what the future held, especially me because the future looked exactly like the present, just me older in prison. Then dead.

In many ways, Show was exactly as he was when he entered at 18, and he'll still be that youth when he leaves at 40. That haunted him. What will he do? What kind of life will he have? After two decades in prison, incarcerated since 18, without job or prospects, how can he succeed? More importantly, what woman would want him? How will he find love?

That's what we all wanted—to love and be loved. But finding someone tormented most men. Not me though; I'd found Sophie. Others searched desperately for someone, or they tortured themselves trying to hold onto the love they'd had before prison.

Eli in the cell next to me tried with two women, his babies' mamas. He'd tell one that she couldn't go to the beach with friends, tried to manage her life, and sought to control the other also. On The Street he could; he was a player, a young handsome guy with personality and moxy, but in prison for eighteen years, he was out of their lives and gone from his sons' lives.

I tried gently to get him to let the women go; he could not possibly control them from inside prison and trying only caused him stress and grief. Older guys told him, *they didn't commit the crime, don't make them do the time*--but he was too young to think of them waiting for him, trying to support their children without his help, women worrying about what *he* would be like when he got out.

Many like Eli were desperate to hold onto their women. Women were their validation as men, proof that they were still alive, wanted, loved, and needed: I'm not a loser; I have a woman waiting for me. And because many equated manhood with babies, they were proud of the number of children they had.

JB, a pit bull puppy on my ball team had five by five different women; he was only 24 and been down 4 years. Social Services had four of the children, his mother the other. He was a handsome dark haired guy who spent most of his time pummeling with Rocky, 23, another pit bull puppy on my team who had three kids.

"One word," I said to them on the ball field. "Condoms."

JB, Rocky, and Eli are white.

Big Show who didn't have a woman kept falling in love with female guards, nurses, secretaries, and even the evil bitch who ran the gym. He wasn't the only inmate who fell in love with female guards. After all, they were the ones with the vaginas, so easily confused with love. The slightest response—a smile!—threw them into raptures. Jealousy too--"That's *my* bitch"—and often violence.

Guys referred to their women as Bitches, Ho's, and My Baby's Mama. My Wife was rarely heard; instead, My

Old Lady—even by twenty year olds like Eli, JB, and Rocky referring to their women the same age.

One day at visitation, a guard told me that Larry's Old Lady asked never to be seated near me again—she had been frightened the whole time. "Do you know her?" the guard asked.

I didn't, but I had noticed her; she looked like a truck driver in drag. Larry, in his forties, small and scruffy, braggart and thief, was no prize himself.

"She says she was your wife's best friend, was at your house often and saw you and your wife fighting. She said she was subpoenaed by the DA to be the star witness against you."

"I never saw that woman in my life. If she'd been Kathleen's best friend, I would have known. If she'd been in my house, I *definitely* would have remembered. If she'd have been subpoenaed by the DA, my lawyers and I would have known."

"*I* know she's lying, but Larry's convinced she's telling the truth. It's love," he said.

It got worse. She escalated her stories which Larry relayed to every guy who'd listen: how Kathleen had confided to her that she was afraid of me, that she had pictures of Kathleen bruised and beaten. They told him that she was playing him, pointed out that she'd been married three times with a husband now even as she came to see Larry. "She's a drama queen. If she's lying to her husband about visiting you, don't you think she might be lying to you too?"

Nope. And there was nothing I could do: calling his Old Lady a psycho bitch would get me stabbed.

Women often formed attachments with inmates who'd gone wrong: star crossed lovers turned into colliding meteors. Prisoners bring out the "bad boy" attraction some women have for men: there aren't cheerleaders for the Chess Clubs, but Hells Angels can't fit all their women on the backs of their bikes.

Gene, in for murdering two women—he tried to burn their bodies to get rid of the evidence—"found" religion, took a correspondence course and became a minister. One day, after saying grace over food that deserved no grace whatsoever, he told me that he was ready to be released. He was rehabilitated. "I've learned my lesson," he said.

"What have you learned?" I asked.

"I learned never try to burn the bodies." A short while later, he bragged about a woman in Texas who had sent him money and wanted to visit. I was dumbfounded. Where did that woman think the relationship was going, and how she did she explain it to her friends? "Of course I have a man—he's temporarily in prison for killing two women and torching their corpses, but he'll be out soon. We'll all get together. We'll do dinner. Maybe barbecue."

But Gene is never getting out of prison.

Perhaps she possessed that reforming nature in women which made her believe she could help Gene who had gone so wrong. Or maybe she believed she was inflammable.

Fame/notoriety draws some women to men—serial killer Ted Bundy got over a hundred marriage proposals. Carruth certainly had his share of women. Rae spent 3-5 hours on the phone daily to them and had problems juggling their visits so they didn't run into each other.

Other men without women found love too, or at least sex, a line often blurred. Someone a lot smarter than I am will have to explain all the nuances of love and sex and define their inclusions and exclusions.

I taught several she-males who demanded to be referred to as girls and addressed as she or her, always in the feminine. Mr. Painter, the teacher/minister, couldn't do it, but the students had no problem. More than a few were attracted to the "girls".

"Tammy", in her forties, thin, with blond hair to the middle of her back that she combed luxuriously, had a pleasing and ingratiating manner. Unfortunately she had a face like Mr. Ed and a nose like my Basset Hound. She told me she was a female in a male body.

At twenty she was convicted of 2d degree murder, served nine years, was released and a year later committed 1st degree murder. Tammy was not your everyday street corner Tranny.

Nevertheless, guys fought over her. Joe, an extraordinarily aggressive young male incarcerated since he was 18--First Degree Murder--would have committed more murders on The Street if someone had suggested he was sexually interested in another male, but at 25 he found Tammy, old enough to be his mother. He fell in love.

I doubt Joe had encountered a she-male before prison; they would not have run in his violent circle on The Street though Tammy certainly could have held her own.

When she showed up in the unit, Joe was bewildered. And captivated, but the taboo he'd grown up with--GUY/GUY: WRONG! QUEER! SIN! DAMNATION!—kept him on the periphery circling Tammy like a tiger circling a lamb, or in this case, the lamb circling the tiger.

Joe and I walked miles discussing the matter. Tammy was like a chocolate chip cookie in a forbidden cookie jar: Joe really wanted the cookie but he didn't want to be caught; he was terrified that others would think him queer.

I advised him to follow his heart not his dick, knowing full well they led to the same place, so of course he hooked up with Tammy after weeks of self-torment. The attraction was too great, and facing the rest of his life without companionship, too much loneliness to bear.

Alas, Joe could not afford to "keep" trophy Tammy. Her never ending demands for cigarettes and canteen goods got Joe into serious debt. He tried to strong arm someone, was snitched on and shipped. Tammy moved on the next day—she had her pick of guys.

Johnny Blood told me of a bizarre encounter with Tammy. She was in the shower; Johnny was next. He waited. And waited. Finally he went to another. Later Tammy apologized. "I'm sorry I took so long, but it's that time of month; you know how it is with girls," she said coquettishly.

"What the fuck are you talking about?" Johnny demanded. "'That time of month'!"

"Oh no, not that," Tammy giggled. "Once a month I shave every hair off my body; I want to be smooth."

"Jesus!" Johnny yelled and ran away—probably a first for him.

One evening on my bunk, Brian, Tammy's new Daddy/benefactor searched under it on his hands and knees. Brian spent all his time with Tammy, sitting beside her, holding her hand, fending off his many competitors.

He held up one of my shower slippers. "Is this yours?" Yes, I said. He held up another. "That's mine too," I said. "What the fuck are you doing under my bunk?"

Then he held up a third slipper. "Not mine," I said. "I only have two feet."

It was his. Brian was in a domestic abuse relationship with Tammy; she had slapped him out of his slippers. He was lucky; it could have been his head under my bunk.

There was little stigma attached to such relationships--in fact long lines to get into one. To be sure, many could not conceive of such contact, yet a lot of furtive curiosity and relief went on in cells and bathroom. I'd see the most unlikely guys slip into a bathroom together. Men without women often turned to one another--the need for warmth, the desire for touch. And sex.

Cory, the then unit librarian, an Army guard at Ft. Meade detailed to NSA security before Don't Ask, Don't Tell, had a list of 90 guys who'd visited him in the library, not to check out books. He delighted in sharing his list. "You're kidding?" I'd say when he'd point to a former liaison, a guy who'd immediately lower his eyes and scurry away.

"Nope," he'd answer, showing me his little black book with dates and details.

This was *known* by guards who'd ignored his library activity because it helped morale and cut down raging testosterone that might otherwise have been directed at them.

Everyone from the warden on down knew about Tammy and other She-males; they were hardly incognito. It made me wonder if officials sometimes "sugared" prisons with them: "Were having problems at Pumpkinville. Send in some pussy to calm them down."

At one time, we had many girls—Tammy, Millie, Precious, Strawberry, Blondie3, and Danyell, a Whitman's sampler of choices—black/white, tall/short, young/old. Guys would run to the chow hall to see Blondie3, six feet and stunning. The most macho guys were appreciative. "God Damn, she's hot!" Big Show would shout, streaking to the chow hall for a glimpse.

A memorable occasion was The Night of The Damsel in Distress.

Millie came to our unit where Tammy had been the lone girl. Millie was early twenties, petite with red hair and the most feminine demure mannerisms—the way she walked, held her hands, crossed her legs. Guys were captivated, but Tammy was pissed; this was more competition than she wanted; they were not "girlfriends".

One night Millie locked her key in her wall locker—whether by accident or design, I don't know, but she couldn't get in and began to weep. I sat at a nearby table writing; Carruth was on the phone; we watched developments with mounting amusement.

Millie's sobs grew louder. Guys crowded around to help, pushing each other out of the way. They tried everything, including using a broom to pry open the door. They literally fought each other to help, especially JB and Rocky, the pit bull puppies.

Tammy observed by the water fountain; her fury could have melted the locker door.

Finally they got it open. Millie was so grateful. JB and Rocky blushed bashfully.

I asked JB next day on the ball field, "What did you think your reward was going to be for getting Millie's locker open?" He glowered, said "Fuck you," and stormed off to left field.

Knowing JB and Rocky well, I doubted they had sexual interest in Tammy, in fact would have been horrified if she'd come on to them publically, though they might have succumbed to a blow job if no one would find out. Millie's appeal was femininity—a beguiling softness they missed and desperately wanted.

"Girls" were accepted, as were punks—males "owned" by other inmates, young males who'd been "turned out" to become sex objects of tougher prisoners. Rabbit, a white slave for Javon, a black athlete was pimped to service others for dope, cigarettes, and canteen items.

Javon made Rabbit blow him on his bunk in the Day Room—wouldn't even throw a blanket over the action. Kenny in the next bunk complained to a guard who told him, "Don't watch." I told him pretty much the same thing: it takes two to make a victim; it's on Rabbit to end it.

Naturally Javon confronted Kenny when he heard about his snitch: "One more word, motherfucker, and you'll be giving me head." Kenny shut up immediately.

I knew several guys who'd been raped…once. They were open about it because there was no shame in being raped by a group pressing a shank to your throat.

Big Tom admitted he'd raped several young guys: "You take what's available."

Then there were "canteen babies" whose hustle was sex; they bartered their only asset—themselves--for coffee, cigarettes, dope, and food. Ricky H had once been the youngest guy in America sentenced to Life in Prison—15; his story had been on Oprah. I met him when he was 26—blond, blue-eyed, well-built, personable. He sold his cock and was happy to fuck anyone who'd pay; he was completely up front about it.

He'd done a terrible thing—murdered an old woman, yet he might have been saved if he hadn't been sent to adult prison with predatory men.

Ricky inadvertently got me in trouble when he asked, "Mr. Peterson, do you know what a CPA is? Have you ever seen a CPA spread sheet of assets and liabilities?"

A CPA spread sheet? Business must be great, I thought. Intrigued, I said yes. He asked if I'd look at one from GaryF, a Chester whose appeal to the state Supreme Court had resulted in an order for the lower court to *increase* his sentence. He'd ingratiated himself to a woman whose husband had died and then he molested the widow's two young sons.

GaryF was paying Ricky for sex and had promised to send money to Ricky's family.

The spread sheet was patently bogus, listing among other assets, $7,000,000 in a checking account in Greensboro. I told Ricky that I had no idea whether Gary was rich or not, but the CPA report was phony: millionaires didn't keep their money in checking accounts.

Outraged, Ricky called Gary a lying faggot pervert (which he was) and threatened physical harm as well as withdrawing his sexual favors. Gary complained to the warden that I had interfered in his life. She confronted me in the unit one day in front of everyone, shaking her finger angrily, commanding loudly, "Mind your business, Mr. Peterson."

Then she lowered her voice and said, "I've seen that CPA report; it's not your affair."

"Do you think he has $7,000,000 in a Greensboro bank account?" I whispered back.

"I don't know and I don't care. *You* don't either!"

She threatened to send me to The Hole unless I promised to mind my own business, which I promised, and which we both knew was a lie. So Ricky went off to find other clients, Gary continued with a string of other young guys, and I continued to not mind my business.

Blondie2 operated on a much smaller scale. He had no use for a CPA spreadsheet, but he could have used a calculator to tote up the blow jobs he gave as he went cell to cell offering his services for a 35 cent ramen noddle soup. He scored enough soup to float a battleship.

Blondie2 was thirty with an extremely large hearing aid on his left ear that looked like a satellite dish. Big Tom said that Blondie could hear him coming better that way.

Once, Blondie mournfully complained that he got no respect. I suggested he raise his prices and take off his ridiculous hearing aid—at least at work.

Curiously, those who bought Blondie2's soups didn't think their participation was homosexual: giving a blow job was queer; getting one wasn't. The same applied to pitching and catching, terms for anal sex--tops and bottoms. Those pitching, tops, were not considered to be in a homosexual act, only catchers/bottoms. Likewise, Daddy's weren't gay, only their punks. So it was for blacks with white "boys", sort of a slavery payback.

Sex in prison is as confusing as it is on The Street, a cauldron that frequently boils over: hearts and minds can be beaten down, dicks can't.

I wasn't immune to the sex siren either. I was in love with Sophie—in Paris, but sex—in here—was another matter. There were numerous handsome macho guys I was attracted to, but I never had sex with them because someone would have snitched, gotten me a write up, been on the news, harmed any chance for appeal, and embarrassed my children.

I always warned young work out partners that they risked talk by associating with me. "But don't worry, I'm not attracted to you," I'd add.

They were insulted. "*Why* aren't you attracted to me? What's wrong with me?"

"You're too fat," I told BillyG who'd played college football. "You're not masculine enough," I told Eli. "You're too old," I told Big Tom. They were all pissed, especially Big Tom. "I don't want to have sex with you, but I want *you* to want to have sex with me," he said.

I laughed. "Spoken like a true prick teasing bitch."

However, I was attracted to Stone Cold, a 33 year old 6'4" blond body builder with an incredible physique;

he'd played AAA baseball until caught trafficking drugs. I saw him often in the gym where he worked, but there was no possibility of anything developing beyond friendship, though he later got caught in a sex scandal with someone else--a judge!

Big Tom had posed shirtless for an ad in a magazine offering pen pals—"friendship"—to prisoners. He got *one* response from a female and a hundred from gay guys offering money for his buff body. Tom asked Stone Cold if he wanted to correspond with them.

Sure said Stone Cold, thinking this an easy way to milk money from gays, so he wrote several and got an enticing offer from a former North Carolina District Court Judge who promised to help with his case, give him money, and leave him a house in his will. The judge was old and wealthy.

"Why, it's Anna Nicole Smith," I'd shout every time I saw Stone Cold after hearing about the judge. He took it well until the Judge came to visit. I arranged for a friend to visit that day because I didn't want to miss the show.

The judge, a very old man, hobbled in with a cane and was seated deferentially at a table because guards knew he was a prominent retired judicial official. When Stone Cold was let into the Visitation Room, the judge squealed so loudly that everyone turned to look. "OH MY GOD, YOU ARE SO GORGEOUS."

Stone Cold crimsoned and tried to flee, but the guard brought him to the judge's table. Looking about in humiliation, he saw me grinning. I blew him a kiss. I knew he wanted to jump the tables to kill me, but the judge grabbed his hands and held them lovingly.

When visitation ended, we met in the back room where inmates were strip searched for contraband, often with a full body cavity check.

"How'd the visit go, Anna?" I asked.

"Peterson, if you say one word about this, I will break you in half."

"Oh c'mon, Gorgeous, he looked like a sweet old guy, and he's obviously infatuated."

"I'm warning you--one word and you are dead meat." He meant it.

Standing next to this naked blond Adonis, thinking back fifty years to when I was a boy on a baseball field baffled by strange yearnings for the shortstop, I shook my head ruefully.

"What's wrong?" he asked as he put on his clothes.

"Nothing. Just thinking. What position did you play?"

"Shortstop."

Of course. He tousled my hair as he left. "Take it easy," he said.

"Yeah. See you later," I said wistfully.

After chow that evening, Big Show and I stood at the fence. We had a ball game the next day. Out of nowhere, he said, "I'm tired of playing 1st Base. How about putting me in at shortstop tomorrow?"

I stared at him a long minute. "This is a joke, right?"

"No. Why?"

"Well, for starters, you weigh 300 pounds, you can barely move, and by the time you bent over for a grounder, the ball would be in the outfield."

Then I laughed and shook my head. "Besides, you're not handsome or buff enough."

"Huh?"

"Forget it, you're not playing shortstop," I said and went inside to call Sophie.

23: GOD

There's a lot of God in prison, or lots of gods, or perhaps none at all. It's very confusing.

Religion in prison—like everywhere—is curious and fraught with explosive tension.

As a Buddhist, God did not interest me any more than it had the Buddha: no way to tell where we came from or where we're going: there is only now. Nevertheless, subsects of Buddhism popped up, adding to Gautama's words like sects of Christianity have added to Christ's teachings—*he* didn't say anything about abortion, birth control, or Hell.

Christians and Muslims were the dominant religions at Nash, but there were also Rastafarians, Native Americans, Vikings, Mormons, Nation of God, and Messianic Jews—just about anything you could imagine: if it could be worshipped, someone did.

Many inmates find religion in prison, but often just to impress parole boards, and they leave their Bibles and Korans at the gate when they go home, only to pick them up again when they return.

Regardless, religion was serious business and caused many disputes, some violent. Why should prison be any different from The Street?

In the cell on one side of mine was Daniel, a Mormon--but he called himself a "Jack" Mormon, which I understand is a lapsed one. Or maybe they tossed his ass out for child molesting. We never discussed religion, but I did with the only other Mormon I encountered.

John was 27, incredibly fit and strong with a wild temper that often got him into serious trouble. Drugs had brought him to prison despite many interventions by other Mormons. As an example of both his anger and physical strength, he ripped the sink off the wall in the bathroom when guards once locked him in.

One day after I'd been moved to a bunk, I was reading and laughing at the play, *The Book of Mormon*. John, on a bunk across from me, came over, polite but miffed. "I've read that book a hundred times; *I* never saw anything funny in it."

I explained this was not *The* book, but a Broadway play. He asked to read it. I warned him that it might piss him off; I didn't want him ripping it in half. Or me.

He loved it, and that began my instruction in Mormonism. He tutored me as we walked endlessly around the rec yard. I listened carefully, sometimes not believing what I was hearing--about aliens, other planets, buried gold tablets, etc.

Finally I went to O'Hanlan, the librarian who had replaced Cory of the NSA. O'Hanlan had a Master's Degree in psychology; he was very smart with a nimble but drug addled mind, down for 162 years for assorted crimes including rape and kidnapping.

"Have you ever talked with John about his religion?" I asked.

"Yes. He comes to the library all the time."

"What do you think?"

"I told him that he was like every Mormon I've met. He's smart, clean, attractive, polite, articulate, but fucking nuts."

I went back to John. "You ever talk to O'Hanlan?"

"Yeah. He told me I was nuts."

I thought so too, but I didn't tell him. Good Buddhist.

Frequently, like on The Street, the line between gangs and religions blurs: Bloods and Crips, Catholics and Protestant, Hindus and Moslems; the list is long. But unlike gangs, religions are encouraged by prison authorities; they get special consideration--a place to meet, dietary allowances, and work holidays.

Messianic Jews pushed those considerations to the limit and drove authorities crazy.

I had never heard of the religion until I noticed two inmates reading and reciting the Torah. They were learning Hebrew. Intrigued, I asked why and they told me about their religion, which seemed a hybrid—Jewish laws, yarmulkes, observing Saturday as the Sabbath, but accepting Jesus Christ as Savior.

After a legal struggle, the Department of Corrections designated Messianic Judaism as a religion entitled to all benefits and protections of other religions.

Jews and Muslims--not a good match, not an easy fit in prison, especially when the race factor was thrown in: the Muslims were black, the Messianic Jews white Chesters.

Emboldened by their designation as a religion, they pushed for kosher meals. After all, Muslims were allowed to observe Ramadan with special meals.

Recalcitrant might charitably describe DOC's reaction to kosher meals, but they relented when Federal District Court did not dismiss their application for kosher meals as frivolous and said it would hear arguments.

God Almighty! It was like the Gaza Strip when word came that Messianic Jews would get kosher meals. Muslims became apoplectic, but when everyone else learned the meals were to be sent in from The Street and would consist of entrees like baked chicken and roast beef, guys went berserk. Trouble escalated when inmates ran to the Chaplain to convert to Messianic Judaism.

"I want that food," several told me. "What does it take to become a Jew?"

"Hope you're circumcised, that's the first requirement," I'd joke.

"For roast beef? Not a problem. I'll do it myself."

And so it went; tensions mounted as the arrival day neared for the first kosher meals.

The authorities were not happy with the required special treatment. Messianic Jews had to eat separately, have special salt and pepper containers, and napkins. Napkins!

The meals were catered from outside and when they arrived, word spread instantly—it *was* baked chicken and roast beef, and green beans and mashed potatoes. Supposedly, each meal cost $7 compared to a $1.50 for other inmates. That's all everyone talked about.

To understand the uproar, one would have to eat prison food—awful! The food is as bad as any conservative Republican would want it to be—as long as prisoners have to be fed in the first place. Perhaps the worst entrée was sweet and sour soy over instant rice. Six slices of white bread daily and kool-aide fill out the court designated minimum calorie requirement.

So kosher meals from The Street—chicken, beef, vegetables! Everybody wanted them.

Then reality set in. The portions were small—very small, certainly not enough to feed the want-to-be Jews; not enough to warrant a circumcision, or even to clip your fingernails.

There it was: want to be special in prison? Go ahead. Now starve, motherfucker.

The crisis passed. The Muslims decided not to pursue kosher meals and everybody else resigned to soy/shit meals.

Native Americans were considered separately—as race and religion. At Nash, most Native Americans were Lumbees, a tribe not acknowledged by the Bureau of Indian Affairs and contested by other tribes, especially Cherokees. A conflict over gambling and casinos—a huge business.

One Cherokee I knew got $10,000 twice a year from casino royalties, but like me, he wasn't allowed to spend more than $40 a week. Pep, a great athlete on another team, was Christian. We got along fine until we went on a religious retreat together; he would have scalped me in earlier days.

DOC granted Native Americans special considerations: Tobacco! In the circle they attended several times a week, they were allowed to smoke; all had pipes. Anyone could join the circle, even blond blue-eyed inmates who looked like Custer. I called them Pre-Tindians.

Of course tobacco frequently left the circle to be hustled on the black market until the Chaplain discovered 20 *pounds* missing from his *locked* safe. After that he and the bald headed chain gang assistant warden monitored peace pipe inhalations, so Native Americans found another hustle--mojos (magical charm bags) and wallets made from DOC faux leather boots stolen from the stockroom. Like on the Street and TV, religion was a good hustle.

Wiccans were a bizarre group, free spirits who never bothered anyone. I kept trying to find out what they believed, but they were even more vague and disorganized than Buddhists. All the ones I knew spent most of the day at a table playing intricate games like Dungeons and Dragons. They asked me to play, but I couldn't do the math.

The eclectic bunch of believers consisted of Rastafarians and Vikings. Everybody seemed to believe in something; it kept them busy, gave them identity and a sense of belonging.

Many guys tried numerous religions, moving from one to the other with ease and rapidity; I couldn't keep up with Carruth's—he even toyed with Jehovah Witnesses!-- but Pops2 was the most mobile.

Pops2 had been down twenty years, soon to be released. He was fifty with long blond hair without much gray; it was his face and eyes that betrayed age and a difficult life. His only support came from his father who pushed a portable breathing machine when he visited, but his father had recently died.

Pops2 was so afraid of release after two decades in prison that he went to the psychiatrist; he had no idea what he'd do or how he'd survive on The Street. She prescribed lithium and Pops fell under its spell. He could barely talk, think, or communicate; he developed the Lithium Shuffle--picture drugged zombies.

Finally we got him to cut back his dosage; he still walked into walls, but he found a better crutch--religion; he tried them all, except Islam--the Muslims wouldn't have him because they knew he wasn't serious, and besides, he'd look ridiculous among them--6'2", blond scraggly hair to his ass, doped senseless. So he went to the Native American circle where he looked just as out of place--the world's biggest Pale Face sharing a peace pipe--but they were more tolerant.

Several of us were sitting at a table when Pops wandered in from some religious ceremony. Big Tom had just read an article in an upscale magazine (anything beyond *People* was considered pretentious) and told us about Hindus. He said (and I disclaim all knowledge of its veracity) that fathers kiss the penises of their new born sons as some kind of blessing.

When Pops stumbled in, Big Tom called him over. "I got a new religion for you. You need to become a Hindu."

Pops, eyes dazed, hair wild, shambled over. "What's a Hindu?"

"It's you. This is your religion. You're meant to be one."

"What do I gotta do," Pops asked.

"It's easy," Big Tom said. "All you gotta do is kiss a dick."

"What?"

"That's it and you'll be saved. In fact, if you kiss all our dicks they'll make you the High Hindu Hoo Doo."

Pops did not become a Hindu, and I do not know what happened to him when he was released. I hope he found a supportive church. Or more lithium.

For a reason that passed understanding, after five years of no contact since the mala beads incident, the chaplain asked me to attend a special three day retreat in the gym called Kairos, a Christian ministry outreach prison program.

Kairos became the talk of our miserable world, not for salvation but for food--*Street* food: pizza, cookies, doughnuts, candy. Everybody wanted to go to the feeding frenzy, but only 50 would be chosen.

Guys started carrying Bibles wherever they went, it was standing room only in the chapel for weeks, and Big Show knelt to pray as he tended flowers whenever he saw the Chaplain.

I didn't care about the food, didn't want to listen to sermons, and I knew the other guys invited—ass kissers and snitches, which made me wonder "What have I done wrong to be included with them?" I felt like Groucho Marx who didn't want to join any club that would accept him as a member.

Nevertheless, I decided to go to the tent show. It would be welcome diversion—anything to break the tedium. However, I feared I'd end up paying for that entertainment, a fear quickly realized: singing! From the first day, every few minutes we had to jump up to sing some idiot hymn and guys ran up constantly to "testify" and praise authorities; it was nauseating. The food was good though; I almost OD'd on sugar--M&M's and doughnuts.

Every morning when we arrived at the gym we'd be greeted by the Kairos staff—fifty ministers and *devout* lay men (one assigned to each of us)—singing praises to God as they stood in a welcoming line slapping our hands like basketball players arriving on the court for the big game. "He's with you. God is here!" they'd shout.

I'd think, He should be. If He knew about the suffering and misery He had caused, He *should* be in this miserable place--punished.

We sat at tables named after the Apostles; mine was The Matthew Table--two Messianic Jews, a Wiccan, a Buddhist (me), a black Christian, and Native American Pep--easily the most eclectic participants, no doubt quarantined from the others.

In many in regards, Kairos was uplifting and thought provoking, though not always in the way organizers intended. Since it was group participation, we were expected to add our thoughts and comments after every story and sermon. Mine were rarely main stream.

When a minister related his own tragic/inspirational tale, I knew better than to say anything. He told the story of his identical twin who died at birth because of severe brain damage; he himself had survived (Praise God) because he was operated on--doctors could only save one. The minister had come to share the good news about Jesus who had saved him.

The audience wept and discussions centered on God's grace. When they turned to me for comment, I said I was going to pass. No, they insisted--tell us what you

330

think; we want to hear your anti-Christ thoughts even if they're blasphemy inspired by Satan.

Pep particularly was interested in what I had to say.

So I asked, "Where was God for your twin who died?"

Gasps from the devout.

"People praise God after escaping some disaster, the only person saved in a plane crash that killed hundreds or an earthquake that killed thousands, but where was God for the doomed? He always gets the praise but never the blame.

"Likewise, ball players credit God with their victory, but nobody blames God when they lose, though I'd love to see a player on his knees after losing a game, point to heaven and yell, 'You asshole.'"

There was total silence, and the next time I said I wanted to pass on commenting, no one pressed me and Pep never spoke to me again.

I think they discussed creating a new table and moving me to it--The Judas Table.

The Baptist minister assigned to guide me through the retreat was Howard; he'd been a Marine in Vietnam also and apparently now being punished for some travesty in a former life: how else explain having to sit next to me and listen to my heresies? Howard was a good and sincere man and I enjoyed every minute with him, but to give you an idea of his Evangelical background, he was minister to two churches--Bear Creek Baptist Church and Turkey Swamp Baptist Church. It wasn't the Vatican or Canterbury.

On the last day (Praise God), we were told to draw up a list of ten people to forgive no matter what they had done to us. God had forgiven us our sins, so we were to forgive those who had trespassed against us. We were to write the names on a sheet of rice paper, drop it in a jar of water, and see our hate disappear just as our sins would.

I said I didn't have ten people to forgive because I didn't hate anyone. In order to forgive someone, I had to hate him for what he'd done to me. That meant thinking about him, but if I thought about him, he owned me. I was not going to let that happen. My belief goes back to Buddha's teaching that hatred is like holding a hot coal to throw at someone—*you* got burned. So I didn't hate anyone enough that I needed to forgive them.

No! I was told--write the names of ten people who wronged you, people such as the DA.

So I searched my mind and realized I really didn't have ten names; I didn't have *any*. The DA did what he thought was right; he was just doing his job. My sisters-in-law fully believed that I had killed Kathleen. I understood their fury—if I believed someone had killed my brother, I would hate him. As for others, I didn't dwell on them or let them rise to a level of such hatred that I had to forgive them, even my sister who had written a long piece on the Internet, "*When your brother is a Murderer.*" She actually did. My own sister!

Thank God mom and dad were dead—it would have killed them to see siblings turn on another. I couldn't even imagine what my grandfather and Nonna would have thought. Family was everything to them. For me too; especially now.

Just before Kairos began, I got a letter from Clayton. When I opened it, a photo fell out. It took a moment for me to figure out what it was: an ultra sound.

Becky had miscarried a year earlier, so for this pregnancy they'd waited until the fetus was viable before telling me, so viable I saw a penis.

I called them that night. Oh my God, I yelled. "I am so happy for you. And he's hung like a little pony."

"That's his foot," Becky laughed. "But it is a boy."

"What are you going to name him?"

"We haven't decided."

"Bob. That's what I'm calling him."

"It will not be Bob."

"He'll always be Bob to me." I taped the photo on the bunk above me so it would be the last thing I saw before falling asleep and the first thing I saw when I woke up. New life. Overjoyed, unable to contain myself, I laughed, punched the air, and couldn't stop smiling. There was no hate in me.

But now, to appease the hate obsessed Christians, I scribbled Adam Sandler on rice paper, tossed it in the bowl of water, and clapped in wonder when it miraculously disappeared. Good Buddhist.

But then those crafty Christians really challenged me, and I failed. They gave us cookies daily, bags of them, all we could possibly want or eat. They were great cookies, home-made by church ladies. The Bear Creek and Turkey Swamp ladies were terrific cooks. No wonder Howard was so fat.

As we left the gym for the last time, we were given a bag of ten cookies to give to an inmate we needed to forgive, someone who had wronged us or someone we didn't like.

I told everyone I'd wait outside for those who wanted to give me their cookies.

I went back to the unit with the bag and wrestled with the problem. I knew I had to give the cookies to Sandman, a guy I truly did not like.

Sandman was liar, thief, and predator, a powerful young guy who strong-armed the old and weak. Most recently he had stolen a bag of coffee from an old man who had saved his salary for two weeks to buy a $3.20 bag from the canteen.

I wrestled and debated for days. I couldn't stand the sonofabitch and I couldn't bear to give him my last ten cookies. But it was all about forgiveness. What kind of Christian would I be, what kind of Buddhist would I be if I didn't forgive him and give him the cookies?

So I finally decided.

I ate the cookies myself.

I decided nothing good would come of giving him my cookies. He would not change his ways; he would only think me weak and stupid, and he would eat my cookies and enjoy them with the coffee he had stolen.

Fuck him. If God wanted him to have cookies, He would have had the chaplain invite him to Kairos.

Bad Buddhist

24. The Hole Yet Again

Bozo, a notorious Chester with hair exactly like the clown's, was told to move from the first bunk in C block where he was watched and protected by guards to one in back where he'd be at the mercy of young fathers like JB and Rocky, the pit bull puppies. Combined they had 8 kids by 7 different women.

Knowing they would beat the shit out of him at every opportunity, Bozo screamed, "You can't move me. I'm a child molester!" And he threw himself on the startled guard's desk.

They didn't move him.

However they did move another Chester; that was my doing to save his life, a good deed I later somewhat regretted.

I couldn't stand Keith; he was a whiney snitching child molesting piece of shit with pot belly, scraggly white hair, awful teeth, and a perpetual sneer. At 50, he'd been in and out of prison since 20 when he was convicted of indecent liberties with a child; he served 5 years.

Soon after release, he got the same charge and was sentenced to 1 year. After that release he got another sex charge, but this time the judge added 6 years for Habitual Felony.

His only saving grace was retardation—mild, but enough to make me *try* to sympathize with him. Everybody hated Keith; it was the damndest thing, and inexplicable--he'd just be standing there and you'd want to hit him. Maybe it was because of the way he stood with that sneer on his face. I never encountered anyone like him; I can't even think of a fictional character so annoying. Of course he was constantly picked on.

Guys would put turds on his bunk, rig packets of condiments—mustard, ketchup, mayonnaise—that would spray him and his bunk whenever he lay down on it, just anything to make his life miserable. Once ants, spiders, and every other insect found on the yard were put in his sheets. When he pulled back the blanket, they sprang out. He screamed and ran to the front desk and wrote a statement accusing JB and Rocky as the perps.

JB and Rocky were best friends, always playing around, constantly chasing and pummeling one another, but most importantly and their saving grace: they were on my ball team.

With many violent crimes, both had been imprisoned off and on since considered adults at 16. Now 23 and 24, they'd spent only enough time on The Street to father kids. Lots of them.

Curiously innocent for once—they'd had nothing to do with the ants and spiders—but just naming them would get them locked in The Hole for investigation, ending their ball careers and dooming my team.

When they heard about Keith's snitch, they decided to drown the "cocksuckering Chester" in the shitter. Everyone encouraged them.

I had to intervene—I really needed JB and Rocky for the next game, so I went to the Sergeant. "You need to move Keith immediately. Get him out of here. Now."

An hour later Keith was in the other block with his soiled sheets—his life and my ball team saved—but after another trip to The Hole, I ended in the same block as Keith.

When the owl MAR was filed, there was massive publicity—all negative. Posters were printed and placed in the post office with a huge picture of an owl: WANTED FOR MURDER. CONTACT DURHAM POLICE.

Stories, columns, and letters to editors were filled with Whooo Hooo, Whooo did it? No one took the Owl MAR seriously and I felt Judge Hudson would not have the courage to buck public/voter opinion by granting a hearing on the motion despite its scientific documentation.

After reading endless articles and letters ridiculing the owl theory, I was sick—my last chance dismissed as nonsense. Worse, as a joke.

Shortly after being moved, I was doing laps one afternoon when I heard "Whooo, whooo, hoooo." I turned to see Keith hands cupped around his mouth. "Whooo, whooo."

I slammed him against the building. "Listen motherfucker, I saved your life once, I won't do it again. One more word from you and you won't make it out of here."

As I yelled, Johnny Blood ambled over. "Everything ok, Crooklyn?"

"You need some stamps?" I asked him, pointing at Keith.

The Terminator bared his teeth and Keith never said another word or made a bird call in my presence again. But

I knew the Owl MAR was dead if even retards were making fun of it.

Nevertheless I hoped against hope Hudson would grant a hearing. I'd become desperate after my favorite former Death Row inmate said, "You need to get out of here, Peterson. Now!" He'd told me this when a crown on one of my teeth came off and I'd seen the dentist.

Al Green was the meanest motherfucker I met in prison: picture Charles Manson; now think vicious. Two years older than me, Al had spent 12 years on Death Row for three murders. He told me there were five more the cops couldn't pin on him. He got off of Death Row on a technicality argued by the crookedest lawyer in Durham, a man I knew well from my column writing days. Such a small corrupt world.

After the crown came off, I'd put in a dental call. A month was the usual wait time to see the dentist who only filled cavities and did extractions—no root canals, crowns, etc., but I felt she might re-cement the crown. However, I worried that if I had to wait a month the crown wouldn't fit back on the tooth, so I asked a guy with super glue if I could borrow a drop to glue on the crown.

He was *very* upset. "How did you know I had it?" he asked. "Who told you?"

After seven years following Gino's advice to observe everything, there wasn't much I didn't know about who did what and who had what. A survival technique.

I shrugged. "I forget. My Alzheimer's getting worse."

He gave me the super glue, but was paranoid about it. "DON'T tell anyone." I didn't understand—this was glue! Not dope or a cell phone. I glued the crown on.

Well of course the next morning the dentist called for me. Seeing the dentist was a major production. Before entering dental you were searched and handcuffed—I suppose because of the sharp instruments which could be stolen, or maybe for fear that a patient in pain would harm the dentist or her assistant.

When I got in, I explained the problem and asked if she could re-cement it. She would be happy too. Did I have the crown with me? Yes. Where is it? In my mouth; I superglued it on.

"You did *what*! You can't do that!" She was wild and explained that she couldn't take it off now without damaging the crown or the tooth. Her assistant ran out of the room.

I told the dentist that when the glue wore off, I'd come back, but as I left dental, I was subjected to a rigorous search and pat down while still handcuffed.

"What's going on?" I asked. "It's routine," the guard answered. Bullshit, I thought.

Back in the unit I asked Al, Why was the guy with the super glue so paranoid? The dentist so upset? Why the detailed search as I left dental?

"Super glue! Jesus, Peterson, you need to get out of here. Now!"

He explained that super glue was considered a dangerous weapon because it could fuck up the locking system if squeezed into it, interfere with prison security, be used to glue guards' hands together, or do other damage. Possessing super glue was a major offense.

As we talked, the intercom summoned me to the Unit Manager's office. The Confederate flag tattooed Mr. Roberts shook his head when I entered. "Ok Peterson, where's the super glue? The warden wants to know where you got it."

"The warden? How does he know about this?"

"The dentist called him. So where did you get it? And where is it now?"

"Where's what? I've already forgotten what we were talking about?"

He laughed. "I'll tell the warden your Alzheimer's is acting up again. Get out."

When I saw the inmate who had the super glue, I told him he better suitcase it; there might be a shake-down search for it, but do it carefully, so as not to glue his asshole shut.

When the crown came off a week later, I put in a dental call and was seen the next morning without incident.

Al was right, I needed to get out. Frau Himmler and the new Warden had intensified their efforts to nail me—the rogue inmate. Every year had gotten worse. When I entered in 2003 I had a job, cell, and kudos for helping students, but by 2010 I had no job, no cell, and was under constant watch.

I drove Frau Himmler crazy. Yet even with her power, she couldn't send me to Pumpkinville unless I committed a serious offense. The worst she could do was put me on a bunk in the day room to share toilets with 59 guys, but I'd adjusted to that. Sending me to The Hole would upgrade me to private cell with toilet.

The only meaningful punishment was to take away my visitors, for seeing my children, brothers, Sophie, and friends was the most important thing in my life, more important every year because they were my last hold on a world slipping away.

But then came the disastrous day when she thought she finally had me.

Once or twice a year, the prison was locked down as 60 to 100 officers swept through conducting contraband searches. In seven years, we were caught off guard just once; all other times bribed or friendly guards warned us in advance. By and large shake downs were a joke; we'd spend the night before hiding our contraband like convict Easter bunnies.

The only shocker came one morning just after chow when Johnny Blood ran wildly into the unit and yelled at me, "They're coming!"

"Who?" I asked nonchalantly, looking up from the newspaper.

He was so pissed at my stupidity he just screamed, "ONE MINUTE! They're outside."

Indeed they were: The Prison Emergency Response Team (PERT), the special strike force old hands spoke of with dread: "Evil motherfuckers."

They came in like a D-Day assault, 75 guards screaming and shoving us on the floor.

After bringing me into the toilet for a complete body cavity check, a young very large guard forced me to kneel in front of my locker as he tore through every item of clothing, each piece of paper and every page of every book. He had USMC tattooed on his arm and his ferocity matched any DI's at Quantico. It took all my will power not to show fear.

At the end of the shake down, while other inmates huddled in skivvies in a corner, he told me to continue kneeling as he conferred with two other massive guards with USMC tattoos; then all three stormed over to me. The guard who had searched my locker slapped his tattoo and snarled, "We were in Iraq, asshole. Show us your books."

I stood unsteadily, wobbled to the locker and handed him a dictionary. He threw it against the wall. "Not that one."

I gave him a thesaurus.

"No," he yelled, hurling that one too. "*Your* books, asshole. The ones you wrote."

Oh, so I handed him two of my books which I kept in the locker to give guys who wanted to read them because Ms. Snow had removed my books from the library when I arrived.

He pointed to my picture on a book jacket with a bio that stated I'd been in the Marines. "I *told* you he was a Marine," he said in disgust to the other two.

They grabbed me, forced me to a table and slammed me into a chair. "You piece of shit, you disgraced the Corps!"

They were wild, but I thought, I can handle this— it's a USMC thing. Leaning back in the chair, I said "I have a Silver Star and a Bronze Star from Vietnam. What I did in the Corps has nothing to do with being here, so fuck off."

That stopped them. One even suppressed a smile; it *was* a Marine thing.

We woofed and yammered at one another for another twenty minutes, then they stood, gave grumpy Semper Fi's and left, taking all my contraband (an officer/enlisted thing): oatmeal, peanut butter, packets of sugar substitute, and arthritis medicine I'd bought from someone because medical wouldn't give me any.

The Naprosyn nearly brought me down. Frau Himmler sought a serious B Charge that could have had me sent to Pumpkinville—possession of unauthorized prescription medication. She tracked down the guard who had found it in my locker and had him write a statement.

She had me at last.

But Semper Fi held. The PERT officer wrote a statement saying he'd found prescription medicine in my locker--the B charge--but he put the wrong date for his search, nullifying it: you can't be charged for items found May 8 if the search was July 21. Bullet dodged. Frau Himmler was wild; this was the fourth time I'd avoided a serious charge. She *knew* I was guilty. I was.

Though happy to have ducked The Hole and pissed off Frau Himmler, I knew she'd win eventually. It happened on my 67th birthday.

My brother Jack visited from Phoenix in October 2010 as he always did on my birthday; out of 900 inmates, only two others had visitors that day. Probably 80% of the guys never got visits, about the same percentage that didn't get mail.

Mail call was the most anticipated daily event--for those who got mail, but sorrowful for most men—passed over, ignored and rejected every day of their lives. Mail Call was as depressing as the visitor's list: it reminded me of Valentine's Day in school when popular kids got Valentines and the unpopular didn't--just mine because my mother had me make cards for everyone.

"But I don't like Suzy or Sam," I'd say. "All the more reason to make them cards," she'd answered. "Think how you'd feel if you didn't get any valentines."

I'd think--maybe I shouldn't be such an asshole; maybe I should change my behavior. But prison was too late to change behavior; those guys were never going to get mail or visits.

When visitation ended the day my brother came, we three inmates remained in the room because afternoon Count had not cleared and inmates were not allowed on the yard until it did.

As we waited to go back to our units, a man in civilian clothes came in to set up chairs for a meeting, a janitor I thought. I'd never seen him before and paid him no attention. I was thinking of my brother, of how much we had shared and how much I loved him; I'd been Best Man at his wedding thirty years earlier. Bill had been my Best Man and Jack had been Bill's.

Suddenly trouble between the civilian and one of the inmates jarred my reflections. Their argument got louder until the civilian screamed at the three of us, "Do you have a problem moving the chairs?"

Startled from reverie, not knowing what was going on, I turned to the guy he'd been arguing with and asked, "Do we have a problem?"

"Fuck yes! It's not my job to stack chairs. They have janitors for that."

So in the interest of inmate solidarity, I said to the civilian, "Yeah, we have a problem."

He screamed, threw up his hands, and ran out of the room.

A minute later, a lieutenant I'd had reasonable dealings with came in with the civilian. Standing over me, the lieutenant asked, "Mike, would you please stack the chairs?'

I pointed to the civilian, "Who is this guy?" The lieutenant rolled his eyes.

I said to the officer, "Lt. Bease, if you give me an order, of course I'll follow it."

Lt. Bease said, "Mike, stack the chairs." So I did; so did the other two inmates.

After count cleared fifteen minutes later, I went back in my unit and was standing in the canteen line when an obese lieutenant notorious for patting down inmates' crotches with disturbing thoroughness cuffed and dragged me to The Hole on two serious A charges—Creating a Riot, and Work Stoppage (like going on strike).

I was stunned. "What's this all about?"

"You disobeyed an order. Captain Lucita said to lock you up."

Frau Himmler! This time she really had me because the civilian turned out to be a former lieutenant who now instructed guards, and it would do me no good to explain (1) I had no idea who the guy was, he didn't identify himself, and (2) he hadn't given an order: "Do you have a problem moving the chairs?" is a question, not an order.

But there was no arguing my case.

My brother had to visit me the next day in The Hole behind Plexiglas.

"What happened?" he asked incredulously.

"A grammatical misunderstanding," I said.

The other two inmates were released from The Hole after less than 24 hours. Five *days* later, Sergeant Gilbert showed up to tell me he was starting an investigation.

"*Starting* an investigation? The other guys have been gone five days!"

His contemptuous gloating expression said it all: Tough shit. Happy Birthday, asshole.

Sergeant Gilbert despised me. He had been a Marine—no doubt a very good one who obeyed all orders and could march well. Mid-thirties, blond, buff and tough, he had the tiniest feet and walked in the prissiest manner. I always stared at his feet when talking to him, which drove him crazy: he knew that I was ridiculing his small feet.

He also could not stand that I flaunted rules such as not going directly back to our unit from the chow hall after meals. I'd wander the yard to socialize and talk to everybody I knew as he'd scream from the unit, "Peterson, come here!"

I'd keep roaming.

"Sgt. Gilbert's yelling at you," guys would say nervously.

"I can't hear him," I'd answer, but as soon as I saw him racing towards me with raised club, I'd start meandering back. I pushed the limits with him as far as I could in every regard.

I was the nail in the Japanese proverb—I had to be hammered down. I understood this: they were running a prison; I was a prisoner. They *had* to break me, and each time I'd dodge their bullet, they'd double down their efforts to get me. Of course they eventually won, for here I was in The Hole again, now facing Sergeant Gilbert.

I learned Johnny Blood was in the Hole on the other side. He'd been caught—snitched on—with weed taped under his bunk. He was waiting to be shipped, probably to I CON again, a scary thought—like injecting a lunatic with steroids then giving him LSD.

I sent him a kite but I don't know if he got it because I didn't hear back.

Realizing this could get ugly—Rioting!—I asked a lawyer friend to intervene, Jim Craven who had volunteered to pursue my case in federal court. A retired Naval Lieutenant Commander and a minister, he'd responded to every request I made of him—pro bono. I never had a better friend. Jim got the charges reduced to Disobeying an Order and Creating an Unsafe Work Environment—one of those "others": (C 99).

Since it would boil down to my word against the officer's, a hopeless defense, I pled guilty and spent two weeks in The Hole. Nothing happened—what *could* happen in solitary confinement? Well, frequently suicide, insanity, beatings, and Death, but I had high profile protection and didn't mind isolation. I'd even come to welcome it as a respite like R&R in war.

I hadn't grown accustomed to heartbreak though: Margaret got married while I was in The Hole. The day of her wedding in New Orleans, I wept that I could not give her away; I wept that she had no mother or father on her most joyous occasion. I'd missed her graduation from Tulane, Martha's from the University of San Francisco, Clayton's from Johns Hopkins, his marriage to Becky, and Todd's to Tara. Losses so great, wounds too deep to heal.

No longer part of their lives, only remembered and missed, I was a ghost growing fainter every year, receding further and further, my life small, isolated, meaningless.

But there was Sophie; I was important to *her*: she wrote of love, the future; she listened to my fears, consoled me, and gave me hope. She became the focus of my life.

When I was sent to The Hole, I wrote that it was like being in the French Resistance.

"That didn't end well for many of them, you know," she wrote back.

Shortly thereafter she had her own problem that would have landed her in The Hole if she'd been an inmate. Visitors didn't have to pass a particularly restrictive dress code, just no thongs, Daisy Duke shorts, or see-through blouses. Sophie was always chic, dressed with flair, a scarf around her neck or waist, stylish gray hair and trim body. She stood out, as though announcing—I don't belong here. Or in America either.

On one visit, I entered the room to see her at a table rigid, eyes flashing, jaw clamped. She was *pissed.* Forever the guilty Catholic, I wondered, what have I done now?

It wasn't me. She stood, we kissed, then glancing angrily at the female officer at the desk, she said "That woman said I wasn't wearing a slip."

"Are slips required?" Too dressy and passé; I wasn't even sure Margaret and Martha owned one.

Then I saw the bullfrogdog Captain in charge of visitation that day enter the room and sit beside the female officer, a faint smile between her jowls.

Seeing her, Sophie smiled back, anger dissipated. "It was a misunderstanding. When I entered, the officer said I wasn't wearing a slip. In France, slip means... like English knickers."

"Panties?"

"Yes. I got very angry. I said, 'Of course I'm wearing a slip.' She said I wasn't and I said, 'What kind of a woman do you think I am?' We started screaming at one another and I yelled, 'Do you want to go in the bathroom and look?' "

Sophie had worked herself into a froth and turned to glare at the officer. "She didn't think I was wearing panties! Can you imagine?"

"Yes, I often imagine that."

"That's when the Captain came in."

"I'll bet *she* doesn't own a slip. She probably free balls it."

Sophie cut me off. "She was nice. Otherwise I might have gone to The Hole for causing a disturbance like you always do, but I explained about slips and everything was fine. Now let's talk about what is happening to you. Isn't it wonderful? We're going to win!"

She meant stunning news in the media, the most encouraging event yet in my woeful saga, a real chance that I could get a retrial and truth finally emerge.

But there was even more wonderful news.

I knew Becky's due date. When it passed I anxiously called every day. Not yet, Clay would say. Then one day there was no answer. I called repeatedly, growing more and more concerned. Finally just before Lock Down, I called Sophie. 3am in Paris.

She answered. Even before I could say anything, she said, "Everything is fine and everyone is still at the hospital. You have a grandson. They named him Drrrrriiium."

"Named him what?"

"Drrrrriiium," she repeated.

"What the fuck kind of name is that?"

"It's a beautiful name. Like the book—Drrrrriiium Gray. Oscar Wilde."

"Oh." It was a beautiful name. Dorian Nathaniel.

With Dorian born, new life, my own was insignificant, but it became more important than ever that I got out. I couldn't have that child visit me in prison: Why's Gramps in the pokey?

For killing his wife and another woman, but he didn't do it.

Then why's he in the pokey?

Do we tell Dorian about injustice? Is that what we teach the young about our judicial system? Or is it better to ignore injustice and just not visit the old reprobate?

I *had* to get out.

And now there seemed a real chance.

25. THE ROAD NOT TAKEN

Wars, pestilences, and politics--who becomes governor or which country is bombed-- didn't interest or concern most guys because they were cast outs in a barbed wired world of shake downs, lock downs, chow calls, hustles, and most of all—fear: for themselves.

But I cared. It mattered for the future of my children and soon to be grandson.

As the only white guy for Obama in 2008 (yet unable to vote), I incurred the wrath of many because *race* always mattered, and I pushed that nuclear button when I made a fly swatter with Sarah Palin's face. Since there were no fly swatters, we had to make our own to combat the summer fly plague; Sarah was frequently splattered with bloody dead flies.

Big Show was outraged; he'd fallen in love with her, so he made an Obama flyswatter. Like many white inmates, he felt conditions would improve under Republicans.

Are you nuts? I asked. We'll be lucky if we're still fed.

However, all of us closely followed judicial news: a law passed or repealed that affected us directly—no more tobacco!—or that the State Bureau of Investigation behind so many of our convictions was under investigation for corruption? News that prisoners might be released?

351

Oh, we cared about that.

The Innocence Project, a non-profit to exonerate those wrongfully convicted was founded in 1992. North Carolina established its own Innocence Inquiry Commission in 2006. If they found merit to an innocence claim, they recommended release to a panel of three judges.

One man I knew well, Dwayne Dail was found innocent in 2007, his rape conviction overturned when DNA evidence cleared him after *18 years* wrongfully incarcerated. Someone else's semen was on the little girl's dress that had been found in a forgotten locker.

I was happy for him, yet his release had nothing to do with me, but bombshell newspaper headlines in January 2010 on Innocence Commission hearings for Greg Taylor definitely affected me.

I first heard of Taylor in 2003 from the sociopath Robert McNeil. He feared Greg might return to Nash and get his TA job back, the one Ms. Snow gave McNeil when Taylor was shipped to another prison shortly before I arrived.

Taylor had been convicted of murdering a prostitute in 1993 on one damning point: SBI Agent Duane Deaver testified that the woman's blood was on Taylor's abandoned SUV found near her body. But 16 years later, Innocent Project attorneys discovered in Deaver's lab notes that his tests had *not* proved positive for blood. It wasn't blood at all! It was paint. Yet Deaver never revealed this and let Taylor be sentenced to Life without Parole.

A few months earlier, a Federal Court had reprimanded Deaver for "misleading" testimony in the trial of another man and overturned his *death* sentence.

Deaver had lied in two 1st Degree Murder cases in which the men got the death penalty; one was executed. In how many other trials had he lied? MINE! I knew during my trial the bastard was lying. Since I was innocent, any "proof" that I killed Kathleen had to be bullshit.

It *was* bullshit—his asinine points of origin in space and him whacking a bloody sponge to get blood splatter on my clothes and shoes. But it worked.

Guilty. Life without Parole. Appeal after appeal denied. Case closed.

In 2010, Greg Taylor's Innocence Commission hearing became media frenzy: **Prostitute murdered! SBI agent lied! Innocent man convicted**!

Though front page every day and on all newscasts, archival newspaper photos and TV footage were not of Deaver at Taylor's 1993 trial: the middle-aged, balding, smug bureaucrat was shown pointing to "evidence"—those points of origin—at *my* 2003 trial that he said proved *my* guilt. The stories were about Deaver and Greg Taylor, but the photos and videos were of Deaver and me.

In February 2010 the Innocence Commission freed Taylor and the Attorney General ordered an audit of all SBI lab cases. Two former FBI agents found over 200 with distorted lab reports that didn't correctly reflect results of potentially innocent men and women in prison. Deaver's work proved the most egregious. He was the prosecution's "Go To" guy for "helpful" testimony—fact *or* fiction: "Tell me what you need? I'll supply it."

Deaver sent innocent men to prison; he let them be executed. For "Atta boys."

During a contempt hearing for him on the Taylor case, Deaver testified that he was merely following orders. He'd withheld exculpatory evidence because it was SBI policy.

The SBI Director was replaced and Agent Deaver fired.

Fired! The main witness against me fired for lying and perjury.

He'd lied about blood on the bumper of Taylor's car--he *withheld* evidence, but in my trial, he *invented* evidence with false experiments.

With all hope gone, suddenly here was hope.

Then despair. The DA would never admit error; a conviction notch would not be un-notched. And so much had to happen to get me back to court: motions, Discovery, new evidence, hearings--the entire system tackled and overcome. Would I even live that long?

My attorney David Rudolf was hopeful Judge Hudson would grant a hearing for the MAR he'd filed based on Deaver's lies. But I was leery: I knew fate's perversity.

I never thought I'd die in war, but how many dead soldiers also believed that? How many go to war thinking they'll be killed? Mike Wunch didn't when he took the road to Con Thien on July 27, 1969.

Forty years earlier, Mike was company commander of A Company, 3rd Tank Battalion in Vietnam where I'd been sent after leading grunt patrols and ambushes for 9 months. He was a Captain, I a First Lieutenant, his executive officer; we were good friends the same age.

Mike had a wife and child and was due to rotate home in less than a week, assigned to the faculty of the Naval Academy, but only a few days before his tour ended, our company was ordered on an operation near Con Thien. Mike didn't want to miss his last chance to see combat.

I told him that he was crazy: Don't take a chance this close to the end. Let me go.

But it was Mike's company. Another reason he wanted to go was to see his friend Oliver North, also a Naval Academy graduate. North was infantry, and tanks, big vulnerable targets, required infantry protection. North's unit would provide perimeter security for our tanks.

Then fate: the NVA attacked that night and Mike was killed, hit directly with an RPG--anti-tank rocket propelled grenade.

Of all the deaths I experienced in war, his hurt most. I couldn't even bring myself to write his widow. I'd start a letter then tear up the empty words: I'm sorry; he was a great guy; I should have been killed instead.

Yet would I have been killed had I travelled that road to Con Thien? Would Mike have lived and I died? Who knows where roads not taken lead? Fate is a coin toss. I became Dad and Gramps instead of him. Con Thien came up heads for me but not for Mike.

But *This* time? A hearing to free me?

I cautioned my children not to get their hopes up. They didn't need the warning; they had experienced the travesty of my conviction. But Sophie was optimistic. "Hudson will grant a hearing. He knows we'll film it; he's not going to miss starring in another movie."

The Attorney General vehemently opposed a hearing. Though Deaver's testimony was 1000 pages of the prosecution's 6000 page case against me, his conclusions 40% of the DA's summation to the jury, the AG said Deaver's work was insignificant. Since it couldn't be defended—he'd fired the bastard for his work—he dismissed it as inconsequential.

The frenzied media were caught in the middle—they'd championed my conviction but had exposed Deaver and the SBI. *Two* evil doers—Deaver and me. Who was worse?

It didn't matter—carrion was carrion; they'd feed on any roadkill; two were even better. A hearing would sell newspapers and boost TV ratings. One of us, I or the DA would lose, but they'd win no matter the outcome. The vile story had new life.

I asked Rudolf how long before I knew if I'll get a hearing? Probably a year, he said.

There was nothing I could do. My fate was not in my hands; I had no control over my future. But days were mine, so I buried my anxieties in staying busy.

MM was an Honor Grade inmate soon to be released--22, 6'6", weighing about 150 pounds. He was dark with good sharp features, but not strong. I'd joke on the weight pile: "I'm three times your age and can lift twice as much."

MM was determined to set his life right after his 5 year sentence for "Discharging a Firearm on Occupied Property" (a house).

"Five years! That's too much time," Sophie said when I told her about him.

"Not really, he was aiming at someone inside and missed; it was a drug deal gone bad."

To prepare for life after prison, MM wanted to take a University of North Carolina correspondence course available to inmates with a violation free record and less than 5 years to serve. He asked if I'd tutor him with the first year English course. I said I'd be happy to.

He was so excited; he was taking a college class! He was in college! But reality crashed down with his first assignment. He came to me in tears. "I can't do it," he said mournfully.

We sat at a table and I asked him to read the passage he'd been assigned to write an essay on. He struggled mightily then pushed the book away in frustration.

"You're dyslexic, aren't you?" I'd seen a lot of it in GED.

He lowered his head. "Yes."

"Jesus, you really are fucked up. You can't lift weights, shoot straight, or read."

He jumped up furiously and was about to swing on me until I said, "It's ok. I'll read the story to you."

He memorized everything I read. We worked together for two months. I'd read the story and he'd write an essay. He'd sit on the floor next to my bunk, his head towering over mine. We'd read his assignment and discuss it. Once I casually mentioned Camus's *The Myth of Sisyphus* and told him about hope, absurdity, Sartre and Existentialism.

For his last paper, he wrote an amazing essay on prison life about Camus and Existentialism with himself as metaphor for Sisyphus.

Alas, just before his final exam, he was taken to The Hole. We'd been working at a table in the Day Room when a female guard went to search his cell. He jumped up and slammed the door shut with her inside. He was so young and playful, and she in no danger--she had a key and her radio--but Frau Himmler charged MM with assault and kidnapping. Kidnapping!

He was shipped to another prison, hopes trampled. Sisyphus indeed.

A better day came when I was summoned to the bald headed chain gang Assistant Superintendent's office. Clayton had sent me *The Hubble Atlas of the Universe*, but it was beyond regulation size so I had to sign a statement saying I had received the book but couldn't have it, nor could I donate it to the library.

While I was in his office, the warden walked in booming, "Ho Ho Ho. What are you doing here, Mr. Peterson?"

"Cooperating with the authorities as usual," I answered.

"Ho Ho Ho," he said, pulling up his pants legs. "It's getting kind of deep in here. But you shouldn't be here at all. After rioting, we should have had you shipped."

"That was such bullshit," I said. "I can't believe what you did. How could you put a sweet little old man like me in The Hole on his 67th birthday?"

The bald headed chain gang guard Assistant Superintendent looked at me levelly. "Peterson, YOU are not a sweet little old man."

I wanted to pump my fist. "Youre goddamn right I'm not," but I nodded meekly and tried to look innocent and contrite, fooling neither of them, of course.

In karmic retaliation, I lost my wedding ring that night. On my bunk reading, I noticed it was gone. I ran up to the shower. I must have lost it there, but I couldn't find it.

Guys stole pencils, stamps, peanut butter--anything; even my Buddhist Mala beads had been ripped off. Certainly no one was going to return a platinum ring they could barter for packs of cigarettes or, I shuddered, whatever else they wanted.

I was mentally beating myself up for being so stupid when a shy young guy who had recently arrived came up to my bunk and said, "Mr. Peterson, did you lose a ring? I found a really nice one when I was cleaning the shower and thought it might be yours."

He handed it to me, a kid who had nothing--no cell, no support, and no friends. He cleaned gross showers for one stamp a day—his only income.

I wanted to hug him but felt he might misinterpret it, so I said, "What can I get you?"

He didn't understand.

"Make out a list from the canteen, $20's worth. I'll get it for you tomorrow."

"No, no," he said. "I can't take anything."

"Listen, kid, make out a list or I'll get you $20 worth of shit you might not want."

"You serious? Twenty dollars?"

"Get me a list."

It took him nearly two hours to come up with his list. He'd write down items, tote up the cost, scratch out an item, tote up the cost, cross something else out, add something, and tote up everything again. Finally satisfied, he brought me the list.

The next day after I got him what he wanted and added a bunch of stamps, I watched him lay the items on his bunk. He selected a candy bar, then carefully put the rest in his locker.

A couple months later during a TV prison interview, the first question from the newsperson was, "You're wearing your wedding ring--why?"

I said it never occurred to me to take it off; I was still in love. Love survives death. I wear the ring today; I've never stopped loving Kathleen. And the ring reminds me of prison. I hope that kid is ok.

Lumbee Locklear isn't.

Most Native Americans were called Chief, but Lumbee Locklear was not the Chief type; he looked and acted like a twelve year old though he was in his early twenties. This was not his first time in prison, but his first time in an "adult" one.

He was always happy and enthusiastic, so young and seemingly innocent that it was like having a little kid around. He'd come running to the weight pile, then sliding, kicking up dirt. Big Tom would say, "Go away, go find a playground with swings and a teeter totter."

Locklear would laugh and then make us laugh. You could not not like him.

Get your shit together, we'd say. One more fuck up and you'll get an Habitual with eight extra years. You'll be a punk. Someone like Big Tom will nail your ass."

He'd grin. "Aw, you know I'm no punk. Besides, I'm never coming back."

Yet we knew he had nowhere to go but back to Pembroke—Lumbee Land we called it--where he always got in trouble. He couldn't stay out of it; he'd follow anyone into anything.

"But what should I do when I get out?" he'd ask.

Get an education! Get a job!

"Yeah, yeah, I will," he'd say eagerly. "I'm going to do that."

But we knew there was no one to make him do it, no help for him on the outside.

When he'd leave the weight pile, skipping away happily, we'd all silently watch him go--a doomed child. Even Big Tom, not remotely sentimental, would shake his head sadly.

Locklear was released a few months later. The following year, he got eight years as an Habitual Felon.

As I waited for Judge Hudson to decide about my hearing, Sophie continued to work on the Owl Theory.

She compiled massive documentation on owl attacks and contacted several raptor experts who confirmed that Kathleen might have been attacked by an owl. One expert, a noted forensic pathologist said the autopsy photographs of the wounds clearly demonstrated that. In addition, she engaged Carla Dove at the Smithsonian who'd identified Canadian Geese as the cause of the airplane crash on the Hudson River. Dr. Dove said prosecution slides definitely showed feathers and blood mingled with her hair.

"Wouldn't you be happier to know that an owl killed Kathleen, something natural rather than if she had been killed by an intruder with a tire iron?" Sophie asked.

Kathleen was gone. Discovering how she died wouldn't bring her back. An owl, a tire iron, or even an act of God might give me freedom, but Kathleen would still be dead.

Yet I would be free. I would be with my children. I would live with Sophie.

But *would* I get a new trial?

26. REVELATIONS

Despite Life without Parole, I never thought I'd die in prison. Of course Luigi in his coffin probably didn't think he'd die either—somebody would get to him in time.

My belief was like Ivan Ilych's: while all men died, he wouldn't. Neither would I. Not a good bet—in Ivan's case cancer, in mine because all my appeals had been denied; we were both doomed—Ivan in his bed, me behind bars.

Then in April 2011, after more than seven years incarcerated, appeal after appeal denied, eight months after Rudolf filed the MAR asking for retrial, Judge Hudson ordered a hearing. He would decide in September whether I got a new trial or died in prison.

Hope! I started the countdown—165 days to go.

A drowning man tossed a life line doesn't think he's saved, he just clutches it desperately. His fear even increases because he knows THIS IS IT, his last chance. That's how I felt: a life line, the last possible hope. My moods careened wildly from elation to terror. I would be Free! No! I would drown.

Clayton and Becky brought Dorian to see me when he was six months old, my son's son, an infant wide awake, bright eyes full on me—a gift, a promise of the future.

It was almost more than I could bear as memories of my son flashed through my mind, holding him as an infant, watching him grow, become a man, and now him holding his son, the future—laughing, crawling, walking, riding a bike, playing ball.

Would I be there to see it?

I gazed at other brown clad men with their children—an hour once a week in a gun guarded room behind razor wire. I knew I could not endure that for the rest of my life. I could not put my family through that. Death was preferable.

We had a lovely visit but when I went back to the unit, I locked myself in the bathroom and cried: for what had been—joy with my sons and daughters, and for what was now—this horror of prison.

After Hudson granted the hearing, seeing Dorian, torn by hope and fear, I developed severe heart palpitations along with sweating and insomnia; I filled out an emergency sick call.

Putting in a sick call was generally a waste of time: one doctor for 900 men came only three days a week. Dr. Bhutto was Pakistani, 80 years old and had lost his medical license in Florida. Although a sweet man...he *was* 80 years old and had lost his license. He was later fired when he came through the security gate with a bottle of gin in his medical bag, completely understandable, but nevertheless illegal.

Sick calls cost $5--one or two weeks' pay. Consequently not many guys put in sick calls. Even if you did, it took days to see a nurse who harassed you and then usually wouldn't let you see Dr. Bhutto. The cost was still $5.

Emergency medical requests cost $7 for the same treatment. However, bleeding and seizures were treated immediately, or something dramatic like when Grandma, a pathetic old queen, whacked off his dick because he had been jilted by his young lover.

That got everybody's attention; every guard on duty that night came to view the carnage. It was a gruesome sight that occurred ten feet from my bunk. I had nightmares for a week after seeing Grandma's bloody dick put in a baggy by laughing guards who brought it to the front desk where it was photographed and never reattached.

At medical, Dr. Bhutto told me that my blood pressure was too high--180/120. All my life it'd been 120/80. Old age and stress, he said. No shit! He gave me ibuprophen. $7.

Sophie saved me: touch and love were so much better than ibuprophen. She visited four times from April to December, stroking my hand, reassuring me that everything would be fine. Don't worry. We will live together in Paris soon.

It had begun to look like we might.

Three TV stations came to interview me. The reporters implied that Judge Hudson would grant a hearing: your story is too good to cancel; it'll be renewed for another trashy season.

Anything to get me out. But would I get out?

My skin started turning black. I had developed the flesh eating disease. Would there be anything left of me for the hearing?

MRSA, a staph infection largely resistant to antibiotics, had become so virulent several prisons had been quarantined. Warnings were posted in all blocks: **WASH HANDS WITH SOAP!** Supposedly that would eliminate infection risk for 60 men sharing four toilets, 120 using four showers, and 900 eating in a chow hall graded Z on any sanitation scale.

Pictures of MRSA infections were displayed on warning posters. When a sore appeared on my leg identical to one in the posters, I put in an emergency medical call. Dr. Bhutto gave me a salve and told me to use soap when I showered, which of course I was already doing.

The sore worsened; it was devouring my flesh— at night in my sleep I could hear the munching. Every morning when I woke I'd check to see if I still had a leg.

Another emergency visit resulted in a biopsy and a precautionary antibiotic.

It turned out that I didn't have MSRA, but *serratia marcesens*, a bacterial pathogen found in moist areas (showers) which fed off soap and shampoo residue. I'd been carefully cultivating the goddamn thing for weeks. Antibiotics and cutting back its soap diet cleared up the staph infection in another two weeks.

I returned to obsessing about my hearing—133 days away—practically living on the weight pile to work off my anxieties.

Thank God for several bizarre incidents, otherwise I might have gone crazy.

When coming in from the rec yard one afternoon, I found a white guy about fifty in the lower bunk beside mine that had been empty for a week, a wheelchair by his bed. I said hi. Slack mouthed, he drooled something.

Now what? I thought. I asked how he was and got another drooled answer.

John the Mormon said the guy had been brought in 30 minutes ago. He couldn't talk or move because he'd had a stroke.

"What's he doing here?" I cried. "He belongs in a hospital! How can he go to the shitter and shower? How's he going to eat?"

"A good Buddhist should be happy to nurse him."

"My ass!" and I stormed to the front desk, déjà vu from the Marines at Zama Hospital where Vic couldn't ring for help because of his amputations. I ranted at the guard. He shrugged. Inmates were assigned by upper staff; he was just following orders.

When I returned to my bunk in disgust, I saw a young Blood gently lift the old guy into his wheelchair and push him to the bathroom. Later he brought him back, helped him eat, and took him to the toilet several more times before lockdown.

The next day I checked with librarian O'Hanlan. "What's the deal with the old white guy and the young Blood?"

"They came in together from another camp. The kid's just helping him."

"Bullshit. What's he up to--is he taking the old guy's money?"

"The old guy doesn't have any. The kid's just helping."

Young black nursing old white man with no strings attached? No way, but SK, a ruthless toothless hairless older Blood shot caller down for murder confirmed the story.

"You going to take care of me like that when I can't move?" I asked. "You going to wheel me to the shitter and wipe my ass?"

"You better have a backup plan, Peterson."

For two more days the young Blood ministered to the old guy. Going back to SK, I gave him 40 stamps and told him to get $10 worth of canteen items for the young Blood, but don't tell him where it came from. I didn't want to be hassled by him or others for more.

SK rubbed the stamps together. "You gonna take care of me like this if I wheel your ass to the shitter?"

"Stamps are my backup health plan," I said.

The next week the old man was shipped to another institution. I don't know if he lived or even if he wanted to: he'd never find someone like Young Blood to care for him.

As the countdown to the hearing dwindled to 47 days, Durham District Attorney Tracy Cline who had replaced the disgraced and disbarred Mike Nifong of the Duke Lacrosse case (he'd lied and withheld evidence; unusual only in that he got caught) launched an unprecedented attack on Judge Hudson. She demanded that he recuse himself for corruption, bias, prejudice and discrimination (they were both black), so Hudson delayed the cases before him (mine!) until another judge heard and decided Cline's accusations.

The hearing was postponed until December 7th; Pearl Harbor Day!

I started a new count down, back up to 119 days. I had become a footnote in my own hearing: the media had a better war to cover than between murderer and corrupt SBI agent—one between Judge and DA.

I was pissed, but relieved too—the battle had only been postponed. I still had hope.

Keaton didn't. Dubbed AK-47 by me, the 60 years old, 6 foot burly former truck driver seemed close to death.

Extraordinarily devout, Keaton spent all day every day reading his Bible. His five children visited regularly despite his crime--shooting their mother, his wife.

When he asked me to read the religious book he'd been working on for years, I said it was not a genre that interested me but I'd take a look. He handed me 300 single spaced hand written pages. I spent a few minutes on the manuscript and handed it back.

"What's wrong?" he asked. "Isn't it any good?"

"I don't know because I can't read it. There are no paragraphs, just a 300 page sentence."

"What's a paragraph?"

I told him, adding, "There's no punctuation either," and I explained about commas and periods and capitalizations.

He took it well, as if it was God's will. Then he told me his story.

Keaton loved his wife but when he discovered she was cheating, he was devastated. Then religious fervor swept him: she was an adulteress. She had sinned against God.

As with many Christians when wrongs need righting, he got his gun--an AK-47, but Keaton had a bum shoulder and couldn't raise his left arm, so he fired the weapon with one hand. When his wife saw him with the

AK-47, she ran out of the house into the fields. Keaton chased her firing with his one good arm. He hit her numerous times and she fell to the ground.

He stood over her, pointing the rifle at her head. She pleaded, "Keaton, don't kill me."

Then he heard God's voice: Don't Shoot! So he didn't fire the coup de grace.

"She lived," Keaton said. "And God forgave me."

"He *did*? God forgave you?"

"Yes. Because I did what He said; I didn't kill her."

"What about your wife? Did she forgive you?"

Keaton shook his head. "Oh no. She testified against me at my trial."

When Keaton moved to another unit, I rarely saw him and only from a distance; he'd lost weight and looked yellowish. Then, 52 days before my hearing, I encountered him in the chow hall wearing suspenders, the only ones I'd seen in prison. They rest of us wore web belts, though many guys let their trousers fall as low as possible on their butts.

I complimented his sartorial splendor. "Love the suspenders. Where'd you get them?"

"I'm ddiiiiiiii," Keaton said in a horse whisper.

I leaned closer. "What?"

"I'm dying." He explained that he had throat and stomach cancer. He couldn't wear a belt because of the pain, so they gave him suspenders.

When I told Big Tom about Keaton, he said, "Did you ask him for his suspenders when he dies?"

Then mortality struck for real on Halloween.

I was down to 37 days, but all Jimmy Passmore's had expired; he died alone and unlamented in his cell.

Though I didn't think I would die in prison, Death had become a reoccurring nightmare. One brought me bolt upright on my bunk. I was very old and desiccated being carried somewhere on a stretcher. I whispered, begged, "Don't stop," because I knew if they did, if they set down the stretcher, I would close my eyes in exhaustion and die.

I wanted them to carry me to my children so I could die with them nearby. Soldiers cry "mother" at the moment of death. They want comfort--not an angel of mercy to save them, just someone who loves them to stroke their brows and hold their hands, to say, "It's all right, my dear. I love you." That's what I wanted. I'm sure Jimmy Passmore wanted that too.

The night before, he had complained of chest pains and numbness in his left arm. He was 62 and had suffered a severe heart attack two years earlier. Tall, thin, sullen, a constant complainer, no one much liked him: he was a child molester convicted of taking indecent liberties with a minor—supposedly his own granddaughter.

We rarely spoke because he was so negative. Life was grim enough without listening to others bitch about it: the food was awful, I didn't need another guy to tell me that; the place was horrible, more commentary wouldn't make it better.

Passmore was the worst complainer, yet despite his sour demeanor, when he described his chest pain and numb arm around 6 pm, I and others said his symptoms sounded like a heart attack. We told him to get to Medical, and I related a couple of heart attack horror stories that I'd witnessed in Unit 2.

"Bowlegs" had legs so bowed The Dwarf could have run between them and rung his balls like a bell. He was black, overweight, and diabetic. When he complained one evening about chest pains and numbness in his arm, I told him those were classic heart attack symptoms. "Go to Medical immediately."

He did. They diagnosed his problem as "gas" and gave him Beano; he went back to bed on his bunk in the Day Room. Around 3am, he was taken screaming in pain to Nash General Hospital where they immediately diagnosed heart attack. We never saw him again.

Another inmate playing basketball in the gym collapsed with chest pains and arm numbness. Guards carried him to Medical where he too was given Beano. That night he fell out of his chair watching the 6 o'clock news, dead before he hit the floor.

"Go to Medical," I told Passmore, "but don't let them give you Beano."

Jimmy went to the front desk to put in an emergency sick call, but guards wouldn't send him, so he went to bed around 7pm.

Lockdown was 11:30. Inmates had to be on their bunks or locked in their cells. We were counted. During the night, guards were mandated to check inmates hourly but often let it slide because no one could escape from locked cells; it was quiet and they could sleep.

At 5:30 am, guards screamed COUNT TIME. Every guy on a bunk sat up groggily, faced forward, and those in cells stood at their doors.

Passmore's cell was on the second floor just above where the TV's were bolted to a pole. A guard knocked. Then he knocked again. And again. Jimmy was not standing before his door. Fully awake now, I feared the worst.

The guard stared through the small window but did not go in his cell; he called the guard checking first floor cells. That guard ran up, looked through the window, then radioed the sergeant who went upstairs, peered in, and said loudly enough for all of us to hear, "Oh shit."

Within minutes the inevitable Captain Lucita arrived; she'd been officer in charge that weekend and supposedly had checked cells Halloween night.

She and the sergeant went into the cell. Guys with an upstairs view saw Passmore naked on the bed except for his socks, stiff in rigor mortis.

Guards were posted in front of the locked cell and yellow crime scene tape strung to keep everyone out, and I suppose, Jimmy in.

"Count Clear" was finally called—everybody accounted for: 899 inmates and 1 corpse.

Chow call was announced but few went; no one wanted to miss this show. I grabbed my books and papers and sat at the table nearest the officer's desk.

Captain Lucita went to the desk and retrieved the officer's logbook with entries for the previous night's guard checks along with her visit to the unit. She left with the logbook.

A little later she returned the logbook to the officer's desk just as the County coroner arrived, a stern stumpy middle aged woman who looked like she'd been born to examine corpses. She went into Passmore's cell with Frau Himmler who herself always looked primed for cadaver duty. In no time, a heated argument broke out with head and finger shaking on the part of the coroner.

Captain Lucita tromped down to the desk, glared at me, brought the logbook upstairs and pointed to a page. The coroner pointed to the corpse and shook her head.

The official word was that Jimmy Passmore suffered a heart attack and died shortly before morning count at 5:30. He had been checked hourly during the night (it was in the logbook) and no problem observed. At 4:30 am, he had been let out of his cell to take a shower (also in the logbook) because he was complaining of chest pains, and then brought back to his cell. He was alive and well at 5 am according to the log book.

The coroner was not buying it--full rigor mortis could not set in that quickly. Furthermore, she knew prisoners were never allowed out of their cells after lockdown. Showers are not generally accepted treatment for heart attacks, and many guys were up early—none saw a guard take Passmore to the shower, which would have been an unprecedented event.

Soon afterwards, we were sent to the rec yard (lest we be traumatized) while the body, stiff as a board, was removed from the cell, hand cuffed to a stretcher.

They were taking no chance that Jimmy was faking his rigor mortis and might escape.

No grief counselors arrived to comfort us. We had no "closure". No one needed any because Passmore was a child molester. Fuck him, everybody said. RIH. Rest in Hell.

After Jimmy's corpse was removed, the unit settled back to its routine of count time, canteen calls, and chow. Everyone moved on to other concerns—hustling tobacco and pills, stamps!, gym call, football, NASCAR, and basketball gambling tickets, fights over the TV schedule, and who would get Passmore's cell.

But I kept seeing Jimmy in that cell. The dreaded coachman had slipped through wire and concrete. Mortality rocked me with fear. I didn't want to die like that, carried out strapped and cuffed on a gurney. I *had* to get out. The hearing *had* to succeed.

But as it approached, DA Cline ratcheted up her attempts to derail it. Every day there were headlines and newscasts: **Judge takes DA Cline to task; Durham DA Cline wants Judge Hudson off retrial; Durham DA seeks to postpone Michael Peterson trial; Cline's motions could stall trial; Grayer Peterson awaits another day in court.**

I was a wreck, unable to sleep and too stressed to even eat from the Christmas package that had just arrived. Once a year, an inmate could receive a food package worth up to $100 *if* his family could afford to buy it for him. Clayton had ordered one for me.

I offered to give Sidewinder anything he wanted from it if he could score me "lean backs" so I could sleep. Lean backs were pills that lowered blood pressure, made you so relaxed you...leaned back, fell down, or didn't even get up; two knocked me out.

Sidewinder, a sweet grizzled little old man my age had a life sentence for killing his father forty years earlier. An accident long ago resulted in a displaced shoulder which brought about a strange sideways walk--hence Sidewinder. I once asked why he'd killed his father. He started a story about Nazis and Hitler, so I said forget it.

Barry was "shelled", someone destroyed by prison or who'd come in crazy--in any case, nuts, but he knew everyone who had pills for sale—he survived on them instead of food.

He didn't want anything from my Christmas package; he wanted stamps to buy pills.

Done, I said, handing him a fistful. He returned with enough lean backs to allow me to sleep at night for the 14 days I had left and for him to stay zwacked during the day.

Barry had no outside support and couldn't keep a job because he forgot he had one. He subsisted on coffee and lean backs; he was very trim. If you gave him a 15 cent coffee packet at 9am, he'd be back at 9:30 and every thirty minutes thereafter, so I'd give him a $3.20 bag on Monday and tell him not to come back until next Monday, but he never knew when Monday was so he'd hit me up every day anyway.

When he couldn't score pills, Barry got a rush with auto-eroticism: he'd go in the toilet and choke himself out. We loved to watch new guards—preferably female--walk past the shitter, stare through the window to see him turning blue as he strangled himself with his T-shirt.

She'd call Code 3 and break in to find Sidewinder splayed on the floor with an erection.

There was always something to divert me. On the weekend before the hearing, I burned myself out on the weight pile, then took two lean backs at night to sleep.

Sunday afternoon the sergeant summoned me inside. "Pack up. You have to be at Receiving for transport to Durham County Jail in 15 minutes."

"What! The hearing isn't until Wednesday. I don't want to go now."

Conditions at Durham County Jail where I'd spent three weeks in 2001 were awful, and I hadn't had a chance to ditch my contraband or say good-bye to anyone.

Two officers brought me to my locker where my contraband was in plain sight—extra stamps, peanut butter, dental floss. They started throwing my gear into two big bags as I tossed the contraband to a friend nearby. "What about my Christmas package?" I asked.

"Take it," said the aptly named Ms. Savage—big, mean, treacherous—a guard I had *the* most contentious relationship with dating back to when I taught GED and had her banned from the classroom for harassing inmates while they studied. We loathed one another.

She tossed all my Christmas items in a bag. "If they don't want you to have it at Durham County Jail, the guards will take it away. It's worth a try."

Stunned by the decent gesture, I thanked her and then she marched me out of the unit. Had I been wrong about guards all these years? No!

The last inmate I saw as I headed to Receiving was Big Show coming back from tending flowers at medical. We hadn't spoken since softball season a year ago when he formed his own team and I had The Dwarf harass him. Both too proud and stubborn to acknowledge one another, we didn't this last time either. I regret that. He was a good guy.

At Receiving, I was given an old shirt and trousers from their *pret a porter* "off the rack" selection of clothes taken from in-processing inmates. Cuffed and shackled then put in the back of a squad car, I returned to Durham travelling the same road I'd taken 8 years before.

This was it I thought staring out the window at farmers in their fields, travelers on the highway, stores, houses, trees—the rest of my life in the balance. I felt like a Death Row inmate walking towards the gas chamber waiting for a last minute reprieve.

I was innocent. The State had wrongfully prosecuted me. They had lied and used false evidence to convict me. I never should have been convicted. I never should have gone to prison. None of the awful things that happened should have happened: all those lost years, missing my children's graduations, marriages, my grandson's birth, my father's death.

I wanted desperately to believe everything would be fine, that I would live out the rest of my life in freedom with those I loved. Was justice too much to ask for?

As the car approached Durham I saw the city's outline with the towering jail its tallest building. My stomach tightened. I felt as I had in combat, exhilarated and frightened.

Was I on my way at last to Con Thien like Mike Wunch 43 years ago not knowing the awful fate awaiting him? Or would the coin toss be in my favor again?

27. THE HEARING

Hustled through the back exit of the nine story white concrete 750 inmate Durham County Jail, I was strip searched in a large sterile holding area while a ferocious female admitting officer inventoried my two bags like a cheetah ripping apart a wildebeest.

Thrusting my razor at me, she snarled, "You can't have this! It's an infraction. I have to write you up."

"I bought it in the canteen at Nash. It's allowed there. The *guards* packed it for me."

Unmoved, she held up my arthritis medication, toe nail clippers, books, pens, and salt packets. "No. No. No. No. No."

Within twenty minutes of arrival, I had numerous infractions and was slammed into solitary, a cell with steel wash basin, lidless toilet, concrete slab bunk affixed to the wall, paper thin mattress, torn sheet, and no pillow; it made Sparta look like the Ritz Carlton.

Stunned by the hostility, I thought, this is not going to end well, but then I realized isolation was probably meant to safeguard me from other inmates and keep me from the media.

Good. I wanted privacy and spent the next half hour happily inventorying my Christmas package which surprisingly I'd been allowed to keep, enough special food—chicken, beef, salmon, cookies, peanut brittle—to last a week and that now I wouldn't have to share with anyone or feel guilty about eating in front of them.

The three weeks I'd spent in Durham County Jail over Christmas and New Year's in 2001/2002 made Bedlam seem like a rest home--non-stop insanity with hundreds of young blacks (DCJ population was 95% black mostly in for drugs) screaming day and night; conditions had not quieted in the intervening decade, and the odor of caged men—sweat, semen, and fear—was the same too.

Nibbling a candy bar, I pressed my face against the window that looked onto a long narrow cell block to see 30 guys gathered around a TV watching the news. Me!

They kept turning to stare at my cell. I went to bed.

At 8 the next morning, shackled, shod with a 10 pound boot, and dressed in a red jumpsuit, I was taken to court in a police van with Michael Dorman—totally psychotic young white with wild hair, only a few teeth, and very confused sexuality.

Accused of murdering a woman whose bones were found in his backpack, Dorman claimed he hadn't killed her, but was just using her bones for sex. We exchanged polite words, and though macabrely curious about his relationship with the bones, I didn't ask for details.

When I'd entered the courtroom and saw my children together for the first time in 8 years, I drew in shocked breath and averted my face to wipe away tears of joy. Sorrow too; they were no longer children. We had aged so much, lost so much.

Suddenly dread struck me and I nearly stumbled on the way to my seat.

What if the hearing failed? Would this be the last I'd see them together? Would their last sight of their father be of an old man in prison garb, chained and shackled?

Forbidden to speak with them, I waved and put on a brave face, but I felt like Tantalus doomed never to get out of his hell, freedom always just beyond reach. Eight years like this.

With everyone staring at me—family, media, supporters and haters—I felt strangely detached, like how animals at a zoo must feel: the curious onlookers had nothing to do with their lives; nothing was going to change.

Waiting with Dorman for our cases to be heard in fiery red jumpsuits like murderous Tweedle Dee and Tweedle Dum, I listened to DA Cline rail against Chief Superior Court Judge Orlando Hudson, demanding that he disqualify himself for prejudice and corruption.

Was she nuts to piss off the judge who would decide her cases? Didn't she know how the system worked? Of course six hours later the obvious was decided: Hudson dismissed her complaint (I'm not corrupt; I am not a crook!) and said he would hear my case in the morning.

I'd jumped off to a good start; the DA and Judge hated one another.

That second night in isolation, I slept fitfully, jarred awake by thoughts of Dorman, his bones, and my fate. In the morning I finally got a shower. Clayton brought a suit that I'd worn at the 2003 trial; it hung loosely and the pant legs dragged on the floor. I'd shrunk.

Slumped on a detention cell bench in an ill-fitting suit waiting to enter court, I tried to muster confidence. The rest of my life was at stake, but even if I won this hearing, a new trial was years away, an uncertain future of endless struggle. I was weary even before the battle.

381

In court, Kathleen's sister Candace, fashionably coifed and dressed for her star turn, demanded to be heard. Eyes ablaze, face twisted in anger, wrapping herself in victimhood—the only victim (no one had suffered as she)—she screamed at me, Rudolf (that was ok), and denounced DA Cline as incompetent, stupid, unprepared, a disgrace, and demanded she be replaced by a special prosecutor from the Attorney General's office.

I almost felt sorry for Cline as she flinched at the verbal assault.

When Candace finished, Hudson merely nodded for Cline to continue, but sirens immediately wailed and pandemonium broke out; the entire courthouse was evacuated for a bomb scare. Except for me; I was tossed in a detention cell so that if the building collapsed, I couldn't escape—I'd be trapped in the rubble.

We never discovered who'd called in the threat.

When court resumed, the hearing was one sided from the outset as Rudolf summoned SBI officials who testified that their own Agent Deaver had lied under oath about his training and credentials; nothing he said could be trusted. He had committed perjury to rob me and others of freedom.

For the next several days, experts attacked Deaver's experiments as "bogus meaningless recreations" conducted to prove a predetermined "guilty" result. They were "garbage"—junk science. Cline didn't bother to defend him. How could she? Her boss, the Attorney General had fired the bastard.

As I listened, I could not fathom what Deaver had done; his actions made no more sense to me than Michael

Dorman with those bones. I wanted to be angry, hate him, but instead of leaning forward in fisted fury, I pushed away from the defense table in disgust. What Deaver did to me and my children was worse than whatever Dorman could do to those bones.

Chained and shackled, dragging the 10 pound boot with all the years and baggage of the past, along with crushing fear for the future up four courthouse flights on the back staircase to avoid the media, I hurt as much as when I'd been med-evaced to Bethesda Naval Hospital in 1970. But then I was 26, doped on Demerol; now I was 68 with a Tylenol.

On the third night I was moved to a cell on the 40 man protective custody block, mostly blacks, numerous screaming queens and several obvious--after 8 years amongst them, I could tell--child molesters: soft and creepy; yucky. Yet I felt comfortable with them; they had become my *compares*. How would I deal with "normal" people in the real world if I got out? What would I have to say to them? What could we talk about?

At 2:15 am, I woke soaked in blood. Panicking, I pushed the panic button and was rushed to the infirmary. A boil on my back had burst. My blood pressure was 190/120. The nurse plied me with so many pills that in the morning I couldn't walk, so deputies put me in a wheelchair.

I spent that day in court like a crippled zombie. My children kept asking Rudolf if I was all right. "He's fine," said my solicitous attorney as I slumped senseless beside him.

That night alone in my cell, I realized exactly ten years earlier at this time, Kathleen and I were watching a movie. We were happy, in love, laughing, but she had only a few hours to live and I the same few before my life unraveled. Ten years!

I buried my face in the pillow and wept. No matter if I got out, those years were lost and she forever dead.

On Friday, the retired FBI agent who had examined 200 suspect SBI cases said the 5 most egregious were Deaver's; 13 of the next 24 were his. Three defense lawyers testified that manipulating evidence to favor the prosecution was Deaver's modus operandi. He was their go to guy for convictions, providing whatever needed for a guilty verdict.

When court adjourned for the weekend, waiting in a holding cell to be returned to jail, utterly drained, I studied drawings on the walls of hearts, crosses, dicks, and vaginas—crude images that seemed to cover everything guys thought about in here. I would have drawn children.

Someone had scratched "I love Amber Thompson."

Who is this girl immortalized on a prison wall? I wondered. I pictured a young woman with teal and red streaked hair, hands on her hips, a smirk on her face, defiant and proud.

Was she there for him when he got out or had she moved on?

Below her name was, "Ho's aint shit."

A spurned lover? Maybe Amber's boyfriend after she left him.

That evening I went to medical to get Tylenol with two child molesters. One said, "They won't let me near my kids." Thank Christ justice works sometimes, I thought. Both smelled. I'd noticed that few men showered, maybe because it was an open stall and these guys modest. Wait till you get to Big Boy Prison, I thought—no modesty there.

At chow I sat with Bones Dorman. He'd been at Nash from 2003-2006 and knew my blown away balls GED student Jay Bird. It's a small world!

Saturday was Margaret's birthday. Thirty years before, I had driven Liz Ratliff to Wiesbaden Hospital for Margaret's birth, an awful snowy night, and I had been there for her next 19 birthdays. My last was her 20th, the day after Kathleen's death, celebrated with a police grid search of our property for a murder weapon. I missed her next ten along with her graduations and marriage.

On Monday, Tom Bevel, author of the major text on blood spatter finished Deaver's demolition: his work was worthless, his "points of origin in space" meaningless nonsense.

That was the end of it. The following day, Clayton's 37th birthday, he got what he said would be his best gift—my freedom.

Judge Hudson overturned my conviction and ordered a new trial. He ruled that Deaver had "Deliberately misrepresented and intentionally misled the Court and jury." Kathleen "had no fracture or other injuries to her skull, suffered no injuries that caused damage to her brain, had no broken ribs, broken bones, or other injuries associated with a beating."

Deaver's experiments were "unscientific and not acceptable." He'd lied and committed perjury, exhibiting "a pattern of bias in favor of the state and against criminal defendants over the course of twenty years." His testimony violated the Fifth and Fourteenth Amendments to the Constitution and denied my Right to Due Process and a Fair Trial.

After 8 years, 2,987 days, I would be freed the following day. Rudolf slapped me on the back, but I sat stunned, unable to grasp the enormity. I'd seen photos of Greg Taylor and others jubilantly pumping fists and hugging their lawyers when they won, but I couldn't. I felt like I had just staggered over the finish line in a marathon—too weary to celebrate.

Eight years earlier when convicted, I'd said to comfort my children, "It's ok, it's ok."

It had been; we'd survived. Now I didn't know what to say. I couldn't explain to them or myself what any of this had meant--Kathleen's death, years of pain and loss, why we all had suffered. No meaning, no lesson. I'd won, but the toll had been so great; we'd lost so much.

Sophie too was there, brimming with happiness. Now we could get on with our lives together; hopes and dreams would become reality. We hugged and I shuffled out of court.

Back in jail I watched the news, a surreal experience sitting with other inmates watching them watching me on TV. My televised image was more real than my presence beside them.

I ate my last dinner at the "Murderers" table, more highly regarded than the lower "Queens" and lowest "Child Molesters" tables: there's always a hierarchy.

My dinner companions were Dorman, the "Black Hebrew" whose four "wives" helped kill the fifth and her child by him because he thought the two year old was gay, and Gabriel, a young white "cowboy" from Texas who'd killed two black athletes in an adult store parking lot.

I was at ease with these guys. We joked and laughed, but I wanted to ask Gabriel, Why did you kill those men?

What made you think your infant was gay? I wanted to ask the Black Hebrew.

Michael Dorman!—what is it with those bones?

Yet I knew there were no answers; nothing made sense: human behavior was inexplicable. Prison had turned out like war—horrible, meaningless.

How do you go home after that? Who can understand what you went through?

The following evening, I packed my few belongings and walked out of jail on a $300,000 bond put up by Patricia and my daughter-in-law.

I was ordered to wear a GPS ankle monitor, given restrictions for travel, and placed on 11pm curfew.

Outside the jail, taking a deep breath of crisp December air, my first breath of freedom in 10 years, I looked to the open sky—stars, the moon—and then all about me. There was no wire. Fear lifted into the night.

My children and year old grandson were waiting. We hugged, and of course, I cried.

I thought the nightmare over, but it was only the beginning of a five year tortuous journey to freedom that didn't end the way I wanted.

IV

2012-2019

28. Freedom

Going into prison was a shock; coming out was a shock, but the adjustment going in was easier and quicker than the adjustment coming out.

Prison was a nightmare haunted by murderers, rapists, thieves, drug dealers, pimps, gang bangers, and child molesters--people, as far as I know, I hadn't encountered at cocktail parties or at parent/teacher nights. At least they didn't *brag* about it or bring shanks.

Nevertheless, I adapted quickly; I was not a pariah, just another outcast: I wore the same clothes as everyone, ate the same food, got up at the same time, went to bed at the same time, and abided by the same rules. Like boot camp, its sole comfort was uniformity: Don't bother to cry, whine, or complain; it won't do any good and everybody suffers the same.

Release was another matter.

Banished from "decent" society in 2003, I was not welcomed back in 2011. Kathleen's and my friends shunned me in prison—didn't write or visit, but I thought a few would reach out after I was released, yet none did: people I'd gone to college with 50 years earlier, friends of decades—doctors, lawyers, Realtors, brokers, professors, businessmen, executives--friends who'd been to our house countless times, whose homes we'd been to, whose children went to school and played with ours, close friends the police talked to and who said I couldn't possibly have killed Kathleen. None contacted me.

Was it fear of contagion for their good names and reputations? Of catching bisexuality?

My reception was socio economic. At rich white Whole Foods where few customers had probably ever had an unpleasant police encounter, I got sneers. At Dollar Tree, Ross for Less, and other stores with more black customers who'd had less happy police encounters, I was warmly received, hugged!, and wished luck against a judicial system they knew through personal experience was rigged against them.

At first, being a pariah among former friends hurt— I was innocent, my conviction overturned!—yet I quickly realized that I didn't want to rejoin my old Street world because I no longer had anything in common with its inhabitants: I was happier spared the pretense of polite conversation or feigned interest in lives I didn't care about.

Prison life had proved easier. It was uncomplicated with simple rules: mind your business; keep your word; don't snitch. I didn't have to worry about food, shelter, clothes or fashion; there were no bills to pay, no mortgage, no taxes. Except for the fear of rape and beatings, it was a stress free life. The only cost was freedom.

Returning to The Street was more difficult even though I had generous help: a wonderful woman offered me a room in her house until I found my own place; my former wife Patricia put up her house as part of my bond— how many ex-spouses would do that? Clayton got me a computer; Todd took me clothes shopping; Margaret and

Martha accompanied me to get necessities I needed—food, toiletries, household items.

With USMC disability retirement and Social Security, I could live comfortably. I rented an apartment in a quiet secluded neighborhood and leased a car.

Nevertheless, re-entry was still so difficult I couldn't imagine how others managed. A little thing like a driver's license poses immense problems: how do you get insurance coming out of prison? A car for the driving test? How will you find a job? Get to one? Get a bank account, a debit card, a credit card? An apartment? What do you do for the deposit? Down payments on electricity, water, cable and Internet? Money for a TV? A computer? A phone? Doctors, dentists, medicine?

After 8 years' incarceration, I got a $55 Release check to return to The Street. $55! $7 a year, two cents a day for food, shelter, necessities. And people wonder at the recidivism rate.

Without money, family, and a few friends to help, I might have had to beg on street corners. But all the corners were taken. At least I was equipped to fight for one: "Put on your boots, motherfucker. This is my corner now."

In 1969, just back from Vietnam and in uniform on my way to see my folks in Denmark, I passed through JFK airport. A young woman crossed the corridor, called me "Baby killer," and spat on me.

Stunned, I reeled into the first bar and ordered a drink. The guy on the next stool patted me on the back. "Hey, Marine, let me buy that." The bartender said, "The drink's on me."

That was my Vietnam homecoming: I didn't know whether someone was going to spit on me or buy me a drink. I was very confused. Wary and uncomfortable all the time.

Returning from prison was worse. Most people and former friends thought I'd gotten out on a technicality, not that the system had convicted me with lies, perjury, and prosecutorial abuse. No one spat, but no one offered to buy me a drink either.

In 1969 I cared what people thought; in 2011 I didn't. I had no interest in them or desire for their company. I had bigger concerns: I was more fragile and wary than I'd expected.

A scene in *Lawrence of Arabia* captures how I felt. Lawrence is in the British Officer's Club just back from his ordeal in the desert. Other officers stare at him as if he's a freak, and he doesn't know how to act. He's awkward and out of place.

Indeed, he *doesn't* belong and never will: too much had happened to him. Like the farm once you leave, it's hard to go back; so it was with me and my world before prison. I couldn't relate to the people of that world; there was total disconnect.

Current events, politics, movies, TV, and Hollywood gossip didn't have anything to do with my prison life. Back on The Street, they still didn't.

The day after release, Clayton and I stopped at Taco Bell for lunch. He ordered and said, "What do you want, Dad?" I stared dumbfounded at the menu. There were so many choices; in prison there were none and no decisions to make.

"Clay, choose for me," I said. "How about a taco salad?" I nodded. "Sounds great," and when it came, I ate it happily, but I would have been happy with anything he ordered.

A few days later, the friend with whom I was staying asked me to run into a grocery store to buy her gluten free crackers. I thought, what the fuck is gluten free?, but I ran in and went to the cracker department. Nothing! The only thing I found was a woman who'd been on the jury that had convicted me. She said hi. I was stunned (shades of JFK and the Marines): my first public outing and I encounter a woman who'd sentenced me to Life without Parole.

What does protocol dictate in such a situation? "Good to see you again, you're looking well," or "What a nice surprise. How's the family?" Or just a simple--"You bitch!"

Mulling that, I sought a clerk. Gluten free crackers? Health Food aisle. I found it and reached for a box then stopped--there were a hundred choices. Jesus! I grabbed one and ran to express check-out for *10 items or Less*. In front of me was the jury woman with a hundred items in her cart. I thought--and *you* convicted me? You're the one breaking the rules. You bitch!

A similar incident occurred when I returned to my old gym. On my way to shower after a work-out, a man in the locker room asked, "Aren't you talking to me anymore?"

I turned. The man, a distinguished looking gentleman from the country club set, was staring at me as if

I had just climbed out of a grave, a look similar to many I'd gotten.

I'd known the man before prison. He was a nice guy, but...no, I didn't want to talk to him. He was part of that world which had rejected me. I didn't want to hear about their work issues, golf games, or kids, and I was not interested in sharing my experience. They had buried me and I was content to stay interred.

"I'm not talking to anyone," I said and continued to the shower.

I didn't even mind when I was asked to leave the restaurant Kathleen and I had frequented many times, a haute cuisine place with flowers and tablecloths; the chef had catered our wedding, swum in our pool. I had gone with the French film crew. The chef bragged about throwing me and my daughter out. He mistook the French producer for my daughter.

Before prison, I lived on 4 acres in a 9,500 square foot house--wife, children, dogs, cars, pool: Zorba's whole catastrophe. In prison I lived in a 9x12 cell, then on a bunk in the Day Room with no freedom or privacy for years.

After release, I moved into a 1200 square foot apartment. I went to bed and got up when I wanted, cooked and ate what I wanted. In the morning, I'd brew coffee and sit in the dining room for thirty minutes, then go to the living room for thirty minutes, then to the porch overlooking a little forest, then to my den, then back to the bedroom. I spent the entire day wandering room to room. Nobody yelled at me, told me to stand up for count, do this or that, go here or there. I luxuriated in freedom and privacy and I didn't want to see or talk to anyone.

Nevertheless, the nightmare that began when Kathleen died did not end with my release. Kathleen was still dead and I struggled with "freedom".

An iconic photograph of Margaret and Martha reacting to my guilty verdict makes Munch's *The Scream* look like minor angst. Beside them, my sons' reactions are a tableau in stoic endurance and bravery. When I was freed, their expressions are happiness beyond description. My own is muted because I had lost so much--the woman I loved, freedom, years without my children, all I owned-- and I had battled for ten years to suppress emotions after Kathleen's death and my own living death among the damned.

What would a photograph of Lazarus coming from the grave reveal—triumph? Relief? Joy? Or maybe just confusion and pain: what was *that* all about? And now what?

That's what I felt emerging from a prison grave, brought into sunlight after interminable darkness, stared at like a freak: confusion and pain.

I had spent one year in war, 1968 to 1969. I was in prison for eight. Both experiences brought fear, boredom, sorrow, separation, courage, humor, even love, but war prepared me for prison: I'd learned to repress as much as I could, show as little as possible, and never show fear.

In prison I spent every day of 3,000 suppressing fear, sorrow, aloneness, grief—the deaths of Kathleen, my mother and father—and rage. It's how I survived.

"I'm fine" is what I wrote in letters and told those who visited. "But how are you really?" they'd ask. "Fine," I'd repeat; it was my mantra. But that was on the surface. I never ventured beyond the shallow end of self because I knew what lurked in the depths—there be dragons: grief, terror, madness: Don't go there.

I cauterized emotions, soldering them like metal because otherwise my wounds of loss and pain would have never sealed; I would have been in constant torment and gone mad.

The Buddha helped, but Sophie helped more: Gautama was abstract, Sophie flesh. She was very gentle the night I got out of prison, but there were unexpected problems.

We thought I would focus on our new life together, but I couldn't.

"You're not here with me," she'd say when we were alone. "You're not *present*."

I wasn't. I had underestimated what prison had done to me. The ankle brace weighed a thousand pounds; it would not let me move forward. It prevented me from thinking of a future.

I needed to be alone to finally grieve for Kathleen, my mother and father, for all that I had lost and missed. I wanted to recapture the past with my children. I wanted to be a father reclaiming lost time more than I wanted to be the partner Sophie deserved and needed in the present and future.

Vulnerable and confused, I needed to recover *me*.

After two weeks, she went back to Paris and we didn't get together for six months.

Under house arrest wearing the ankle monitor with the Damoclean sword of retrial over my head, I ate real food and wore real clothes. I listened to music. I saw the moon and stars for the first time in nearly a decade. But I had trouble making decisions—where to go, what to do, even what to eat; prison hadn't allowed choices. Now I had too many. Paralyzed by indecisiveness, I'd sit alone in my apartment unable to confront the world beyond my door.

And I cried a lot. Everything made me cry—the love of my children; my grandson; a sunset; the moon; sports on TV; Verdi; Bach! At a ballet, tears streamed down my cheeks. What is wrong with me? I wondered, then realized it wasn't the beauty of the performance, but the memory of past ones and the realization that I thought I'd never see another--I'd given up all that, but here it was before me: Beauty. Joy. Art.

So it was with everything I thought I'd lost forever—my children, touch, love; I was unable to grasp their return. I had been strong and harsh and cold so long, but now I didn't need to be, yet I could not shake the demons of loss and deprivation suddenly unleashed.

I was a physical and emotional wreck, PTSD of course, so I went to a VA psychiatrist, a smug middle aged bland man to exorcise what I knew lurked in those depths of self I'd been avoiding. Without even making an entry in the open notebook balanced on his knee, he suggested I join a group session for anger and grief.

Group anger? *Group* grief? I just spent eight years in group anger and grief with hundreds in the groups—it was called *prison*; that's the last thing I need.

"Well, what do you want me to do?" he asked without sympathy or concern.

"I want you to unfuck my head. I want you to put everything back together."

I told him that I felt like crying all the time.

"Well, go ahead and cry," he said, closing his notebook.

I just stared at him. Then I walked out. That was the end of my treatment. I was pissed for days--until I realized he was right. There was nothing wrong in crying. It was a catharsis I needed to handle on my own. All I had to do was rip open the wounds, plunge the depths, combat the dragons, and write about what had happened since Kathleen's death: my trial and prison. So I started this book, but I could not finish for six years--that's how long it took for my case to be resolved.

For two of those I wore an ankle monitor, had restrictions on travel with an 11pm curfew which Todd thought was too lenient: At your age Dad, you should be in bed by 10.

I was on pre-trial supervision longer than anyone in North Carolina history.

Re-trial was scheduled for 2013, 2014, then 2015, 2016, and finally May 2017, though with discovery, experts, continuances, and delays, trial was still another year or two away.

For five years I lived a low profile life; I read, wrote, watched TV, and went to the gym.
My children and grandchildren came frequently; we spent holidays and Christmases together.

Sophie returned after six months separation and we began to plan the future again. We would live happily ever after in Paris.

We joked and laughed when she came every few months. We were *so* good together.

When Judge Hudson ended ankle monitoring and removed my travel restrictions, we went to Baltimore to see Clayton, Becky, and my grandsons, then to New York, Savannah, Charleston, Phoenix, the Grand Canyon, and California.

All the while, my case dragged on. No end seemed in sight, so in 2014, with very mixed emotions, I offered to take an Alford Plea to end the ordeal for myself, family, and Sophie. Just get it over so we can move on with our lives.

An Alford Plea allows a defendant to profess innocence in court though the result is a guilty conviction. The West Memphis Three, innocent men in Arkansas, one—Damien Echols—facing execution on Death Row, did this.

The DA rejected my offer because Kathleen's sisters-in-law demanded that I admit in court that I killed her. I said that would never happen, so we proceeded to trial.

Though the plea would have ended the matter, deep down I was pleased because I wanted to prove my innocence and felt confident I would win at retrial.

The first trial had been a travesty: the SBI had lied, withheld and invented evidence, used junk science; The medical examiner who'd testified Kathleen had died of blunt force trauma had lied—she didn't believe it; Judge Hudson admitted that he had erred in allowing testimony about Liz Ratliff's death and wouldn't allow it at re-trial; the NC Supreme Court had ruled that the search of my computer with gay pornography was unconstitutional; there was no murder weapon, no motive. THERE WAS NO MURDER.

I was eager for a re-trial and even more convinced I would be acquitted when new discovery emerged: the SBI had seized Kathleen's clothes from the police but never tested them for DNA. They tested mine and Todd's, but not Kathleen's.

Why hadn't they tested her clothing?   Were they afraid they'd find someone else's DNA?
When we sought to test them, we discovered that after Kathleen's clothes had been returned by the SBI to the Clerk of the Court, the boxes containing them had been mysteriously ripped open and contaminated. They could never be tested, thus ruling out any possibility of proving a third person had attacked Kathleen.

Finally, bloody feathers and hair ripped from Kathleen's head had been found clutched in her right hand. Had she have been attacked by a raptor/owl, a theory some experts believed but which police and prosecutors had ridiculed? Had there been feathers on her clothing?

Hoping at re-trial to discover who ripped open and contaminated the evidence boxes and if there had been a raptor attack, I was ready to go to trial when the District Attorney suddenly offered an Alford Plea in February 2017: Manslaughter with time served.

Too Late! Why accept a plea when I was innocent and a re-trial would prove it? I told Rudolf I wasn't interested.   Tell the DA and the sisters to go fuck themselves.

"You *sure* you want to risk re-trial?" he asked. "Consider carefully, Mike. Do you trust police and prosecutors? A jury? You sure you want to put your life and freedom in their hands?"

15 years earlier I believed that if police arrested someone, that person was guilty. If they shot someone, it was justified. Now I knew better; police and prosecutors do anything for a conviction. That's what they did in my case. Why wouldn't they do it again?

I could hear Nonna: "Fool me once, you're the fool. Fool me twice, *I'm* the fool."

I was innocent in 2003 yet had been convicted. The police brought in Duane Deaver who with bogus experiments and no proof declared that I had beaten Kathleen to death even though there was no murder weapon, no motive, and no history of domestic violence.

How could there be a conviction when there was no evidence and I was innocent?

Because evidence and innocence didn't matter as much as Blood! Pornography! Homosexuality! Lying SBI agents and medical examiners! Weeping perjuring sisters!

I'd been a fool in 2003 to think a scientific defense could counter a mud slung prosecution. The jury, offered a choice between a medical text and a trashy novel, chose trash.

When the DA offered the Alford Plea, Deaver was gone, but the culture he'd thrived in continued—police would do anything to convict.

Nothing had changed in the judicial system either. The DA who'd convicted me had been promoted to judge. Convicting defendants in high profile cases is a good career move for DA's—they become judges, governors, congressman and senators.

DA's and judges are not elected to be "soft on crime;" they're rewarded for convictions. It's their *job*. The toughest most harsh win because that's what voters want.

And Deborah Radisch had become more important and powerful than ever. She was now the *Chief* Medical Officer.

The criminal justice system is geared to convict defendants. That's its raison d'etre. The police have carte blanch too—even when videotaped beating or killing someone. And juries? Too often they're like blood thirsty Forum crowds.

Did I want to risk another trial knowing they'd do the same thing again? Should I risk freedom to fight for an uncertain exoneration that might take years, or should I cop to a crime I didn't commit and walk away?

For once Nonna's words were no help: on one hand, Never give in; on the other, Don't gamble. Should I choose the door where I knew The Lady was, albeit ugly—freedom with a conviction—or risk The Tiger, maybe death in prison?

I went back and forth, growing more and more depressed at the thought of a conviction for a crime I didn't commit, but at the same time I didn't want to put my children, grandchildren, and Sophie through another fight that might drag on for years. Should I take the Plea or fight?

I couldn't sleep, threw myself on the sofa during the day, didn't go to the gym, moped and felt sick. I decided to leave it to my children and Sophie.

Todd said, "People who believe you're innocent always will. Those who think you're guilty won't change their minds. So what's the point fighting? Why bother? Move on with your life. Better to look ahead than behind because there's not much ahead--you're 73, Dad."

Clayton said, "You're playing a game at a crooked table. You'll never win. Pick up your chips and go home. You're too old to fight another battle. You're 73, Dad."

Margaret and Martha agreed, so did Sophie: Take the Alford Plea. Salvage your life.

I was *pissed*; 73 wasn't too old to fight: you're never too old to right a wrong. I couldn't bear a conviction, couldn't stand the DA winning. The thought made me sick at heart.

Nevertheless, I caved in. I didn't end it with a bang, but a whimper. It was the most difficult decision I ever made.

Three things decided it for me. The first was one of my father's favorite quotes: "Discretion is the better part of valor." Of course he'd never read Henry IV and the only Falstaff he knew was the beer, but Shakespeare's words swayed me. Fighting is not always the best solution. What was served by the Charge of the Light Brigade? They died, the battle....was Balaclava won or lost? Who remembers save a few? Did it matter to the dead on either side?

The second was what my wise Gunnery Sergeant in Vietnam said about an enemy held ridge we were told to take. "It's dirt, Lieutenant. Not worth anybody's lives— ours *or* the gooks. Fuck the Major's orders. Just say you didn't hear them." Had commanders at Hamburger Hill to our south in the A Shau Valley followed Gunny's advice, hundreds of men would not have died.

Finally, there was the unchanged judicial system. The DA, police, and medical examiner would do everything to convict me again; the sisters would never recant--they'd double down their lies. The same tactics would be used to get the same result.

So gnashing my teeth, I told Rudolf I would take the plea. I told my children to stay home because this was not cause for celebration. I didn't want them to witness the capitulation.

On February 24, 2017, before reporters, TV cameras, the BBC, and the French film crew, Judge Hudson asked me if I understand that by taking an Alford Plea, I was maintaining my innocence but would be found guilty of Manslaughter.

I said yes.

That ended it. After sixteen years, the case was resolved.

Finally free, I walked out of court disgusted with myself.

I got a passport and went to Paris to start my new life.

29. KARMA

Here there is supposed to be a happy ending: Love Triumphs. But it didn't. In the end, I did not leave my family and country to live in Paris with Sophie.

On her last visit to America in October 2016, three months before I took the Alford Plea, I told Sophie what had been tormenting me since a Skype call we'd had in August. She said she'd spent the day clearing out a closet in her house for my clothes.

She was clearing out a closet? Suddenly Paris was no longer fantasy; I had a clothes closet there.

In prison, Paris—the future—had been a dream, a fantasy of sex with Sophie, walking along the Seine together, going to patisseries and parties. Life. Fun. An American in Paris. Me!

I loved Sophie, that was real, but Paris was a dream because I lived in a barbed wire world of concrete: Bloods; The Hole; Frau Himmler.

My children were not in my dream future, nor a closet in Paris with my clothes; it was just Sophie and me in a fantasy world with the Eiffel Tower and Arc de Triumph as backdrop.

 The closet broadsided me with reality; the dream grew ugly tentacles: I was 73, didn't speak French, couldn't afford Paris, and had no friends there. I'd lose free military retirement medical care for hip, shoulder, and cataract surgery I'd soon need. There'd be no gym, Dallas Cowboy games or Duke Basketball. I wouldn't have a car;

I couldn't get an English Bulldog (Sophie said it wasn't possible at her place). MY CHILDREN AND GRANDCHILDREN WOULDN'T BE THERE.

Of course I can swim the ocean to be with you, boasts the man to his lover. Of course I will be brave and heroic thought Henry Fleming in *The Red Badge of Courage*. But at the ocean's edge—the water is so cold, the distance so far; when the battle begins, those bullets kill. Reality sweeps dreams and heroics aside: I might drown; I might get shot.

Of course I wouldn't drown or get shot in Paris. What was wrong that I suddenly had reservations? I loved Sophie. *Why* was I having second thoughts?

Because at long last, for the first time since Kathleen died, I was content: I liked being alone most of the time; I liked my children and grandchildren visiting when they could and me visiting them when I wanted; I loved Sophie coming every couple months for several weeks. I was happy with the way things were.

But how could I tell her this after all she had done for me? After all we had planned? After all that I had said for years? I would break her heart.

I agonized for weeks; I couldn't work, I couldn't sleep. Yet I could not get over this truth: I did not want to live in Paris for the rest of my life. I did not want to be an ex-pat in France. There were many things wrong with my country (soon to get much worse), but I'd been a Marine; I loved America. MY CHILDREN AND GRANDCHILDREN WERE IN AMERICA.

Sophie had a lovely home near Montparnasse about the size of my apartment not far from the Luxembourg

Gardens and Seine. She lived with her 24 year old son
Felix who stayed home all day playing music with his
friends. I wouldn't be living just with Sophie, but once
again with people I had not chosen to live with; I was too
old to live in a youth hostel.

Long ago, an old friend married a German when
they were young. She, from a wealthy Philadelphia family,
was a student studying in Heidelberg; he had just joined the
diplomatic corps. When she got pregnant, they debated
where to raise the child. He wanted to live in Bonn, she in
Philadelphia. Unable to resolve the problem, they
divorced. He later became ambassador to an African
country, she married the chairman of the Duke English
Department; the child lived in America, spoke German, and
became a doctor.

"Jesus, Bootsy, why didn't you decide where to live
before you got married?"

"We were young and in love. Nothing else
mattered. After Serge was conceived, we lived apart the
rest of our lives, but it worked out nicely. We're still
friends." she said.

I thought theirs might be the solution: I could live in
Paris a few weeks or months, and Sophie could continue
coming to America. We would be together but with
separate lives.

I had lost eight years with my children during my
imprisonment. At 73, how many good years did I have
left? However many, I wanted to be with them and my
grandchildren. I wanted to remain an American going to
the gym, watching football and basketball, having free
medical care; I wanted a Bulldog. Not unreasonable

requests, I thought, while Sophie would have her son, her house, her work, her friends, and France—in Paris.

I told my children who knew about my plans to live in Paris (and who'd never said a word) that I was having second thoughts. Their reactions were Mars/Venus.

My Martian sons said: Do what you think is best, Dad. We'll support you. Case closed.

My daughters from Venus had stronger views. Good, said Margaret and Martha. We lost you all those years in prison; we don't want to lose you again.

You wouldn't be losing me, I said; I'd just be in Paris. That's 6,000 miles from us on the West Coast, they said. How often would you make the trip? We can't afford to fly there often. What about Todd in Mexico? Clayton, Becky, Lucian and Dorian in Baltimore? How long could you stay? How much would the trips cost? What about holidays? Emergencies?

Becky was relieved too. I want you in Dorian's and Lucian's lives. You're Gramps; they love you. You're important to them. We see you nearly every month now; you're only a few hours by car. How often would your grandchildren see you in Paris?

Margaret, Martha, and Becky were practical about love too. You need a companion; Sophie's wonderful. You should arrange to be with her part of the year, but you need to be by yourself sometimes, and other times you need to be with us.

When Sophie came in October for three weeks, I told that I was having reservations about Paris. Living there was going to be more difficult than I had imagined.

She wept for a week. "But you said for years that you could do it. You said you loved me. We made plans. How can you say now that you can't do it? Don't you love me?"

"Of course I do, I just don't think I can live in Paris full time."

For Sophie it was solely about love. If I loved her, I would go to Paris and live with her. If I couldn't do that, I didn't love her enough and she did not want to be with someone who could not commit completely to love. It was all or nothing.

She wanted to end our relationship right then, but I convinced her to stay another two weeks. I said we could work it out. I said I would go to Paris and try.

She doubted it'd work because she thought I had already made up my mind.

I had, but maybe in Paris I could convince her to try living together part time.

As I awaited my passport, my brother Bill called to ask if I'd go with him to Italy for two weeks—sort of a "Last Hurrah" together.

Are you dying? I asked.

No, his granddaughter, my grandniece Ashlyn, was finishing a dance course in Arezzo; he wanted to see her graduation. He was renting a car, but Bill had no night vision, NO sense of direction, and GPS baffled him. In the army, he couldn't read a map. He wanted me to help drive and navigate.

We would meet in Florence, drive to Arezzo, then to La Spezia and Venice, fly to Marrakech, and end up in

Paris where he'd fly back to Reno and I would stay with Sophie.

Florence! Venice! Morocco! France!

Of course, I said. I really *was* free. I would see the world again.

I told Sophie I'd be in Paris shortly. I packed my bags and left with great anticipation.

Bill was as funny and wonderful as ever, but Europe had changed dramatically since I'd last been in 2000. Florence was overrun with tourists and Venice even worse: massive cruise ships in the harbor disgorged crowds so thick that it made the city impossible—two hour waits to get into St. Mark's and the Doge's Palace for ten minute visits. La Spezia and Quinta Terre were just as bad. We eagerly escaped to Marrakech, but I got violently ill drinking water and was still sick when we arrived in Paris.

Not wanting to see Sophie in miserable condition, I queasily toured the city with Bill. Soldiers and gendarmes with automatic weapons were everywhere; only Saigon fifty years earlier had been this armed and fortified. And the people! The noise!

It seemed the Orient had been evacuated and all of them were in the Louvre taking selfies in front of the Mona Lisa. I couldn't stand it. I was homesick already.

At Sophie's house at last, she could not understand how I had been in Paris three days without contacting her. Sick was not an excuse, she said.

It wasn't—I had just been putting off the inevitable, which she surmised immediately.

Her home was lovely, fabulous for Paris, Manhattan, or LA, but not large. Downstairs was a living/dining room, a tiny kitchen, and a toilet. There was also a small garden. Upstairs were three small bedrooms, Felix in one, a friend of his and his girlfriend in another, Sophie and I in the third--five of us sharing a toilet.

Because Felix was having a large party that weekend (I arrived Thursday), Sophie booked a house in Normandy for three nights.

We stayed two. That's all it took to realize our relationship was over: I said I could not live in Paris in her house; she said she did not want to be with me if I wouldn't.

We wept, she for the failure of love, me for my inability to be the partner she deserved, for what I was doing to her, for what I was losing—her love: Her. For not loving her enough after all she had done, after all we had planned. For being a failure.

We drove back to Paris Sunday. I checked into a hotel. She said Don't call, Don't write, but we didn't part bitterly: the long relationship—13 years—had a dignified death, a sheet discreetly pulled over its corpse.

One evening before I flew home, I walked the streets of Saint Germaine. Near San Michel I found where Patty and I had stayed before we had children, a 50 Franc a night dive in 1972, now a 300 Euro a night boutique hotel.

Young lovers filled sidewalk cafes, drinking, smoking, and laughing. I did not belong.

I had been madly in love twice, first with Patty. We married at 22, had two sons and travelled the world. I dedicated *A Time of War* to her because she had suffered all my sorrows and carried me through terrible tragedies. My second love was Kathleen. I'd given myself to her completely and would never get over her death. I could not love Sophie like I had loved Patty and Kathleen, not enough to give up my country, my children, and my grandchildren.

Prison and age had shriveled my heart; it had made me selfish. I wanted to live the rest of my life on my own terms. I didn't need a lover. At seventy-four I didn't have energy or interest to pursue that passion. Being Dad and Gramps was enough.

When young, I swore I'd live life to the fullest without regrets, not realizing I was living it then with regrets by not being true to myself. I should have embraced the fantasy about the shortstop as my reality; I should not have hidden who I was. Now was too late. An unscalable mountain of mistakes and regrets—should have beens and if onlies.

A monk asked, "What is the Way?" The Master answered, "An open-eyed man falling into the well."

I think it means: avoid the mistake that fool ahead of you just made.

Good luck: too many fools to watch and too many wells to fall into. I drowned long ago.

But I may be wrong about that koan altogether.

Karma is a bitch.

http://www.behindthestaircase.com/

EPILOGUE

Netflix and Aftermath

Netflix and *The Staircase*

I did not learn that the French filmmakers had sold their documentary *The Staircase* (which they began filming in 2002) to Netflix until February, 2018, long after the sale.

Before airing the documentary in June, 2018, Netflix representatives warned the family that it might find a large audience, and from their past experience said it could result in heavy media coverage and lots of attention. They suggested that we go "dark" on social media.

We did, but we were not prepared for the overwhelming public response.

Questions answered

The Staircase heavily favors the defense. Did I receive money from the French film crew or Netflix?

The Staircase was conceived by director Jean de Lestrade as the first explorative documentary of an American trial. In February 2002, he approached me, DA

Jim Hardin, and Judge Hudson to film a trial from the defense, prosecution, and judge's point of view. No money would be paid to anyone. We agreed to this, but a month into filming, the DA and Judge Hudson bowed out. I didn't. That is why the documentary emphasizes the defense point of view—I was the only participant. I received no money.

Jean also approached Kathleen's daughter Caitlin and her sister Candace numerous times for interviews, but they refused.

Did I kill my first wife?

For seventeen years there have been rumors that I murdered my first wife Patricia, the mother of our sons Clayton and Todd. Patricia is alive and well. She attended my trial and all hearings to support me. She posted bond for me twice. We remain good friends and see each other frequently to attend cultural events together.

Were Margaret and Martha my Daughters?

For seventeen years there have been Internet rumors that I fathered Margaret and Martha. They are the biological children of George and Elizabeth Ratliff. I became their guardians after George and Liz died in 1983 and 1985 respectively. The District Attorney, hoping to prove that I was their biological father, did DNA testing in 2002 which proved that I was not their father. Had DNA tests proved that I was, it would have featured prominently at my trial.

What about the Owl?

Since the Netflix movie, there has been much discussion as to whether Kathleen had been attacked by an owl and died as a result.

I do not know and have no idea whether a raptor Owl attacked Kathleen.

The lacerations on the back of Kathleen's scalp look like what the talons of an owl might cause, and small feathers were found in Kathleen's hand during the autopsy. I feel certain that Kathleen brought out the balsa wood deer to decorate for Christmas that night after she left me at the pool and before going to bed, but I do not know if an owl attacked her.

My attorney David Rudolf now believes that an owl attack is the most plausible explanation for Kathleen's lacerations.

The only one way to prove if that happened would be an exhumation to determine whether there is owl DNA in the wounds or in her scalp.

If Kathleen's daughter and sisters want an exhumation, I would authorize it as the next of kin.

Did Kathleen know about my bisexuality?

Kathleen and I never spoke of my bisexuality. I did not tell her that I was bisexual or that I had had relations with men. Once she told me that she had had a lesbian relationship with a friend. I believe she told me this to encourage me to talk about my sexual relations, but I didn't.

Kathleen often spoke about the Latin and Math courses she took as a high school senior. She placed out of her high school classes, so was sent to nearby Franklin and Marshall College for courses. She said that as the only woman in the Latin class, the professor delighted in having her read aloud and translate the homoerotic poetry of Catullus. She said the men in the class were embarrassed but she wasn't. She said it all seemed perfectly natural to her.

I think Kathleen knew about my tendencies. It was understood but not discussed.

Who owned the house?

1810 Cedar Street was in my name alone. I bought it in 1993 with a down payment of $250,000, money that I had received from my books.

Did Kathleen find Internet Porn?

The District Attorney stated throughout the trial that Kathleen found Internet porn on my computer after her midnight call to a colleague in Canada. The colleague had sent material to my computer because Kathleen needed to review the documents for a conference call in the morning.

Finding the Internet porn supposedly resulted in a fight in which I murdered Kathleen. However, the DA's own computer expert stated that the computer had not been accessed after 4pm the afternoon she died, and the file sent to her had never been opened. Nevertheless, the DA in his closing argument argued that Kathleen found the Internet porn and this provoked my assault on her. That was untrue.

Were there Financial problems?

The DA suggested that because we had around $130,000 in credit card debt (which included the cost for Kathleen's leased Jaguar), we were in financial trouble and that this was a motive for me to murder Kathleen.

However, the DA's financial expert testified that Kathleen was deferring 80% of her income (about $150,000), the maximum allowed, to a savings program and that we were not in financial trouble. Indeed, we were worth nearly $2,000,000, living within our means, and could have paid off the credit card debt at any time simply by reducing the amount deferred.

Kathleen and I used the credit cards to get airline reward points and encouraged the girls—all three of whom had American Advantage Cards—to charge their college expenses. We had so many miles that we used them to go to the Orient and Bali for a month.

Another financial motive was suggested that because Kathleen had a million dollar insurance policy with her company Nortel that she took out when she was married to Fred, I killed her for the money. But I was not the beneficiary of the policy—her first husband Fred was. I assumed he collected the money, and I hope he gave it to Kathleen's daughter Caitlin.

What about the Blowpoke?

Kathleen and her first husband Fred Atwater had been given a fireplace tool called a blowpoke by Kathleen's sister Candace Zamperini. After Kathleen's and Fred's divorce, Kathleen kept the blowpoke. It was in our house on Cedar Street. It had been used a few times to fan flames in the fireplace.

However, no one in the family saw the blowpoke after 1997. It simply disappeared. Even Kathleen's daughter Caitlin stated she had not seen the blowpoke for years before Kathleen died. Pictures and video of the fireplace showed all the fireplace tools *except* for the blowpoke. Our housekeeper and handyman said they hadn't seen it.

After Candace informed the DA that it was missing, she convinced him that it was the murder weapon.

Near the end of the trial, my son Clayton was working on his 1966 Ford Mustang in the basement. He saw the blowpoke in a corner, covered with cobwebs. He showed it to his sister Margaret and they got me. None of us touched the blowpoke. I immediately called my attorneys. They came over immediately. They called Judge Hudson and he came to the house to see it. It was photographed and tested. Tests proved that it was not dented and had no trace of blood on it.

After my trial and conviction, it was learned that the police had discovered the blowpoke in the basement during one of their initial searches in 2002, but dismissing it as a possible murder weapon, they placed it in a corner where it stayed until discovered at the end of my trial.

The police said nothing to the District Attorney who throughout the trial emphasized that it was missing and the police had never found it despite thorough searches.

The Website

http://www.behindthestaircase.com/

The book is free on the website, and there are more stories, plus photos and videos. I strongly urge you to visit.

The website will be updated periodically.

http://www.behindthestaircase.com/